THE PROVINCE
OF
THE LAW OF TORT

THE PROVINCE
OF
THE LAW OF TORT

(Tagore Law Lectures delivered in 1930)

BY

PERCY H. WINFIELD, LL.D. Cantab.
Hon. LL.D. Harvard

*Rouse Ball Professor of English Law; Fellow of St John's
College, Cambridge; of the Inner Temple,
Barrister-at-Law*

CAMBRIDGE
AT THE UNIVERSITY PRESS
1931

CAMBRIDGE UNIVERSITY PRESS
Cambridge, New York, Melbourne, Madrid, Cape Town,
Singapore, São Paulo, Delhi, Mexico City

Cambridge University Press
The Edinburgh Building, Cambridge CB2 8RU, UK

Published in the United States of America by Cambridge University Press, New York

www.cambridge.org
Information on this title: www.cambridge.org/9781107635586

© Cambridge University Press 1931

This publication is in copyright. Subject to statutory exception
and to the provisions of relevant collective licensing agreements,
no reproduction of any part may take place without the written
permission of Cambridge University Press.

First published 1931
First paperback edition 2013

A catalogue record for this publication is available from the British Library

ISBN 978-1-107-63558-6 Paperback

Cambridge University Press has no responsibility for the persistence or
accuracy of URLs for external or third-party internet websites referred to in
this publication, and does not guarantee that any content on such websites is,
or will remain, accurate or appropriate.

PREFACE

THIS book comprises the lectures delivered as Tagore' Professor in the University of Calcutta, 1930. Its aim is neither to construct a perfect definition of tort nor to isolate entirely the Law of Tort, for either task is impossible. Any attempt to separate completely one topic in the Common Law from another is likely to yield artificial and unpractical results which may be compared to wrenching a limb from a living organism rather than to detaching a part from a machine. The real object of the lectures was to trace the *liaison* between tortious obligation and other regions of the law, and, paradoxical as it may seem, it is suggested that the Common Law has gained greatly in effectiveness by the absence of clearly marked barriers on the boundary of any one of the subjects analysed. This may make exposition rather difficult, but a good test of an adequate system of law is its satisfactory working by the Bench and practitioners for those who have to obey it; and, in the main, the Law of Tort satisfies that test, not only in what may be reckoned as strictly part of its contents and of nothing else, but also in those portions of it which overlap other legal territory.

The space allotted to one of the topics may seem disproportionate. The chapter on Quasi-contract is much longer than any other and is, in effect, a short monograph on that part of the law. But in view of what is said on pp. 116–119, it may be doubted whether abridgment was feasible. I confess that at one point in my preparation of the lectures I found it difficult to resist the

vi   PREFACE

temptation to concentrate on Quasi-contract and to include nothing else. There is need of a good English law textbook on it, and, given that, it ought to be taught as a post-graduate subject in the English law schools.

I welcome this opportunity of repeating my sincere thanks to the managers of the foundation which was the occasion of these lectures; and to all my friends in Calcutta for the extraordinary kindness which I experienced there.

P. H. W.

1931

CONTENTS

Preface . . . . *page* v

Index of Statutes viii

Index of Cases ix

Chap. I. Definition of Tort. General Remarks   1

   II. General Historical Outline . . 8

   III. Tort Defined 32

   IV. Tort and Contract . . . 40

   V. Tort and Bailment . . . 92

   VI. Tort and Breach of Trust . . 104

   VII. Tort and Quasi-contract . . 116

   VIII. Tort and Crime 190

   IX. Tort and the Law of Property . . 204

   X. Tort and Quasi-delict . . . 208

   XI. Statutes of Limitations and Judgment 219

   XII. Other Definitions of Tort . . 229

General Index 245

INDEX OF STATUTES

Stat. Westminster II, 1285 (13 Ed. I. c. 24), 12–14
Stat. of Limitations, 1623–1624 (21 Jac. I. c. 16), 219–228
Capiatur Fine Act, 1693–1694 (5 & 6 W. & M. c. 12), 52
(Joinder), 1696–1697 (8 & 9 W. III. c. 11), 56
Civil Procedure Act, 1833 (3 & 4 W. IV. c. 42), 56, 57, 145
Fatal Accidents Act, 1846 (9 & 10 Vict. c. 93), 89
Common Law Procedure Act, 1852 (15 & 16 Vict. c. 76), 58, 146
—— 1854 (17 & 18 Vict. c. 125), 236
Mercantile Law Amendment Act, 1856 (19 & 20 Vict. c. 97), 220
(Punishment of Frauds), 1857 (20 & 21 Vict. c. 54), 98
Ecclesiastical Dilapidations Act, 1871 (34 & 35 Vict. c. 43), 235
Prevention of Crimes Act, 1871 (34 & 35 Vict. c. 112), 194
Judicature Act, 1873 (36 & 37 Vict. c. 66), 195, 220
Real Property Limitation Act, 1874 (37 & 38 Vict. c. 57), 227
Conspiracy and Protection of Property Act, 1875 (38 & 39 Vict. c. 86), 194

Children's Dangerous Performances Act, 1879 (42 & 43 Vict. c. 34), 84
Summary Jurisdiction Act, 1879 (42 & 43 Vict. c. 49), 202
Married Women's Property Act, 1882 (45 & 46 Vict. c. 75), 231
County Courts Act, 1888 (51 & 52 Vict. c. 43), 43
Trustee Act, 1888 (51 & 52 Vict. c. 59), 225, 226
Sale of Goods Act, 1893 (56 & 57 Vict. c. 71), 68
Dogs Act, 1906 (6 Ed. VII. c. 32), 212
Probation of Offenders Act, 1907 (7 Ed. VII. c. 17), 202, 203
Criminal Appeal Act, 1907 (7 Ed. VII. c. 23), 195
Prevention of Crime Act, 1908 (8 Ed. VII. c. 59), 194
County Courts Act, 1919 (9 & 10 Geo. V. c. 73), 43
Administration of Estates Act, 1925 (15 & 16 Geo. V. c. 23), 145
Supreme Court of Judicature (Consolidation) Act, 1925 (15 & 16 Geo. V. c. 49), 195, 236
Workmen's Compensation Act, 1925 (15 & 16 Geo. V. c. 84), 91

INDEX OF CASES

Abbotts v. Barry, 170, 171
Addis v. Gramophone Co., 79
Allbutt v. General Council, etc., 24
Alton v. M.R. Co., 75
Ambrose v. Kerrison, 174
Andrews v. Hawley, 176
Anon (1502), 152
— (1697), 156
Ansell v. Waterhouse, 61
Ashford v. Thornton, 27
Ashmole v. Wainwright, 143, 168, 186
Astley v. Reynolds, 168
Atcheson v. Everitt, 190
Attenborough v. Solomon, 112
Att. Gen. v. Bradlaugh, 193
— Radloff, 195
Austin v. G.W.R. Co., 70, 71

Bahama Islands, Re, 197
Baily v. Birtles, 50
Barber v. Brown, 157
Barber Surgeons of London v. Pelson, 180
Barclay v. Pearson, 140, 160
Barlow v. Browne, 136, 137
Baron v. Husband, 135
Batard v. Hawes, 164
Batthyamy v. Walford, 150, 179
Bavins v. L. & S.W. Bank, 145
Baylis v. Lintott, 78
— Bishop of London, 130, 132, 157
Benningsage v. Ralphson, 46
Bentley v. Episc. Eliens., 197
Birch v. Wright, 176
Black v. Siddaway, 136
Blacker v. Lake & Elliot, 75
Bodega Co., Re, 130
Bonnel v. Foulke, 157
Boson v. Sandford, 60
Boulter v. Clark, 86, 87
Bovill v. Hammond, 185
Bowden, Re, 226
Bowen v. Hall, 34
Bower v. Peate, 36
Bradford Corporation v. Ferrand, 130
Bradshaw v. Beard, 174
Bretherton v. Wood, 61

Brittain v. Lloyd, 161
Brocklebank v. R., 141, 173
Brooke v. Bool, 35
Brown v. Boorman, 65–66
— Dixon, 61
— Howard, 221
Brunsden v. Humphreys, 228
Bryan v. Clay, 179
Bryant v. Herbert, 69, 77, 227
Buckland v. Johnson, 228
Buddle v. Wilson, 60
Burnell v. Minot, 163
Burnett v. Lynch, 144

Cabell v. Vaughan, 62
Camillo Tank S.S. Co. v. Alexandria etc. Works, 167
Cavendish v. Middleton, 157
Chamberlain v. Williamson, 54
Chandler v. Vilet, 220
Child v. Sands, 55
Chinery v. Viall, 80–81
Christopherson v. Bare, 86, 87
Chung Chuck v. R., 194
City of London v. Goree, 179–180
City of York v. Toun, 126, 179
Clare C.C. v. Wilson, 44
Clark v. L.G.O. Co., 75
— Urquhart, 34, 80, 81
Clarke v. A. & N.C.S., 68
— Dickson, 171
Clark's Case, 87
Clifford v. O'Sullivan, 194
Cobb v. Beake, 135–136
Coggs v. Bernard, 95, 101
Collen v. Wright, 177–178
Columbus Co. v. Clowes, 81
Cooth v. Jackson, 130
Couch v. Steel, 146
Courtenay v. Earle, 65
Cowling v. Beachum, 160
Cutter v. Powell, 158

Dale v. Hall, 61
Dalston v. Eyenston, 46
— Tyson, 46
Dalyell v. Tyrer, 72
Dann v. Curzon, 84, 85–86, 89
Darlston v. Hianson, 46

INDEX OF CASES

De Freville *v.* Dill, 69
De Mattos *v.* Gibson, 105–107
Decker *v.* Pope, 163
Deering *v.* Winchelsea, 164
Denison *v.* Ralphson, 46
Denton *v.* G.N.R. Co., 69–70, 153
Denys *v.* Shuckburgh, 224
Derbyshire C.C. *v.* Borough of Derby, 199
Derry *v.* Peek, 70
Dewberry *v.* Chapman, 156
Dickson *v.* Clifton, 48, 61
Dunlop Pneumatic Tyre Co. *v.* Selfridge & Co., 107
Dupleix *v.* De Roven, 150
Duppa *v.* Gerard, 179
Dutch *v.* Warren, 158, 187

Earle *v.* Maugham, 162
Eason *v.* Newman, 15
Edgar *v.* Knapp, 163
Edmunds *v.* Wallingford, 162, 165
Edwards *v.* Bates, 185
— Mallan, 69
Ehrensperger *v.* Anderson, 157
England *v.* Marsden, 165
Everet *v.* Williams, 90
Exchange Banking Co., *Re*, 226

Falcke *v.* Scottish Imperial etc., Co., 151
Feltham *v.* Terry, 48, 144, 146
Finlay *v.* Chirney, 52, 54
Five Steel Barges, 156
Fleming *v.* M.S. & L.R. Co., 78
Foster *v.* Stewart, 121, 140, 145, 174–175, 186
Foulkes *v.* Metrop. D.R. Co., 71, 73
Fraser *v.* Balfour, 35

Game *v.* Harvie, 95
Garbett *v.* Veale, 185
Gelley *v.* Clerk, 95
Gibbs *v.* Guild, 220
Giles *v.* Edwards, 156
Gladwell *v.* Steggall, 69
Gloucestershire Banking Co. *v.* Edwards, 220
Gore *v.* Gibson, 166
Govett *v.* Radnidge, 61
Grant *v.* Gold Exploration Syndicate, 167, 185
Gray *v.* Gee, 34

Green *v.* Duckett, 168
— Greenbank, 68, 80, 214
Grendon *v.* Bishop of Lincoln, 82
Griffinhoofe *v.* Daubuz, 161

Hadley *v.* Baxendale, 41–43
Hambly *v.* Trott, 49, 50, 51
Hardie & Lane *v.* Chiltern, 117, 176
— Chilton, 173
Harington *v.* Hoggart, 160
Harvey *v.* Archbold, 185
Hastelow *v.* Jackson, 140, 160
Hayn *v.* Culliford, 70
Hegarty *v.* Shine, 90
Heilbut *v.* Nevill, 176
Hill *v.* Perrott, 48, 170, 171
Hitchin *v.* Campbell, 134
Holmes *v.* Hall, 156
— Williamson, 163
Holt *v.* Ely, 170
— Markham, 132, 155
Hooper *v.* Treffrey, 138
Horne *v.* Widlake, 82
Hovenden *v.* Milhoff, 166
How *v.* Winterton, 226
Howard *v.* Harris, 100
— Shepherd, 72
— Wood, 169, 172
Howell *v.* Batt, 135
— Young, 221–222
Howlet *v.* Osborne, 95
Hulton *v.* Hulton, 231
Hunter *v.* Walsh, 184
Hyman *v.* Nye, 66

Inchbald *v.* Western etc. Co., 158
Indermaur *v.* Dames, 34, 36, 243–244
Irving *v.* Wilson, 145
Isaack *v.* Clark, 150

Jackson *v.* Rogers, 152, 153
Jacobs *v.* Morris, 130
Johnson *v.* Johnson, 130
— R.M.S.P. Co., 162
Jones *v.* Carter, 138

Kavanagh *v.* Gudge, 85
Kelly *v.* Metrop. R. Co., 71–72
— Solari, 131
Kettlewell *v.* Refuge Assurance Co., 170
Keyse *v.* Powell, 227

INDEX OF CASES

King v. Leith, 145
Kirkman v. Phillips, 224

Lagos v. Grunwaldt, 160
Lamine v. Dorrell, 48, 144, 170
Laycock v. Pickles, 167
Legge v. Tucker, 68
Leglise v. Champante, 55
Les Affréteurs eto. v. Walford, 107
Lethbridge v. Phillips, 100
Lilly v. Hays, 137
Limpus v. L.G.O. Co., 215
Lightly v. Clouston, 48, 121, 140, 145, 174, 175, 186
Lindon v. Hooper, 48, 143, 144, 170, 187
Lloyd v. Burrup, 181
Lodge v. National Union, etc. Co., 130
Loes Case, 95
Longchamp v. Kenny, 158, 184
Lord Strathcona S.S. Co. v. Dominion Coal Co., 105–107
Lubbock v. Tribe, 167

McGruther v. Pitcher, 106
Malcolm v. Scott, 136, 137
Manby v. Scott, 165
Mann v. Owen, 194
Marriot v. Hampton, 131, 132
Marsack v. Webber, 164
Marsh v. Keating, 170
Marshall v. York, etc., R. Co., 62, 70, 71, 73
Martin v. G.I.P.R. Co., 73
Marzetti v. Williams, 79–80, 213–214
Mason, Re, 220
Mason v. Dixon, 53
Mast v. Goodson, 47
Matthew v. Ollerton, 87
Mavor v. Pyne, 158
Mayor of London v. Hunt, 180
Max v. Roberts, 60
Milburn v. Jamaica, etc. Co., 183
Miller v. Atlee, 130
Mellor v. Denham, 199
Meux v. G.E.R. Co., 73
Meyer v. Everth, 176
Mogul S.S. Co. v. McGregor, Gow & Co., 194
Molton v. Camroux, 166
Monro v. Butt, 159

Moore v. Bushell, 136
Moses v. Macferlan, 128, 129, 130, 131, 142
Mosley v. Fosset, 94

Nadan v. R., 194
Nash v. Inman, 182
Neate v. Harding, 141, 135, 170

Orton v. Butler, 145, 146
Osborn v. Gillett, 75
Oughton v. Seppings, 135, 141, 170, 175

Palmer v. Wick, etc. Shipping Co., 210
Parker v. Bristol, etc., R. Co., 186
— Green, 198
Pasley v. Freeman, 13, 34
Pearson (S) Ld. v. Dublin Corporation, 84
Perkinson v. Gilford, 50
Phillips v. Homfray, 52, 145, 176, 186
— London School Board, 130
Pickas v. Guide, 95
Pinchon's Case, 49
Pippin v. Sheppard, 69
Polemis, Re, 41–43
Pontifex v. M.R. Co., 78
Powell v. Layton, 60, 61
— Rees, 170, 176
Pozzi v. Shipton, 62
Prickett v. Badger, 158, 188
Provincial Cinematograph, etc. v. Newcastle-upon-Tyne, etc., 195

Quirk v. Thomas, 209

R. v. Ashwell, 98
— Coney, 84, 87, 88
— Daly, 198
— Denmour, 98
— Kerswill, 199
— Lovett, 202
— McDonald, 98
— Paget, 199
— Robson, 97–98
— Steel, 195
— Tyler, etc., 200
— Whitchurch, 196
Read v. Hutchinson, 176
Redmond v. Wynne, 84

xii   INDEX OF CASES

Rees *v.* Abbott, 57
Rhodes, *Re*, 125, 166
Rice *v.* Read, 176
— Shute, 56, 57
Riches *v.* Bridges, 95
Robbins *v.* Fennell, 137
Robson *v.* Biggar, 196, 198
Roche *v.* Hepman, 220
Rodgers *v.* Maw, 144, 170
Rogers *v.* Price, 174
Rowland *v.* Divall, 156
Rumsey *v.* N.E.R. Co., 171–172
Rylands *v.* Fletcher, 34, 36, 215, 243–244

Sachs *v.* Henderson, 77
Sadler *v.* Smith, 160
— Evans, 143
Schibsby *v.* Westenholz, 150
Seaman *v.* Burley, 196, 198
Seaton *v.* Benedict, 165
Sharpe, *Re*, 221
Sheppard *v.* Baillie, 56
Sherrington's Case, 52
Shuttleworth *v.* Garnet, 126, 181
Sinclair *v.* Brougham, 112, 130, 138–141
Six Carpenters' Case, 89
Slade's Case, 124
Smith *v.* Airey, 127
— Hodson, 145
Sollers *v.* Lawrence, 179
Sorrel *v.* Smith, 34
Southwark etc. Water Co. *v.* Hampton U.D.C., 198
Speake *v.* Richards, 154
Spottiswoode's Case, 163
Starke *v.* Cheeseman, 126
Starkey *v.* Bank of England, 177
Steele *v.* Williams, 173
Steljes *v.* Ingram, 66, 77, 154
Stephens *v.* Badcock, 135
Steven *v.* Bromley, 159

Stone *v.* Rogers, 156
Stuart *v.* Wilkins, 67
Sumpter *v.* Hedges, 159
Symons *v.* Darknoll, 94

Tarry *v.* Ashton, 36
Tattan *v.* G.W.R. Co., 60, 78
Taylor *v.* Bowers, 140
— M.S. & L.R. Co., 77, 209
Tobacco Pipe Makers Co. *v.* Loder, 181
Tollit *v.* Sherstone, 72
Towers *v.* Barrett, 131, 158
Turner *v.* Stallibrass, 69, 77, 101, 227

Valentini *v.* Canali, 133
Valpy *v.* Sanders, 228

Walker *v.* Rostron, 137
— Witter, 150
Warbrook *v.* Griffin, 153
Watson *v.* Russell, 136
Weall *v.* King, 67, 214
Weld-Blundell *v.* Stephens, 42–43
Weston *v.* Downes, 158
Wheatley *v.* Low, 45, 95
Wilkinson *v.* Verity, 225
Williams *v.* Cartwright, 44
— Everett, 136
— Jones, 150
Williamson *v.* Allison, 67
Winkfield, The, 102
Winsmore *v.* Greenbank, 34
Winterbottom *v.* Wright, 74–76
Wolmershausen *v.* Gullick, 164
Woodhall, *Ex parte*, 195
Woodward *v.* Mayor of Battersea, 84
Wooley *v.* Batte, 165

Young *v.* Marshall, 135, 141, 145, 169

INDEX OF YEAR BOOKS

33 Ed. I (R.S.), 8–9; 82
33–35 Ed. I (R.S.), 238; 123
22 Lib. Ass. pl. 41; 45
Pasch. 41 Ed. III, f. 10, pl. 5; 122
Hil. 48 Ed. III, f. 6, pl. 10; 21
Hil. 14 Hen. IV, f. 21, pl. 27; 58
36 Hen. VI, f. 9, pl. 5; 123

39 Hen. VI, f. 44, pl. 7; 123
4 Ed. IV, f. 8; 234
Trin. 11 Ed. IV, f. 6, pl. 10; 66
Mich. 12 Ed. IV, f. 13, pl. 10; 93
Hil. 2 Hen. VII, f. 11, pl. 9; 93
11 Hen. VII, f. 6, pl. 23; 59

Chapter I

THE DEFINITION OF TORT.
GENERAL REMARKS

IN dealing with many branches of English law one regrets that definition should be necessary at all. It is not because one objects to definition on principle, but because our system has at the back of it a long unscientific history which makes a neat framework of it almost impossible. This is peculiarly true of the topic of these lectures—so true that a quite legitimate question at the outset is, "Why need any definition be attempted?" There is no doubt that the law of tort has been well taught and understood with tolerable ease for a long time, though no two teachers or writers of textbooks are agreed as to its exact contents. Moreover, it is a branch of the Common Law which has, as a matter of practice, been adequately kept in touch with the needs of the community. Is there any reason, then, theoretical or practical, why one more effort should be made to determine its province? The answer to this may be taken under the two heads indicated. For theoretical purposes, it is advisable in order to make exposition in teaching more scientific. There is no need to labour the point that a student has a right to know at the beginning of his reading what it is that is under discussion and how he is to distinguish it from other chapters of the law. Besides, every law school worth the name nowadays makes jurisprudence a part of its course and, if the form of the law is to be improved, the analysis of tort will be forced on the student's attention there, whatever attitude of *laissez faire* may be adopted by writers on the law of tort. A case is therefore made out for definition so far as theory goes. On the practical side, arguments in favour of it

THE DEFINITION OF TORT

are quite as strong, if not stronger, and it is singular that this point should have been somewhat ignored hitherto. There has been no lack of perception that a tort is different from a crime, or, according to another line of analysis, that a civil proceeding is different from a criminal proceeding; or, again, that a tort differs from a breach of contract and from a breach of trust; but little trouble has been taken to explain *why* there is any practical need to distinguish a tort from the two last-named divisions of the law. Again, the relation of breach of bailment to tort and to breach of contract has been treated too brusquely, and it was not until Sir Frederick Pollock's book on the *Law of Torts* that real light was thrown upon the puzzling way in which the law of tort and the law of property overlap. But more lamentably neglected than any other boundary has been that between quasi-contract on the one side and tort on the other. In the United States the reproach is much less merited, for two monographs of good repute exist on the subject and a special course is given on it in the Harvard Law School and in many other American universities. If its scientific treatment has been scanty in England, we can plead in excuse, if not in justification, the intricacy of its history; indeed that has been so exasperating in its judicial hesitations and blinking of facts that one is tempted to deny any possibility of treating it scientifically. Finally there are regions of the law scarcely named, much less fully explored, that lie beyond the law of tort, but are yet closely akin to it. Such is quasi-tort or quasi-delict— terms that are almost total strangers to the Common Law, and that encounter quite as much abuse at the hands of the theorists as ignorance on the part of the practitioners.

Now the practical reasons for separating liability in tort as sharply as possible from liability arising from crime, from contract, from trust, from bailment, from

GENERAL REMARKS

the law of property, from quasi-contract, and from quasi-tort will appear in greater detail on a further examination of each of these branches of the law in relation to the law of tort. But, without anticipating the matter of later lectures, it is enough to pick out some salient practical differences which pervade the majority of such topics when contrasted with tortious responsibility. First, there is the variation in remedies. We shall see that an action for unliquidated damages is the characteristic remedy for a tort. Criminal redress has nothing in common with this, though it will be seen when we come to deal with it that in one respect there is a startling resemblance between the two. And though actions for unliquidated damages are quite possible in other branches of the law, yet there are other modes of getting satisfaction as well, and sometimes damages are not appropriate at all in such branches.

Secondly, statutes of limitation often fix different periods of time for barring a remedy or (where that is their effect) for extinguishing a right. Tort, crime, trust, contract and property differ notably here, and one of the first things that any practising lawyer has to consider is whether his client's claim is too stale or not.

Thirdly, the law of status, or, if that term be regarded as too full of ambiguity, the law relating to variation in personal capacity, is not by any means the same in tort as in some other parts of the law. Kings, trade unions, lunatics, minors, corporations, and married women are all subject to different rules under different headings of the system.

These examples will serve, but they are certainly not exhaustive. Death has different effects on different kinds of liability. Again, vicarious responsibility, if not peculiar to the law of tort, occupies a much larger space in it than elsewhere. Then a right of action in tort is in general incapable of assignment. There seems, there-

THE DEFINITION OF TORT

fore, to be no lack of practical reasons in support of the necessity of defining liability in tort. But there is yet another consideration which hovers on the border line between the theoretical and the practical. It is well known that for some years past the case law of the United States of America has been in process of semi-official restatement. This must be sharply distinguished from codification. Restatement of case law takes no account of statute law and is thus not concerned with the whole law. Nor does it profess to do more than to state in reasonable compass and in systematic order rules which the Courts of the separate States and the intermediate and final Courts of Appeal may adopt, if they think fit, as fairly representative of existing judge-made law. Several parts of the law have already been almost completely epitomized in this way. Much of the law of tort has been restated, and it is not without significance that the preliminary part of it, which will presumably contain the essentials of tortious liability in general, has yet to come. Now something of the same sort may be done at some future time in England and, if we try now to mark the bounds of the law of tort, that will be of some help to draftsmen who may have to restate, or perhaps even to codify, the law. It should be added by way of emphatic protestation that the English law of tort is not at present in a condition in which it can be profitably codified or restated, and that the urgency of the problem is nothing like so great as it is in the United States, where some fifty jurisdictions of first instance staffed by judges of very varying ability have made the case law so enormous in bulk and so difficult to ascertain that there is a serious risk of resorting to the curious mode of assessing juristic opinions which was adopted by the Valentinian Law of Citations.

But if there are practical reasons in plenty for constructing a definition of tort, there are also practical

GENERAL REMARKS 5

difficulties in the way of doing it. No completely satisfactory definition has yet been given, and it would be either vanity or optimism to expect complete success where every one else has achieved less than that. The impossibility of it has been pointed out on both sides of the Atlantic. "It is well to state at the outset", said Mr Addison in his *Law of Torts*, "that there is no scientific definition of a tort."[1] So too the learned editor of the late Sir John Salmond's *Law of Torts*.[2] Clerk and Lindsell open their *Law of Torts* with a definition, but they add in the next breath that it is impossible to define the general term, tort, otherwise than by an enumeration of particulars, and they say later that it is also impossible to lay down any general principle to which all actions of tort may be referred.[3] American writers are even more emphatic. Mr Street says in his *Foundations of Legal Liability*:

No definition of tort at once logical and precise can be given. The reason for this is found in the fact that the conception belongs to the highest category in legal thought. Any logical definition of tort must specify the conditions under which delictual liability arises. But there is no typical tort, and in the nature of things it is impossible that a specification of the circumstances under which delictual liability is imposed should have finality.[4]

On the other hand, some of the boldest plans for reconstructing the framework of the law of tort have originated in the United States.[5] It must be confessed that in certain instances they have gone so far beyond anything that practitioners are at present likely to accept that it would be perilous to teach them in the law schools here.

[1] 8th ed. (1906), 1.   [2] 7th ed. (1928), 7 note *g*.
[3] 8th ed. (1929), 1, 3.   [4] (1906), vol. i, Introd. xxv.
[5] E.g. Jeremiah Smith in 30 *Harvard Law Review* (1917), 241–262, 319–334, 409–429.

6 THE DEFINITION OF TORT

But they do at least mark progressive thought, and that is preferable to the view which deprecates definition because exactness in it is impossible. The real obstacles are of two kinds. The first, which has been already noted and of which more will be said almost immediately, is the dead hand of history. It still rests upon the law, but since the copious statutory reforms in procedure of the nineteenth century its burden is much less. The second is more subtle and troublesome because it is not so perceptible. It is that no clear-cut exclusive definition of tort is possible until the complementary task of settling the limits of other fields of the law has been accomplished. This is particularly true of the law of property and far more so of that equatorial belt between contract and tort which shades off into quasi-contract on the one side and into quasi-delict or quasi-tort on the other. As to the former, the law of tort overlaps the law of property and no property lawyer seems to think that it is quite as much his duty to map out what belongs to him as it is incumbent on his brethren in the law of tort to settle the extent of their own claims. As it is, what can a jurisprudent say of the law of personal property? When Joshua Williams wrote his *Law of Real Property* in 1845 he gave the legal profession a classic, but when he followed it up three years later with the *Law of Personal Property* he presented them with a legal pound filled with an incongruous collection of strayed topics— limited companies, ships, bankrupts, actions *ex delicto*, common carriers and the like, or, rather, the unlike. If he had been a man of less learning, the book, or at least its choice of subjects, might have perished with the first edition. But his reputation carried it as an *hereditas damnosa* to the present generation and inspired several other learned lawyers to produce books with the same title. As to quasi-contract, in England, it is not so much an *hereditas damnosa* as an *hereditas jacens*. There is

GENERAL REMARKS

much work still to be done upon it, though Harvard has ably shewn us the way. At present it is regarded here as territory which is more useful for the deportation of undesirable ideas than for colonization. Until it is properly settled there is not much prospect of completely defining tort.

But these difficulties are not insuperable, and even if it is too much to expect complete definition, useful working ones have been put forward. The very critics of them have helped towards something better by pointing out that there is less fault to find with some definitions than with others. None can yet be claimed as canonical, and indeed portions of the subject-matter are at present too intractable to be forced into any mould. Some of this intractability is historical, and this leads us to a brief general historical outline of tort, reserving special matter of this kind for particular topics which are to be distinguished from the law of tort.

Chapter II

GENERAL HISTORICAL OUTLINE

THE segregation of the law of tort from other parts of the law is quite modern. We know of only one monograph in England on the topic earlier than Addison's book which was first published in 1860. In 1720 an anonymous publication appeared entitled, "Law of actions on the case for torts and wrongs, viz. 1. Trover and conversion of goods. 2. Malicious prosecutions. 3. Nusances. 4. Disceits or warranties. 5. On the common custom against carriers, innkeepers, etc. With select precedents". It seems to have been a small book of no special reputation.[1] Indeed, until the latter half of last century no literary effort worth the name was made in England, and the same tale comes from the United States. There, as late as 1853, a legal author of high standing could find no law-book publisher willing to issue a book on the law of torts. He was told that there was "no call for a work on that subject, and there could be no sale for it".[2] Six years later, Francis Hilliard seems to have overcome this objection. In 1859, his work on the *Law of Torts or Private Wrongs* was published in Boston.

But if tort was late in its development as a compartment of the law, the word was familiar early enough. As the Old French "tort" in the eleventh century it has equivalents in Provençal, Spanish and Italian. Derivatively it signifies "wrong" and springs from "tortus" meaning "twisted" or "wrung". In an entirely un-

---

[1] No copy is available to me. Clarke, *Bibliotheca Legum* (1819), 261, states it to be only a new title for "Law of actions. A methodical collection of all adjudged cases", 1710 or 1711.

[2] 30 *Harvard Law Review* (1917), 247.

GENERAL HISTORICAL OUTLINE 9

technical sense it appears as late as Spenser's *Faerie Queene*.[1] Even in legal literature it had a convenient vagueness.[2] The treatise entitled Britton (c. 1290) is one of the earliest of our law books written in French, and one of the chapters, headed "De plusours tortz", treats of a miscellaneous collection of wrongs which vary from the construction of unlicensed castles to the cooking of stale meat for sale.[3] They have nothing in common except that none of them is particularly heinous; great offences like murder, burglary and arson have chapters of their own. Elsewhere in Britton "tort" seems to mean nothing more than "unlawful".[4]

Again, in trespass a common form plea of the defendant usually begins by a denial of "tort and force and all that is against the peace",[5] and "tort" indicates little more than "wrong". At a much later period it still retains this sense, and is equivalent to any legal wrong.[6] Coke in his commentary upon Littleton defines it in the same way,[7] and the compilers of law dictionaries in the seventeenth and eighteenth centuries and even as late as 1835 merely repeat that tort is a French word for injury or wrong.[8] The reports tell the same tale. Tort is used in a case of 1625 to cover all the wrongs alleged against the defendant in an action on the case where he

---

[1] "It was complaind that thou hadst done great tort
　　Unto an aged woman, poore and bare."
[2] Pollock and Maitland, ii, 512 note 2, 534 note 2.
[3] Ed. Nichols (1865), i, 77–85.
[4] *Ibid.* i, 296: "Car a tort apele eyde de la ley, qi a la ley est contrarie". Coke's rendering of this is justified, though he has syncopated the passage. Co. Litt. 158*b*.
[5] Pollock and Maitland, ii, 608; see many examples in *The Court Baron*, Selden Society, vol. iv (1890).
[6] See the examples of 1586, 1609 and 1622 given in the *NewEnglish Dictionary*.
[7] Co. Litt. 158*b*.
[8] Cowell, *Interpreter* (2nd ed. 1684). T. Blount (3rd ed. 1717). Giles Jacob (10th ed. 1782). T. E. Tomlins (4th ed. 1835).

10 GENERAL HISTORICAL OUTLINE

is charged with having broken his contract, committed conversion and, in effect, abused a bailment.[1]

But it is not in the word "tort" that the germs of the department of law now known by that name are to be sought. "Trespass" is its earliest source. In Edward I's time this includes nearly every wrongful act or default, whether it were what we should now call a crime or a tort. It is first heard of in John's reign and it becomes common at the end of Henry III's reign just after the conclusion of the Barons' War[2] in which Simon de Montfort was so prominent and in which he lost his life. Very likely the writ of trespass was one of the agencies in restoring the kingdom to decency after the litter of lawlessness and disorder which every civil war leaves behind it. The action of trespass commenced by the writ was quasi-criminal; that is, it was aimed at serious and forcible breaches of the King's peace. Though it was begun by the injured individual, it ended in the punishment of the defendant as well as in the compensation of the plaintiff. It was more popular than the appeal of felony, because the same exactitude of pleading was not required, and the detested trial of battle was inapplicable. Its scope was also wider, and damages were obtainable.[3] Its usefulness is testified by the fact that in the fourteenth and fifteenth centuries it was deliberately borrowed by some statutes as the appropriate remedy for certain offences. Criminal appeals were obsolescent, there was no organized police force, the judges were often corrupt except in the central courts and were not always trustworthy there.[4] Hence the action of trespass developed speedily. In a loose sense almost any wrongful act or default was at first regarded as a trespass or

[1] *Whyte* v. *Rysden* Cro. Car. 20.
[2] Maitland, *Equity* (1909), 342–344; *Collected Papers* (1911), ii, 154.
[3] Holdsworth, *History of English Law* (3rd ed. 1923), ii, 364.
[4] *Ibid.* 453.

GENERAL HISTORICAL OUTLINE 11

transgressio. It would include even such a serious thing as a felony. But in a narrower sense it was contrasted with felony and signified a less grave wrong. Trespasses were either criminal or civil, if one may anticipate the technical distinction between crime and civil injury which at that period was not at all clearly drawn; indeed it was not until 1694 that the defendant in trespass ceased to be liable to fine and imprisonment, though by that date this was only theoretically true. Criminal trespasses were what we should now call misdemeanours and were punishable upon presentment either before local courts or before the royal justices.[1] As to civil trespasses, an allegation that they were committed *vi et armis* was necessary, though the "force and arms" need be but very slight. They might be (i) trespasses to the person and from these sprang assault and battery and torts of the like nature; (ii) trespasses against goods, or trespass *de bonis asportatis*; (iii) trespasses against land, such as *de clauso fracto*, or breaking another man's "close". Now the writ of trespass was well enough so far as it went, but its limitation is that it applies only to direct harm. And here it was supplemented by the well-known writ of trespass upon the special case. That would cover injury that was indirect or consequential. The trite illustration of the difference between trespass and case is that if I throw a log upon another man's land, that is trespass, for the injury is direct; but if he stumbles over it when it is there and is hurt by it, that is trespass upon the case. The injury is indirect or consequential. Maitland placed the date of the origin of this writ as about 1400. Professor Plucknett points out that as early as 1390 trespass and case are distinguished in a Year Book of Richard II.[2] Moreover, long before

[1] Pollock and Maitland, ii, 510–511. Maitland, *Equity*, 343.
[2] *History of the Common Law* (1929), 283. *Year Books 13 Richard II* (Ames Foundation, 1929), 104. Maitland, *Equity*, 360.

12   GENERAL HISTORICAL OUTLINE

this, the Statute of Westminster II, 13 Edward I, c. 24 (1285), commonly called the Statute *in consimili casu*, had not only emphasized the need of new writs, but had established means for creating them, subject to one notable limit. The words of the translation of the Statute must be given in full, for there is one puzzling point about their interpretation which seems never to have been realized, much less solved.

> And whensoever from henceforth it shall fortune in the Chancery, that in one case a writ is found, and in like case falling under like law, and requiring like remedy [is found none], the Clerks of the Chancery shall agree in making a writ, or shall adjourn the plaintiffs until the next Parliament, and the cases shall be written in which they cannot agree, and be referred until the next Parliament; and by consent of men learned in the law, a writ shall be made [that it may not hereafter happen that the King's Court shall fail] in ministering justice unto complainants.[1]

The clerks of the Chancery, the *officina brevium*, had evidently been turning away people who applied to them for the only thing by which a civil action could be begun—a writ.[2] Henceforward they can vary existing writs to cover claims analogous to them, but, if they cannot agree, they must refer such cases to the next Parliament. It seems to be implied, though it certainly is not expressed, in the Statute that the clerks are also to refer to Parliament cases where no analogy to an existing writ exists, as well as cases upon which they cannot agree. Maitland thought that little use was made of the power given by the Statute to the clerks of the Chancery except to vary the writs of trespass so as to suit special cases.[3] But this is somewhat inconsistent

---

[1] *Statutes at Large.*

[2] Sir Frederick Pollock, however, considers that the Statute did not confer new power, but regulated and restrained an indefinite power of framing writs which had been claimed by the royal officers. *Torts* (13th ed.), 551 note *a*.   [3] *Equity*, 345–346.

GENERAL HISTORICAL OUTLINE 13

with the rapid growth of *Registrum Brevium* between 1285 and about 1390 when the distinction between trespass and case is emerging. If the Register was not swelled by writs of trespass on the case until this latter date, what sort of writs did account for its increasing size? It is submitted that many of them must have been due to adaptations made under the Statute of 1285, and indeed close personal acquaintance with the development of one particular writ—that of conspiracy—confirms this suggestion.[1] The point, though its importance is historical only, is that it has been rather hastily assumed that some actions in tort are traceable to trespass upon the case when it is possible that they are directly due to the Statute of 1285, instead of coming from it indirectly by way of trespass upon the case.[2] In other words, the Statute may well have been their parent and not their grandparent. One of these doubtful instances is the modern tort of deceit. In early times deceit merely indicated swindling a court of justice in one way or another, but in the modern form in which we know it, it was recognized in *Pasley* v. *Freeman* (1789).[3] Whether it is to be regarded as remedied by an action upon the case or by an action of trespass upon the case is not clear. In *Pasley* v. *Freeman*, Lord Kenyon C.J. and Grose J. regarded the old writ of deceit as independent of trespass upon the case. Fitzherbert in his *Natura Brevium* is confusing upon the point, but his classification of writs is little more than by rule of thumb. Maitland puts deceit under trespass upon the case,[4] but he

---

[1] Winfield, *History of Conspiracy* (1921), chap. ii. See too the author's article on "Writ" in the current ed. of *Encyclopædia Britannica*.

[2] Blackstone's attribution of writs of trespass upon the case to both the Common Law and the Statute of 1285 (*Comm*.iii, 122–123) is a mere guess.

[3] 3 T. R. 51.

[4] *Equity*, 346. *Contra*, Jenks, *History of English Law* (4th ed. 1928), 139. Ames, *Lectures on Legal History* (1913), 442–443, is ambiguous; but possibly because the point is not in his mind. Blackstone, *Commentaries*, iii, 123–124, speaks merely of "an action on the case".

14   GENERAL HISTORICAL OUTLINE

cites no authority for so doing. We should incline to the other view, and prefer to reckon deceit and trespass upon the case as distinct in origin and to hold that variations of the writ of deceit were quite possible by virtue of the Statute of 1285 and that they actually occurred.[1] There is no reason to suppose that other writs were not evolved in similar fashion. Trespass upon the case has unquestionably been responsible for many of our modern torts; but action upon the case in its simplest form, without the intervention of trespass and based merely upon the Statute *in consimili casu*, was perhaps a more fruitful source of new wrongs than has been commonly supposed. However, it would be unprofitable to decide between the competing claims of these two roots of legal development, and in fact there is not enough material to make nice discrimination possible. When once the writ of trespass upon the case was recognized, the clerks of the Chancery, if they were willing to allow a variation of a writ, would scarcely trouble themselves to answer the theoretical question, "If we issue this writ, are we adapting the writ of trespass upon the case, or are we acting upon the Statute of 1285 as our primary authority?" The numerous Abridgements and Digests of the law from Statham onwards leave us equally puzzled as to whether the caption "Action upon the case" had any exact meaning to the compilers. With most of them it seems to have included actions of trespass upon the case, but that throws no light on the historical problem which has just been mooted.

Between the two of them, however, it is safe to say that to trespass upon the case, and case *simpliciter*, we owe most of our law of tort. The part which the former played in the development of the law of contract need be noticed here only to remind us that *assumpsit* was

[1] Holdsworth, *op. cit.* iii, 429, regards the boundaries of trespass and deceit on the case as a little difficult to define.

GENERAL HISTORICAL OUTLINE 15

established about the year 1500. Later, more must be said of this in differentiating tort from contract and quasi-contract.

One or two important illustrations may be given of nominate torts which have sprung from one or other of these sources. The tort of conversion is, of course, traceable to trover, and trover in its turn goes back to detinue *sur trover*. This was the "new found haliday" that upset the conservative Littleton in 1455.[1] Now detinue in origin has nothing to do with trespass, and it follows that the germ of trover must be "case" and not "trespass upon the case". It must be confessed that a student will find it hard to reconcile some of the statements as to the growth of trover into conversion, but that does not concern us here.[2] Another tort which is of late origin was born of either "case" or trespass upon the case. Which of these was the parent is a problem of no importance and it is very improbable that it can be solved. For negligence as an independent tort came into being in the early nineteenth century[3] and by that time the centre of gravity in legal procedure had shifted almost entirely from the writ to the declaration. The framing of new writs had ceased, and what the Courts concentrated attention on was not so much the document which summoned the defendant as the details of

---

[1] Y.B. Trin. 33 Hen. VI, ff. 26–27, pl. 11. Ames, *op. cit.* 82 and note 4; and 83.

[2] It is difficult to ascertain from the historians the date at which trover may be regarded as established. Maitland, *Equity*, 365, says it "begins to appear about the middle of the sixteenth century". Holdsworth, *op. cit.* iii, 351, says it was settled by that time that an action of trespass on the case [trover] lay against a bailee and one who was a finder or who had come by the goods otherwise. His citations do not support this; nor, as to the finder, is this consistent with Ames, *Lectures*, 85 (*Eason v. Newman*). What seem to be confused are the *origin* of trover and the development of its *scope*.

[3] 42 L.Q.R. 184, 195.

16   GENERAL HISTORICAL OUTLINE

the claim which was made against him.[1] Much the
same applies to other nominate torts which have come
into being during the eighteenth and succeeding centuries. But of these we can speak more fully when we
have marked the stages by which the English system
has advanced from a period in which isolation of tort as
a separate branch of the law was impossible to a period
in which it is discernible, if not completely definable.
We need go no farther back for the first of these periods
than Sir Henry Finch's Νομοτεχνία, which was first
published in law-French in 1613. It deserves serious
attention, for not only did Blackstone owe a good
deal to it, but it also represents the only attempt at a
scientific discourse on the law in the century between
St German's *Doctor and Student* (1st ed. 1523) and
Coke's *Institutes* (1628–1641). Finch's style is crabbed
and much of his arrangement appears to be confused.
But these are faults which start to the eye of a modern
critic whose duty it is to recollect the difficulties inherent in Finch's task. Nothing will be gained from his
book, and a wrong value will be set upon it, unless it is
borne in mind that any attempt to give a rational account
of our law as it stood at that time shewed conspicuous
courage, and that the very reason why his effort was
successful in his generation was because later standards
would judge it to be a partial failure. For if it had presented a satisfying scientific plan of our law, it would
have been useless as a practical demonstration of it.
Finch did his best with matter that was in several respects intractable. Where he broke down, no man could
help breaking down. He was not writing jurisprudence
in vacuo, but was endeavouring to elicit some theory of a
body of law of which he was a distinguished practitioner.[2]

[1] *Encyclopædia Britannica* (current ed.), article "Writ". Holdsworth,
op. cit. viii, 248–249.
[2] Winfield, *Chief Sources of English Legal History*, 330–332.

GENERAL HISTORICAL OUTLINE 17

The book was translated by its author and republished in English in 1627 after his death. This is no mere matter of bibliographical curiosity, for there are serious differences between the two editions. It has been said that the English version, being the product of second thoughts, is a great improvement on the French,[1] but this is by no means invariably the case.[2] The treatise is in four books. The first takes a general view of the law. The second is taken up chiefly with "Possessions" and as a possession is "whatsoever may be injoyed", we can roughly identify it with "property". The third book comprises "justice in the punishment of offences"; the fourth begins with courts, passes to writs, and handles the divisions of actions. It is with these last two books that we are mainly concerned, and it will simplify discussion if analyses of them be appended. They are founded on the 1627 edition with a record of the more serious variations in the earlier publication.

In order to assess the value of Finch's classifications, it is necessary to look at them from two points of view:

(1) The substantive law.

(2) The law of procedure.

If he had attempted to deal with (1) without trying to co-ordinate it with (2), he would have spoiled the book as an account of both theory and practice, whatever merit it might have achieved as a development of theory only. Procedure was, at the period of which he wrote, not so much a vehicle for carrying the plaintiff's claim to success as an integral part of the claim itself. Or, to vary the metaphor, it was rather what its skin is to an animal than what clothes are to a human being.

Now Finch attained useful results in working out the scheme of (2) in connection with that of (1).

[1] Holdsworth, *op. cit.* v, 399.

[2] E.g. Book II, chap. XVIII, is much more intelligible in the earlier, than in the later, edition.

18 GENERAL HISTORICAL OUTLINE

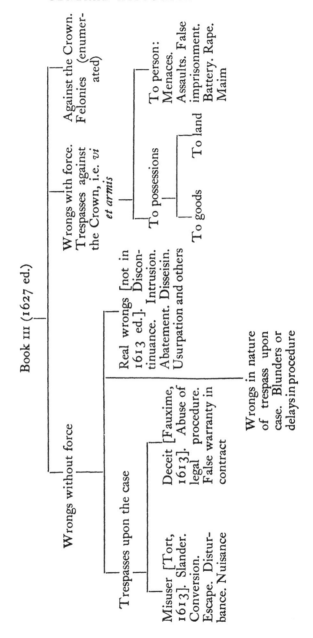

GENERAL HISTORICAL OUTLINE 19

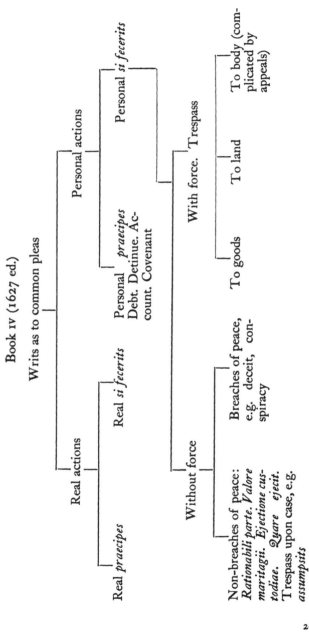

20   GENERAL HISTORICAL OUTLINE

As to (1), most of what we should call "torts" appear in his "Wrongs without force" and "Wrongs with force" (*ante*, 19). When he dealt with the procedural side of law, he forged a link between (1) and (2) in his "Personal actions" under the sub-heading "Personal *si fecerit te securums*". The characteristic of a personal action is that it claims damages.

Of any definition of "tort", Finch is quite innocent. He divided the law (if we may paraphrase his arrangement) into Property, Wrongs, and Procedure. If he had been pressed to say what "tort" meant, he would probably have replied, "any unlawful injury to person or to property". In his mind no technical signification attached to it. It was a mere doublet of "unlawful wrong". We shall find many ragged edges in Finch if we seek to mark off torts, as we understand the phrase, from crimes, breaches of contract, breaches of bailment and breaches of trust.

(i) First as to crimes. A broad view shews that his "Offences against the Crown" may be segregated as pure crimes. They are felonies. The only complication with respect to them is on the procedural side, and that is due to the fact that appeals of felony were in the nature of private litigation. At the opposite pole, one can isolate as civil wrongs his "Wrongs without force". The hitch here is that wrongs like deceit and conspiracy were breaches of the peace. Midway between these poles are "Wrongs with force". They are capable of being treated either as wrongs against the Crown or as wrongs against a private person. As Finch says of Trespasses, "The torts here...are all manner of trespasses... *vi* or *contra pacem*; for, though at the suit of the King they are offences against his crown and dignity, yet as regards the party, they are mere personal torts".[1]

---

[1] 1613 ed. Book II, chap. XIV.

GENERAL HISTORICAL OUTLINE 21

It thus appears that there is a considerable overlap of crime with tort. But after all that is so at the present day. Where we are more fortunate is in the sharper separation of civil from criminal remedies.

(ii) Breaches of contract and breaches of bailment. Here Finch simply reflects the confused thought of his era about a legal idea—contract—which was perplexing because of its rapid growth.

He classed contracts and bailments under "possession" and, in effect, under a sub-heading, "Transfer of personal chattels".[1] From Book II, chap. XVI, the title of which is "Of personal charges, and torts", we learn that acts (i.e. transfers) special to them are their pledging or their receipt to the use of another, and that receipt to the use of another is by bailment or otherwise. His description of bailment bears a resemblance to the present definition of it.[2] Then comes what he has to say about contract. "Personal charges are obligation and covenant, both by deed; and *assumpsit* which is by parol." For *assumpsit* there must be good consideration. He develops this, and says that "the torts are in detaining the goods, not rendering an account, not performing a contract, covenant, *assumpsit*, or the like". He slips in at the end of his discussion of bailments and contracts a reference to "certaine (as it were) contracts in law, though not arising from the speciall agreement of the parties". They are what would now be called quasi-contracts.

One might have expected that Finch would have added more about *assumpsit* in Book III under "Trespasses upon the case", but there is nothing approaching it except a few words about "if a smith cloy my horse";[3]

---

[1] Here the 1627 ed. makes such intricate nonsense of the 1613 ed. that one suspects posthumous garbling by the publisher or editor.

[2] It is much the same in both editions.

[3] The reference is to Y.B. Hil. 48 Ed. III, f. 6, pl. 10.

22 GENERAL HISTORICAL OUTLINE

and in Book IV there is a bare reference to *assumpsits*.[1] Indeed, in handling contract and bailment, Finch made little further progress than St German who wrote nearly a century earlier.[2] Both authors seem to telescope property and obligation, or rights *in rem* and rights *in personam*.

(iii) Breaches of trust. Finch is almost silent about trusts, and that has been noted as one of the defects of his book.[3]

To sum up, the only characteristic of Finch's equivalent to modern "torts" is that they were redressible by personal actions, and the mark of a personal action was its claim for damages. Usually, too, the particular form of personal action applicable to torts is a *si fecerit te securum*, not a *praecipe quod reddat*. The *si fecerit* writ proceeds upon the assumption that the defendant has already done something wrong, while the *praecipe* merely tells the sheriff to bid the defendant to do or permit something and no further steps against him would be taken if he obeyed. But here again there are loose ends in Finch's classification. First, some torts are redressible, at least primarily, by "real actions". These are what he calls "real wrongs" and they include "Discontinuance", etc. The difficulty of classifying them was due to the possibility of claiming not only restitution but, in some cases, damages as well.[4] Secondly, the

---

[1] Ed. 1627, p. 304. See table *ante*, p. 19.

[2] *Doctor and Student* (ed. W. Muchall, 1787), Dialogue II, chaps. XXIV, XXVIII: "It is not much argued in the laws of England what diversity is between a contract, a concord, a promise, a gift, a loan, or a pledge, a bargain, a covenant, or such other. For the intent of the law is to have the effect of the matter argued, and not the terms". Dial. II, chap. XXIV, p. 176.

[3] Holdsworth, *op. cit.* v, 401.

[4] Finch was not confident about his own arrangement here. "Real wrongs" do not appear in the 1613 ed. Blackstone, *Comm.* iii, 167, describes them under the general term "Ouster" and says the universal remedy is "the restitution or delivery of possession...and, in some cases, damages also for the unjust amotion". *Ibid.* 174.

GENERAL HISTORICAL OUTLINE 23

inclusion of *assumpsits* under "Personal *si fecerit te securums* without force" puts *assumpsits* in some queer company, and to a modern eye emphasizes the great difficulty that the lawyers of that era had in perceiving the difference of contract from tort. Thirdly, Maitland pointed out the importance attached by Finch to the division of actions into *praecipe quod reddats* and *si fecerit te securums*.[1] No doubt Finch made this dichotomy a useful starting-point for a rough distinction between contract (debt, detinue, account, covenant) and tort; but the distinction is rough because *assumpsit* goes under tort. Nor must it be forgotten that Finch's main division of writs is "Real actions"—"Personal actions". If, as Maitland says, that cardinal division was of little account, the *praecipe—si fecerit* division was of still less for our purposes.

Of the institutional writers who succeeded Finch, Coke does not help us, for the methods which he pursued in composing the *Institutes* precluded the necessity for attempting an analysis of tort. But Blackstone in his *Commentaries* certainly improved upon Finch. He divides "wrongs" (which he describes merely as privations of rights) into public and private. Public wrongs, which in effect signify crimes, are treated in Book IV; private wrongs in Book III. But a considerable portion of this latter book would have to be redistributed to make its arrangement square with that of modern exposition. The first two chapters are taken up with the redress of such wrongs by the acts of the parties and by the operation of law. The next four are occupied with an account of the Courts. Chap. VII to XVII are those which are really cognate to private injuries as a branch of the substantive law. Chap. XVIII to XXVII conclude the book and deal with procedure in a civil action.

[1] App. A to Pollock, *Torts* (13th ed.), 586–587. Finch is responsible for these Anglicized plurals.

24   GENERAL HISTORICAL OUTLINE

Chap. VII deals with private wrongs remediable in Ecclesiastical and Maritime Courts; and it certainly shews that Blackstone did not shrink from including such injuries under private wrongs, and, if we make the recovery of unliquidated pecuniary damages the test of a tort, we must admit that there were ecclesiastical torts (e.g. withholding of tithes where there was no dispute as to the right to demand them),[1] and that there were, and still are, maritime torts. This is worth noticing, for the tendency in some quarters nowadays is to exclude from the law of torts civil injuries which are cognizable in courts other than those of Common Law jurisdiction as it existed prior to the Judicature Acts. It is questionable whether this is justifiable. At any rate no support for it is to be procured from Blackstone. His treatment of the prerogative writs of *procedendo*, *mandamus*, and prohibition at the end of Chap. VII is less happy, and it will save repetition if we briefly dispose of it before we put forward our own definition of tort. *Mandamus* is often an effective writ for restoring an injured person as nearly as may be to his position before he was injured, without, however, awarding him pecuniary damages. A typical instance is that of a practitioner who alleges that he has been struck off the register, without lawful cause, by the General Council of Medical Education.[2] His chief grievance is not so much that he has suffered damages as that he is subject to very serious disabilities unless his name be restored to the register. He may succeed in doing this by procuring the issue of a writ of *mandamus* to the General Council; but he does not thereby claim damages, and the possibility of doing this is an essential element in an action of tort. However much writers disagree on other points, they are unani-

[1] *Comm.* iii. 88–89.
[2] E.g. *Allbutt* v. *General Council of Medical Education* (1889), 23 Q.B.D. 400.

GENERAL HISTORICAL OUTLINE 25

mous on this one. Is a claim upon a *mandamus* therefore an exception to the general rule, and can it be said that it is founded on tort, though there is no demand for damages? No, for the writ is granted only to ensure the performance of a *public* duty.[1] It belongs to public law, whereas, vague as this division is, it is generally conceded that the law of tort falls within private law. *Mandamus* is consequently not a remedy in tort at all.

Chap. VIII and its successors handle the remedies of private wrongs in the "public and general courts of common law". At the outset of his discussion of private wrongs, Blackstone links them with the trichotomy of actions into personal, real and mixed.[2] But his development of the substantive law is not smothered by procedure. Indeed, it is surprising how clear and readable his narrative is when we recollect that most of the great procedural reforms had still to come. Most of the torts which are familiar to us are analysed with a poise and clearness that compare favourably with the jejune and highly technical descriptions to be found in Finch. This is not to say that there are not plenty of puzzling classifications in Book III. They will appear after we have noted Blackstone's definition of personal actions.

"Personal actions", he says, "are such whereby a man claims a debt, or personal duty, or damages in lieu thereof: and, likewise whereby a man claims a satisfaction in damages for some injury done to his person or property. The former are said to be founded on contracts, the latter upon *torts*, or wrongs....Of the former nature are all actions upon debts or promises; of the latter, all actions for trespasses, nusances, assaults, defamatory words, and the like."[3]

Real actions were also remedies for some private wrongs;

[1] Shortt, *Informations, Mandamus and Prohibition* (1887), 231–232. Blackstone's definition of *mandamus* is accepted by the author; *ibid.* 223–226.
[2] *Comm.* iii, 117.   [3] *Ibid.*

26 GENERAL HISTORICAL OUTLINE

in them the demandant claimed title to some species of real property, but they were unpopular owing to their inordinate delays and the meticulous care needed in their management, and they were becoming obsolete in Blackstone's time.[1] They can be ignored in ascertaining his conception of the law of tort. But mixed actions cannot so easily be brushed aside. They were for the recovery of real property coupled with a claim for damages. Waste is an example and there is a good deal about it in Book III. It is one explanation of the fact that even nowadays waste is a topic in books on the law of torts as well as in those on real property.

But injuries to real property bulk more largely in Blackstone's "private injuries" than in our law of tort. Chap. x to xvi cover them, and here it was impossible for him to escape from the domination of remedies. If we are better off than he was in this respect, we seem to be just as far from deciding the relation of the law of property to the law of tort, chiefly because we cannot make up our minds whether the main basis of law is Right or Duty. However, a personal action (i.e. an action for damages) may be regarded as the main Blackstonian test for a private wrong. So far we get a fairly visible line between it and a crime, though there is no definition of tort. It is true that two possible elements of confusion occur. Blackstone inherited from Finch the distinction between private injuries without force or violence (e.g. slander, breach of contract), and those with force and violence (e.g. battery, false imprisonment), and he makes it, at least in theory, one of considerable importance.[2] But it was really a legacy that he need never have accepted. The only practical use which he makes of it is to call attention to the fact that injuries with force and violence are also crimes.[3] He

[1] *Comm.* iii, 117–118.   [2] *Ibid.* 118–119.
[3] *Ibid.* 121–122.

GENERAL HISTORICAL OUTLINE 27

certainly says that in strictness (presumably in the same civil proceeding) a fine ought to be paid to the King for a trespass *vi et armis*, as well as a private satisfaction to the injured party; but while that held good in Finch's time, it had long ceased to do so before Blackstone lectured.[1] Hence this blurring of the line between civil injury and crime had disappeared, for though a wrong like battery might be both actionable and indictable, the proceedings were entirely different in each case. The other intrusion of civil proceedings into criminal was the appeal of felony, but it was very little in use[2] and its employment would probably have astonished Blackstone's generation nearly as much as it did the public in 1818.[3]

But if civil injuries and crimes were distinguishable with tolerable clearness, the differences between tort on the one hand and breach of trust, breach of contract, and breach of bailment on the other were not sharply drawn. English law was not yet ripe enough for this. The jurisprudential position of uses and trusts gave Blackstone little trouble because it never occurred to him that they needed analysis in relation to other legal conceptions. They figure under modes of conveying things in his second Book and under proceedings in Courts of Equity in his fourth Book.[4] As to breach of contract, it is redressible, like any other private wrong, by a personal action; but Blackstone's account of contract is a rather scattered affair which appears not only in Book II under "Rights of Things"[5] but also in Book III under "Private wrongs".[6] Still, it is detachable from obligation arising from tort by being reckoned as a *chose in action* or a species of property.[7] This is not

---

[1] *Ante*, p. 11.   [2] *Comm.* iv, 312–313.
[3] *Ashford* v. *Thornton*, 1 B. & Ald. 405.
[4] *Comm.* ii, 327; iv, 431, 439.   [5] *Ibid.* ii, 396–397.
[6] *Ibid.* iii, 154.   [7] *Ibid.* ii, 396–397.

28 GENERAL HISTORICAL OUTLINE

convincing, but shortly afterwards he gets the true foundation of it as "an agreement upon sufficient consideration, to do or not to do a particular thing",[1] and this element of agreement at once marks it off from tortious liability. Bailment he regarded as merely a species of contract of common occurrence.[2] When, in a later Book, he came to develop the difference of express contract from implied contract, he got some odd results in his effort to conjure *assumpsit* into some compact shape. Express contracts were easily disposed into debts, covenants, and promises.[3] But implied contracts included two main varieties,[4] the first of which would now be relegated to a museum of political antiquities. It was the social contract, which Blackstone accepted in general as an adequate account of the relation of the subject to his ruler, and in particular as the legal reason why a man should pay a judgment debt or a penalty to a common informer. The second main variety had six subdivisions. The first two of these may now be regarded as ordinary contracts. The next, the duty to repay to another his money which has been had and received, is now reckoned as quasi-contractual. The fourth (the obligation of A to recoup B who has expended money for A's use at A's request) is probably contractual if it is binding at all. The fifth (account stated) is perhaps no more than an incident in the proof of a real contract. The correct classification of the sixth is still a matter of acute controversy. It consisted of what Blackstone called the "class of contracts, implied by reason and construction of law" which "arises upon this supposition, that every one who undertakes any office, employment, trust, or duty, contracts with those who employ or entrust him, to perform it with integrity, diligence, and skill".[5] Current opinion is almost

[1] *Comm.* ii, 441. [2] *Ibid.* ii, 446, 451. [3] *Comm.* iii, 154.
[4] *Ibid.* iii, 159 *seq.* [5] *Ibid.* iii, 165.

GENERAL HISTORICAL OUTLINE 29

unanimous that Blackstone was wrong in calling this "implied contract", and in almost entire disagreement as to what he ought to have called it; but of these last four subdivisions, more hereafter.[1]

We can sum up the results obtainable from Blackstone by saying that he regarded what we now style a tort as a civil injury usually (but not invariably) remediable by an action for damages, that it is distinguishable in his *Commentaries* from crime and breach of contract, but that the relation of contract itself to bailment and quasi-contract is still ill-developed because the limits of these subjects were not clearly perceived—much less fixed—by the eighteenth-century courts. As for trusts, their implication with other parts of the system did not present itself to Blackstone.

We have indicated that, thanks to Blackstone's remarkable abilities as an expositor, his chapters on private injuries of a tortious kind were well abreast of the scientific side of English law. *Assumpsit* was the most refractory topic in this part of the *Commentaries*, but its treatment there, though not without difficulty for a later generation to whom forms of action are of little account, is infinitely superior to what will be found in the contemporary alphabetical Abridgments of the law. Viner, in the second edition of his *Abridgment* (1791–1794), has a single page on "Tort", and the seven references there connote no closer meaning than "legal wrong".[2] If we want anything more fruitful than this, we must seek it under quite different titles.[3] Moreover, treatises of the early nineteenth century were not a step farther forward than Blackstone. In Chitty's *Practice of the*

---

[1] Chap. VII.

[2] Vol. xx, 305. In Bacon's *Abridgment* there is no such title.

[3] E.g. "Actions (joinder)". Cf. Bacon, *Abridgment* (7th ed. 1832), vol. i, 58, "Actions in General (C) In what cases distinct things may be had in the same action".

30   GENERAL HISTORICAL OUTLINE

Law, the author emphasizes the importance of ascertaining whether a private injury is "a tort without contract, or a mere breach of contract, or of what other precise nature".[1] He goes on to say that torts affect the person absolutely or relatively, or personal or real property, and what he includes thereunder is very much what is to be found in the law of tort now. No further separate treatment of the meaning of "tort" appears in his work. "Contracts in general" are a minor species of "Rights to personalty". In "Rights of persons" both criminal and civil remedies are inserted. So too, under other heads, remedies are a cross-section through torts and crimes. The whole work is overlaid with procedure. Still, Chitty was writing for practitioners in London, not lecturing to students at Oxford.

If we wonder why it was that for more than half a century after Blackstone there was scarcely a single effort made to work out in detail, and to improve upon, his institutional methods, the solution is not difficult. The complexity of actions in the courts has been regarded as one of the obstacles that blocked progress. No doubt there is something in this, but be it remembered that Blackstone himself surmounted it. What is much nearer the truth is that legal education had perished in the Inns of Court and was scarcely reborn in the Universities. As for the Inns of Court, a young man, "with no public direction in what course to pursue his inquiries, no private assistance to remove the distresses and difficulties which will always embarrass a beginner", was expected "to sequester himself from the world, and by a tedious lonely process to extract the theory of law from a mass of undigested learning; or else by an assiduous attendance on the courts to pick up theory and practice together, sufficient to qualify him for the ordinary run of business".[2] For the Universities, there

---

[1] 2nd ed. (1834), i, 12–13.   [2] Blackstone, *Comm.* i, 31.

GENERAL HISTORICAL OUTLINE 31

was the Vinerian Chair at Oxford, but Blackstone's immediate successors in it were men of no great mark. At Cambridge, the Downing Professorship of the Laws of England was not founded till 1800, and its first occupant was credited with nothing more original than an edition of Blackstone's *Commentaries*. There was Bentham, of course, but he was more instructive to an ardent, not to say impatient, law reformer than to any one who wished to evolve a theory of our law that bore some relation to legal facts.

Enough has been said in this chapter to shew the general historical difficulties that have made perception of tort as a technical division of the law such a tardy affair. The special historical obstacles which make its severance from contract and other branches of the law a troublesome matter even now will be explained in their proper place.

Chapter III

TORT DEFINED

WE have reached a point where a definition of tort appropriate to current law must be attempted. The chief aim of these lectures is to determine the province of the law of tort, and we cannot mark the boundaries between it and other regions of the law without hazarding at the outset some positive description of tort itself. Hazardous it is, for it may be doubted whether complete definition is possible. It is as well to emphasize here that, if one is to be framed at all, it must be in reasonable touch with the law as it is and not simply as it ought to be; and one characteristic of the English practitioner is his suspicion of unfamiliar terms. It is suggested that the following definition is less open to criticism than any other.

Tortious liability arises from the breach of a duty primarily fixed by the law: such duty is towards persons generally and its breach is redressible by an action for unliquidated damages.

Other possible definitions must be considered in the last chapter. It would be unwise to discuss them here, as that would assume a close acquaintance with quasi-contract and associated topics, all which follow after this chapter.

We have referred to "tortious liability" and have not tried to define a "tort", and this seems to be a fitting place to settle what is the foundation of liability in tort. Is it based on the principle that (1) all injuries done to another person are torts, unless there be some justification recognized by law; or on the principle that (2) there is a definite number of torts outside which liability in

TORT DEFINED   33

tort does not exist? According to the first theory, if I injure my neighbour he can sue me in tort whether the wrong happens to have a particular name like assault, battery, deceit, defamation, or whether it has no special title at all. According to the second theory, I can injure my neighbour as much as I like, without fear of his suing me in tort, provided my conduct does not fall under some rubric like assault, battery, deceit, defamation. If the first principle is the correct one, the courts have full power to create new torts, or (more consistently with judicial caution) to extend the law of tort without any baptismal ceremony for each extension. But the second principle presents us with a row of pigeon-holes, each labelled with the name of a particular tort, and if an injury cannot be fitted into one of these, whatever the plaintiff's remedy may be, he has none in tort.

Sir Frederick Pollock has consistently adopted the first view.[1] The chief British champion of the second was the late Sir John Salmond.[2] He says: "Just as the criminal law consists of a body of rules establishing specific offences, so the law of torts consists of a body of rules establishing specific injuries. Neither in the one case nor in the other is there any general principle of liability".

I have been at some pains to shew elsewhere that, with all deference to the high authority of Sir John, the first view, and not the second, is the one which is more consistent with the English law of tort.[3] There is no need to repeat the arguments there set forth, but it may be as well to summarize them. Incidentally, the learned editor of Salmond's book seems to concur in them, so that the necessity for enlarging upon them is still further

[1] *Law of Torts* (13th ed.), 21–23.
[2] *Law of Torts* (7th ed.), § 2 (3).
[3] 27 *Columbia Law Review* (1927), I–II.

W P   3

34 TORT DEFINED

diminished.[1] The greatest difficulty in the way of those who support the second, or "inexpansibility", theory is the development of the law of tort itself. From first to last it has steadily grown upwards and outwards. Innominate torts concealed behind the convenient shelter of "action upon the case" have become nominate torts, and at the present day it may safely be said, not only that there are specific torts in search of specific names, but also that the general principle forbidding the infliction of unjustifiable harm upon one's neighbour is a lively root for further development. Here are some of the nominate torts whose introduction can be definitely traced in our history: malicious prosecution (*temp.* Elizabeth); unlawfully enticing away a wife from her husband (1745);[2] the converse tort of enticing away a husband from his wife (1923);[3] deceit (1789);[4] negligence (early nineteenth century);[5] the rule in *Indermaur* v. *Dames*[6] as to dangerous structures (1866); the rule in *Rylands* v. *Fletcher* (1868);[7] malicious inducement of breach of contract (1881).[8] Whether there be an independent tort of conspiracy or not, only another decision of the House of Lords can tell us. Their latest pronouncement leaves open the possibility of such a wrong[9] and it has the advantage of a recognized name waiting for it. Much the same considerations apply to the "invasion of personal privacy", a tort which has been recognized as such in some jurisdictions in the United States and which is well known in India in Gujerat and the North-West Provinces. In England, it

[1] *Law of Torts* (7th ed.), 64.
[2] *Winsmore* v. *Greenbank* Willes, 577.
[3] *Gray* v. *Gee* 39 T.L.R. 429. [4] *Pasley* v. *Freeman* T.R. 51.
[5] 42 *Law Quarterly Review*, 184–201.
[6] L.R. 1 C.P. 274; 2 C.P. 311. [7] L.R. 3 H.L. 330.
[8] *Bowen* v. *Hall* 6 Q.B.D. 333.
[9] *Sorrell* v. *Smith* [1925] A.C. 700. So too the *dicta* in *Clark* v. *Urquhart* [1930] A.C. 28, 51–52, 76.

TORT DEFINED

is probably only the House of Lords which now has a free hand to pronounce judicially in favour of its existence.[1] On the other hand, one or two other torts are still innominate and their existence is doubtful or not completely established. Thus it is not clear whether an action for damages will lie for maliciously causing the retirement of a naval officer. The House of Lords left this point open in *Fraser* v. *Balfour*.[2] Another tort of recent origin, if indeed it really exists at all, which has no definite name, is attributable to *Brooke* v. *Bool*.[3] It is worth some attention as illustrating both the vitality of the law of tort and the judicial caution attending its development. *A* let to *B* a lock-up shop adjoining a house in which *A* resided. It was arranged that *A* might enter the shop after *B* had left it at night, to see that it was secure. One night, *C*, the lodger of *A*, told *A* that he suspected a gas escape from the shop. *A* and *C* entered the shop. *A* examined the lower part of a gas-pipe with a naked light. Nothing happened. *C*, who was a much younger man, got on the counter and did the like to the upper part of the pipe. An explosion occurred which damaged *B*'s goods. *B* sued *A* for negligence. *A* admitted that he welcomed *C*'s help in examining the upper part of the pipe. A Divisional Court held, in an unconsidered judgment, that *A* was liable on any one of four grounds: (1) *C* was *A*'s agent, invited and instructed by *A* to act as he did. (2) *C*'s act was done in the course of proceedings over which *A* had control. (3) *C*'s act was done in pursuance of a joint enterprise concerted by *A* and *C*. (4) *Per* Talbot J.: *A*, having undertaken on or near another's property an operation involving danger to that property, unless proper precautions were taken, was under a duty to take

[1] 47 *Law Quarterly Review* (1931), 23–42.
[2] (1918) 87 L.J.K.B. 1118.
[3] [1928] 2 K.B. 578.

36   TORT DEFINED

reasonable care to avoid actual danger [? damage] to property resulting from it, and he could not escape liability for breach of this duty by getting any one else, whether agent, servant, or contractor, to discharge it for him.

It is this fourth ground (supplied, be it noted, by one only of the two judges) which looks very much like the recognition of a new tort. No one would quarrel with the justice of holding a defendant liable in such circumstances, or with the reasonableness of making this the basis of his liability. But the novelty of it is seen when we try to fit it under any existing tort. It is not merely negligence, for it includes liability for the default of an independent contractor. It falls short of responsibility under the rule in *Rylands* v. *Fletcher*, for *A* would not have been liable if he had shewn "proper care" or "reasonable care", and, moreover there was no "escape" of anything from the occupier's land. It is near the duty set up by the rule in *Indermaur* v. *Dames*, but differs from it in scope. In fact, if it exists, it is a new tort, and the balance of probability is in favour of its existence. For there were several previous *dicta*[1] and perhaps even one earlier decision[2] that indicated the formation of the rule.[3]

There does seem to be, therefore, a respectable body of opinion and practice in favour of the view that the law of tort is based upon a general principle that all harm to another person is presumptively unlawful. And from this standpoint it is a matter of small import whether we speak of the "law of tort" or the "law of torts". The contents of that compartment of the law

[1] They are reducible to an opinion in a considered judgment of the Q.B.D. delivered by Cockburn C.J. in *Bower* v. *Peate* (1876) 1 Q.B.D. 321, 326.

[2] *Tarry* v. *Ashton* (1876) 1 Q.B.D. 314. But it is doubtful what exactly was the *ratio decidendi* in this case.

[3] Cf. 45 *Law Quarterly Review*, 1.

TORT DEFINED

consist at any given moment partly of nominate torts, partly of innominate. "Law of tort" is perhaps the more accurate expression as indicating the existence of unoccupied territory which is bit by bit and from time to time being recognized as the source of fresh liabilities in tort. The recognition is sometimes by the legislature, but more frequently by the judges.

The main argument the other way is that there are many instances of *damnum absque injuria*. The man who is ruined by fair business competition, or who is injured by a merely spiteful act of his neighbour, or who acts to his damage upon a telegram never intended for him, has no action in tort. This is true enough, but the fallacy lies in the inference that, because the law will not give a remedy in every case, it will therefore never give a remedy in a new case. To say that all unjustifiable harm is actionable is a totally different thing from saying that all harm is actionable. The first proposition fully admits the possibility of many circumstances in which an injured person can recover nothing. There never was a time when a plaintiff who asserted a new cause of action could be sure of getting the courts to admit its existence; and that is just as true now as it was nine centuries ago. The courts have power to create new remedies for tortious injuries, but whether they will create them or not is a matter of judicial discretion. They may well be slow in creating them, for their primary duty is to get rid of the case before them, and, for the rest, they have to consider many other things besides the stark fact that the plaintiff has been injured before they concede him a remedy. Logic, history, what Judge Cardozo calls *mores*, the general needs of the community—all these have to be taken into account. "Public policy" under one name or another has been a weighty influence in the growth of Anglo-American law.[1] It may well be

[1] 42 *Harvard Law Review* (1928), 76–102.

38   TORT DEFINED

that the plaintiff is asking for more than any court will give him, because he has forgotten or underrated the competing interests of other people, or because it is the legislature, and not the judicature, whom he should approach. All these reasons, or any of them, may suffice to make the allowance of a new remedy unwise. That is one source of *damnum absque injuria*. Another is connected with the plaintiff's loss of an action for a tort which is already well recognized. Every such nominate tort has its specific legal ingredients and if the plaintiff cannot establish them all he will recover nothing. It is not every blow that is a battery, nor every lie that is a slander, nor every detention that is a false imprisonment. It may be worth while to cite once again a parallel from medicine.

Certain specific remedies are fitted to cure only certain specific diseases; and no remedy of any sort may be applied to procure an abortion, to satisfy a craving for drugs, or to end suffering by depriving the patient of life. But these limitations do not prevent a medical practitioner from creating new remedies for the alleviation or the cure of human ills.[1]

It is worth while to notice how the Civil Codes of France and Germany treat the basis of what corresponds to tort in those countries. In the French *Code Civil*, Art. 1382 postulates a general liability in tort in the broadest terms. "Tout fait quelconque de l'homme, qui cause à autrui un dommage, oblige celui par la faute duquel il est arrivé, à le réparer."[2] The German *Bürgerliches Gesetzbuch* states liability in a mode which, though it is more specific than the French code, is nevertheless framed as a general prohibition against wrongdoing. Art. 823 provides that any one who, in contravention of

---

[1] 27 *Columbia Law Review* (1927), 11.
[2] So too the Italian *Codice civile*, Arts. 1151–1152. See too *Progetto di Codice delle Obbligazioni e dei Contratti* (Roma, 1928), pp. lxxxi *seq.*, and Art. 74.

law, intentionally or negligently injures the life, body, health, liberty, ownership, or any other right of another person, is liable to compensate that person for the ensuing damage. Art. 826 enacts that any one who intentionally causes damage to another in such a way as to offend "gegen die guten Sitten" is liable to make good the damage to that other. An exact English equivalent to "gegen die guten Sitten" is difficult to find, but perhaps the best description of the phrase is "unsocial conduct". Between them, Arts. 823 and 826 cover the domain of possible torts, except that Art. 824 fills up what was regarded as a lacuna in Art. 823 by dealing with attacks on the honour and credit of another person, and Art. 824 makes seduction of a woman a tort. Of course, these general propositions in the two codes will not, standing by themselves, help us to say of any particular injury whether it is a tort or not; much less do they countenance any idea that every conceivable injury to another person is redressible by an action. We have to know a good deal more about such terms as "dommage", "faute", "widerrechtlich", "Schade", before we can determine exactly what harm is unlawful; and in both systems the literature is sufficiently copious on these points.

Chapter IV

TORT AND CONTRACT

AT the present day, tort and contract are distinguishable from one another in that the duties in the former are primarily fixed by the law, while in the latter they are fixed by the parties themselves. Moreover, in tort the duty is towards persons generally, in contract it is towards a specific person or specific persons.

It has been pointed out already that the necessity of distinguishing tort from other forms of liability is a practical affair and not merely a lecture-room adjunct. Some reasons in support of this have been given, such as differences in remedies, in the effect of lapse of time, and in variations in the law of personal capacity.[1] More can easily be added in differentiating tort from contract. Some notable distinctions exist with respect to the award of damages. Exemplary or vindictive damages are possible against any tortfeasor, but the general rule is the other way in the law of contract. A satisfactory reason for the difference is rather hard to find. In the measure of damages, tort and contract parted company pretty early, but whether this divergence applied to exemplary damages is another matter, for until 1695 the courts would not interfere at all on the score of excess of damages. As late as the nineteenth century there are signs that they could be awarded for breach of contract. However, the rule is now settled firmly enough and perhaps its best justification is that common experience shews that men are much less likely to outrage the feelings of one against whom they break a contract than those of one upon whom they inflict a tort.[2] Exception-

[1] *Ante*, pp. 2–4.
[2] Salmond and Winfield, *Law of Contracts*, 510–511.

TORT AND CONTRACT 41

ally, exemplary damages may be awarded in an action for breach of promise of marriage.[1]

Again, as regards remoteness of damages, the rules in tort and in contract are disparate in at least one important respect. According to *In re Polemis*,[2] the test for deciding whether damage for negligence is too remote is that if any reasonable person would have foreseen that the act complained of would cause damage, then the defendant is liable for all damage directly traceable to his act; and damage is indirect if it is due to "the operation of independent causes having no connection with the negligent act, except that they could not avoid its results".[3] Another way of putting the same thing is to say that the damage is too remote if the chain of causation is interrupted by a *nova causa interveniens*, though neither formula, standing by itself, will throw much light on what is "indirect" or what is a *nova causa interveniens* in any particular case. There is good reason to suppose that the rule deducible from *In re Polemis* is of general application in the law of tort and is not confined to negligence. But in the law of contract the defendant is not so extensively liable. According to what is known as the rule in *Hadley* v. *Baxendale*,[4] where there are special circumstances in a contract which are wholly unknown to the defendant, he is not liable for damages solely due to those special circumstances, though he is liable for general damages; for if he had known of the special circumstances, he might have declined to enter into the contract without special provision as to the amount of damages, and it would be very unfair to deprive him of that advantage.

---

[1] Salmond and Winfield, *Law of Contracts*, 510–511. The liability of a banker who dishonours his customer's cheque is not a true exception.

[2] [1921] 3 K.B. 560.

[3] *Ibid.* 577 (*per* Scrutton L.J.).

[4] (1854) 9 Exch. 341, 354–355.

42 TORT AND CONTRACT

These rules, whatever difficulties may arise in their application, are easily grasped and, in a special course of lectures, might have been summarily dismissed but for one circumstance. Until 1927 it had escaped notice that the relation of *In re Polemis* to *Hadley* v. *Baxendale* needed some explanation. *In re Polemis* arose in connection with a charter-party, and it is scarcely necessary to say that a charter-party is a contract. Yet it has been consistently treated in textbooks as a decision on remoteness of damage in the law of tort, and with equal consistency books on the law of contract took no account of it. Can it be reckoned as derogating in any way from the rule in *Hadley* v. *Baxendale*? That case was not cited *In re Polemis*. Upon the whole, however, there seems to be no real conflict between the two decisions. There were alternative claims *In re Polemis* for damages for (*a*) breach of contract, (*b*) the tort of negligence. But in the Court of first instance Sankey, J. was content to rest his judgment on the claim in tort.[1] He treated the litigation before him as "a case of mere damages by negligence of the respondents' servants". It is possible, but not certain, that the Court of Appeal took the same view. If so, no shadow of doubt is cast upon the rule in *Hadley* v. *Baxendale*. It was never considered, but it was never impugned. It would be rash to conclude even on this line of reasoning that the difficulties raised *In re Polemis* disappear,[2] but it is safe to say that, if it applies to the law of contract, then it does so only subject to the qualification set up by the rule in *Hadley* v. *Baxendale*. And the later decision of *Weld-*

---

[1] (1921) 26 Com. Cas. 281. 37 T.L.R. 696.

[2] This book was too near completion to take adequate account of Dr A. D. McNair's article on *In re Polemis* in *Cambridge Law Journal* (1931), where the documents are printed. The learned author has no doubt that *In re Polemis* must be confined to the measure of damages in tort.

TORT AND CONTRACT 43

Blundell v. *Stephens* is some prop for this argument.
There Lord Sumner said:

The damage must be such as would flow from the breach of duty
in the ordinary and usual course of things. That is the general
rule, both in contract and in tort, except that in contract the law
does not consider as too remote such damages as were in the con-
templation of the parties at the time when the contract was made.
Subject to that, only such damages can be recovered as were
immediately and naturally caused by the breach.[1]

Some of the discussion which I have developed here was
raised elsewhere,[2] and it may be wound up with the
comment of Sir Frederick Pollock that "the Court of
Appeal could not now overrule *Hadley* v. *Baxendale* if
it would, neither is it credible that the House of Lords
would if it could".[3]

Another practical difference between an action in
tort and an action upon contract is in the award of costs
in the County Court. There has been some litigation
about this distinction but much less than one would
have anticipated.[4] In turn it has led to a secondary distinction as to costs in a High Court action. If an action
is brought there which might have been sued in the
County Court, costs, in certain circumstances, will be
awarded on the lower scale of the County Court instead
of on the higher one prevalent in the High Court.[5]

---

[1] [1920] A.C. 956, 979.
[2] Salmond and Winfield, *Law of Contracts,* 506–507. It has roused
some comment in Scots law as well as in English law: Gloag, *Law of
Contract* (2nd ed. 1929), 697. A friendly critic describes it as a "bogey":
The Bell Yard, June 1929, p. 44. Quite possibly it is, but I have done my
best to lay the ghost before it haunts the student or worries the practitioner.
[3] *Law of Torts* (13th ed.), 37–39.
[4] The County Courts Act, 1888, s. 62, uses the antithesis "action of
contract", "action of tort". The Act of 1919, ss. 1, 2, 11, varies it with
actions "founded on contract", "founded on tort". But both antitheses
occur in earlier Acts.
[5] County Courts Act, 1919, s. 11. Odgers, *Pleading* (10th ed. 1930),
372–373.

44 TORT AND CONTRACT

Next as to joint wrongdoers. As a general rule there is no right of contribution among joint tortfeasors, but the rules as to contribution among co-contractors are not nearly so simple. In general, however, a co-contractor who has been cast in damages can claim recoupment against his fellow-contractors.[1] Again, judgment against one joint tortfeasor bars any action against the others, but there are several cases in which judgment against one co-contractor will leave his co-contractors liable.[2] Finally, where there are joint tortfeasors, each, any, or all of them may be sued, but where there are co-contractors, in general all must be sued. Another procedural difference between contract and tort appears in the rules as to service of a writ outside jurisdiction.[3]

It is almost impossible to give an intelligible account of the relation of contract to tort at the present day without frequent reference to the history specially affecting them. A brief reminder of early outlines will not be amiss before we pass to later and more intricate details. Until the introduction and extension of the action of *assumpsit*, the action of debt and the action of covenant were the chief Common Law remedies for contract. The seeds of confusion were scattered pretty early, for "the action of debt was very amorphous in its character. It was proprietary; and this in early days was perhaps its leading characteristic. But...it was sufficiently contractual to be capable of being used to enforce certain varieties of contract; and it had also a certain delictual element".[4] When *assumpsit* came and spread from misfeasance to nonfeasance, more tares were sown in the

---

[1] *Laws of England* (Halsbury), vii, §§ 958 *seq.*

[2] *Annual Practice* (1928), p. 348: note to Order 19, rule 15 ("joint contractors").

[3] *Ibid.* (1928), Order 11, rule 1 (*e*) and (*ee*), pp. 92–93, 94 (especially *Clare C.C.* v. *Wilson* (1913) 2 I.R. 89), 98 (especially *Williams* v. *Cartwright* [1895] 1 Q.B. 142, 145).

[4] Holdsworth, *op. cit.* iii, 425.

TORT AND CONTRACT 45

field of classification, for *assumpsit* was a special kind of trespass on the case or deceit on the case and thus delictal in origin. By the end of the seventeenth century it is distinguishable into (i) special (or express) *assumpsit*, where there is an executory contract; (ii) *indebitatus assumpsit*, where the contract is implied; and (iii) the old action of *assumpsit*, which was the parent of both of these and was based on the simple idea that if one person caused damage to another by misperformance of a duty which he had undertaken to perform he was liable. Now the special *assumpsit* in (i) may easily be confused with the older *assumpsit* in (iii), but it had a different aspect, which led to practical consequences. A single example will suffice. In 1348, in one of the earliest cases on *assumpsit*, a defendant (who would certainly now be described as a bailee) had undertaken to transport safely the plaintiff's cattle across the Humber and, owing to overloading of the boat, the cattle had perished. It was held to be no answer to an action upon the case that the plaintiff could have sued upon covenant or upon trespass.[1] This is an example of *assumpsit* of the third kind. But in the seventeenth century it was decided that a bailee could be held liable on a special *assumpsit* of the first kind.[2] Thus different remedies were available for the same claim, the one distinctly delictal in character, the other contractual. Again, *indebitatus assumpsit* figured not only in genuine implied contract, but played an important part in the development of quasi-contract and of this more will be said in a later chapter. It introduced a further entanglement of contract with quasi-contract, not to say of tort with both of these. Nor was that all. Debt, which was beset by several procedural niceties, was driven to the wall by *indebitatus assumpsit* and, as a remedy upon simple contracts, was thrust out

[1] 22 Lib. Ass. pl. 41.
[2] *Wheatley* v. *Low* (1624) Cro. Jac. 668.

46   TORT AND CONTRACT

by it. Thus tort, contract, and quasi-contract were woven together in a skein, the threads of which are hard to trace scientifically.[1] Maitland suggested three different lines of investigating the difference between actions in tort and actions on contract in comparatively modern times:

(1) As to joinder of actions.
(2) As to survival of actions.
(3) As to joint liability.[2]

We can pursue these in detail.

(1) *Joinder of actions.* It was said by the court in 1681 in *Denison* v. *Ralphson*,[3] "Causes upon contract which are in the right, and causes upon a tort cannot be joined", for they require several pleas and several process; and again in 1694 it was adjudged "that an action on a tort and on a contract cannot be laid together".[4] And the importance of the distinction was marked by Lord Chief Baron Gilbert in a book much recommended by Blackstone. He admitted that it might not be the best possible division, but had no doubt that it was a guide as to what could, or could not, be contained in one declaration.[5] Substantial reasons for the non-joinder of certain actions were variation in process and in the fines paid for taking out the writs which commenced the actions. In debt the old process was by summons, attachment and distress, and the fine payable to the King for procuring the original writ was proportionate to the sum claimed. But in trespass the process was by *capias*, because the tortfeasor might be supposed to fly from justice, and the

[1] See generally Holdsworth, *op. cit.* iii, 412–454.
[2] Pollock, *Law of Torts* (13th ed.), App. A, pp. 589–592.
[3] 1 Vent. 365. Reported *sub nom. Benningsage* v. *Ralphson* 2 Show. 250.
[4] *Dalston* v. *Eyenston* 12 Mod. 73. Also *sub nom. Dalston* v. *Janson* 1 Salk. 10; 1 Ld Raym. 58; *Dalson* v. *Tyson* 3 Salk. 204; *Darlston* v. *Hianson* Comb. 332.
[5] *History and Practice of Civil Actions* (3rd ed. 1779), pp. 2–8.

TORT AND CONTRACT

court set a fine upon him in proportion to his offence and levied it by *capiatur*.[1] Hence, there was no objection to joining several trespasses in the same action. So too with several actions on the case, provided they were of the same kind; e.g. action for fraud on the delivery of goods and on the warranty of the same goods, for both arose from contract. On the other hand, *assumpsit* and trover against a carrier could not be joined, for, though both were actions upon the case, yet trover was founded upon tort, *assumpsit* upon contract. That is clear enough. But an action against a common carrier upon the custom of the realm could be joined with trover.[2] That was because the action upon the custom of the realm against a carrier goes back to a period long before *assumpsit* had become a general contractual remedy, and when its foundation upon delict was clearly perceptible. Indeed, this action upon the custom of the realm against innkeepers and common carriers may have been prevalent before *assumpsit* came into existence. In any event, it was delictal in origin, not contractual.

All this lore about joinder of actions is dead and gone long ago, but it was worth exploring in order to discover what test the courts adopted for deciding whether a given claim were in tort or on contract. And the result is completely disappointing. There is not a trace of any reasoned distinction of the one from the other. The judges and writers constantly assume that the distinction exists and never say what it is.[3] Considering the tough historical knots in the grain of our law of contract, it is not surprising that they cut no deeper than

[1] This is once again the distinction to which Finch attached some importance, between the *praecipe quod reddat* type of action and the *si fecerit te securum. Ante*, pp. 19 *seq.*

[2] Bacon, *Abr.* (7th ed. 1832), i, 58–59. Bacon borrowed a good deal here from Gilbert's book.

[3] E.g. *Mast v. Goodson* (1772) 3 Wils. 348.

48 TORT AND CONTRACT

was necessary for getting rid of the case before them. At least they did try to simplify the law as to joinder of actions and as to allowing alternative actions on the same set of facts; but this was notable more with respect to *indebitatus assumpsit* and its bearing on quasi-contract than in connection with any neat separation of tort from contract. The cases will be noticed when we come to talk of quasi-contract.[1] But it may be added here that, if the law was even at the end of the eighteenth century too much implicated with historical matter to make scientific classification advisable or even possible, it was nevertheless this same historical overlapping of tort, contract and quasi-contract that for practical, as distinct from theoretical, purposes made it easier for the courts to multiply remedies for the benefit of plaintiffs. The law might be tough for the jurisprudent, but it was plastic for the practitioner.

(2) *Survival of actions.* Here again, it is vain to attempt to elicit any scientific test for distinguishing tort from breach of contract in the decisions down to the end of the eighteenth century. The courts were aware of *a* distinction between actions *ex delicto* and actions *ex contractu*, and they made some use of it in this connection. But what the distinction was the reader is always left to infer and, whatever it was, it seems to have been no better than a source of embarrassment to the judges, who really solved the question of what actions would survive and what not, by a line which cut across contract and tort instead of dividing them, and which left contract and a particular species of tort on the one side and the residue of torts on the other. Once again the literature of the topic makes it clear why it was practically

---

[1] E.g. *Lamine* v. *Dorrell* (1704) 2 Ld Raym. 1216. *Dickon* v. *Clifton* (1766) 2 Wils. 319. *Feltham* v. *Terry* (1772) Lofft, 209. *Lindon* v. *Hooper* (1776) 1 Cowp. 414. *Lightly* v. *Clouston* (1808) 1 Taunt. 112. *Hill* v. *Perrott* (1810) 3 Taunt. 274.

TORT AND CONTRACT 49

impossible that the division, contract and tort, should have been of much real use in developing the law.

The subject may be discussed under two heads, which are natural partitions and are adopted in the old digests of case law.[1]

(i) What causes of action against the deceased survive against his executors?

The earlier history of this I have treated elsewhere,[2] and here I need only say that the highly penal character of trespass prevented the survival of any remedy for it when once the delinquent was dead. Then towards the end of the fifteenth century the phrase *actio personalis moritur cum persona* begins to be talked about in the courts, and in the seventeenth and eighteenth centuries that is the centre of gravity around which the discussions revolve. The maxim, if it can be called one, is, and always has been, a mischievous fractional truth which would have done a great deal more harm if any lawyer had accepted it literally; but fortunately none did. While, however, its limits were being fixed, frequent reference was made to the difference—whatever it was—between actions *ex delicto* and actions *ex contractu*, and thus it becomes of interest for present purposes. The maxim did not apply to *assumpsit*. That was settled in 1611 in *Pinchon's Case*.[3] And the annotator of that decision inferred (rather prematurely as will be seen later) that *any* action upon contract would survive, and he certainly had Lord Mansfield's opinion in his favour.[4] But still most of such actions did survive, and we should expect as a logical antithesis that actions in tort perished with the tortfeasor. This, however, was certainly not the general rule. What then was the criterion? We need

---

[1] E.g. Viner, *Abr.* (2nd ed. 1792), Executors, xi, 123, 244.
[2] 29 *Columbia Law Review* (1929), 239–254.
[3] 9 Rep. 86*b*, 87*a*, 89*a*.
[4] Note in 1826 ed. vol. v, 161. *Hambly* v. *Trott* (1776) 1 Cowp. 371.

W P   4

50 TORT AND CONTRACT

not pause to investigate a certain amount of groping after a test in earlier cases,[1] for it was threshed out in the twice-argued decision of *Hambly* v. *Trott*,[2] which settled the law then, and which, allowing for procedural reforms, represents it now. The plaintiff sued an action of trover against an administrator *cum testamento annexo* for conversion of goods alleged to have been committed by the testator in his lifetime. The defendant pleaded not guilty. Verdict for the plaintiff. The defendant moved in arrest of judgment that this was a personal tort which died with the plaintiff. Lord Mansfield, who delivered the considered decision of the court, made a cardinal distinction between (*a*) survival with respect to cause of action, and (*b*) survival with respect to form of action. As to (*a*),

where the cause of action is money due, or a contract to be performed, gain or acquisition of the testator, by the work and labour, or property of another, or a promise of the testator express or implied...the action survives against the executor. But where the cause of action is a tort, or arises *ex delicto*...supposed to be *by force* and *against the King's peace*, there the action dies; as battery, false imprisonment, trespass, words, nuisance, obstructing lights, diverting a water course, escape against the sheriff, and many other cases of the like kind.[3]

As to (*b*), where the defendant could have waged his law, no action in that form will lie against him, but other actions have been substituted upon the very same cause, and these will survive. No action will lie against the executor, where the declaration must allege *quare vi et armis et contra pacem*, or where, as in the case before the

[1] E.g. *Perkinson* v. *Gilford* (1639) Cro. Car. 539, which formed some sort of an authority for an unsuccessful attempt by Raymond in *Baily* v. *Birtles* (1662) T. Raym. 71, to argue that it was "misfeasance" as opposed to "non-feasance".

[2] (1776) 1 Cowp. 371.

[3] At p. 375.

TORT AND CONTRACT 51

court, the plea must be that the testator was not guilty; for "the cause of action arises *ex delicto*; and all private criminal injuries or wrongs, as well as all public crimes, are buried with the offender".[1] The court held it to have been settled that trover and conversion by a testator did not survive against the executor, that the plea of not guilty was decisive, for it purported to put in issue the guilt of the testator, and that judgment must be arrested.[2]

Now *Hambly* v. *Trott* is valuable to us in a negative sense. It shews the futility of the "contract-tort" demarcation for ascertaining what actions will survive, and, as no scientific analysis of those terms appears in the report, it might be thought that all further interest in the case vanishes. But that is not so. It demonstrates clearly *why* at that date such demarcation was destitute of practical value. For, let the court try to draw what line it might in substantive law, it must, as it actually did, go on to point out the cobweb of procedure overlying any such distinction. How can you get any distance with a theoretical distinction when you are forced to ask in addition, "Could the party have waged his law in this action?" "Must he plead not guilty?" Moreover, Lord Mansfield scarcely made up his mind as to whether trover were *ex maleficio* or not. At the second hearing he thought it was so in form only, but that in substance it was an action to recover property,[3] but in the decision he regarded the plea of not guilty as making it *ex maleficio*. Yet another element of confusion as to the survival of remedies was a cross-division between torts and crimes. "Private criminal injuries" (or "private crimes") is a phrase twice used in the decision,[4] and it shews us an echo of the criminal aspect of trespass, though the theoretical fine and imprisonment to

[1] At p. 375. [2] P. 377.
[3] P. 374. [4] Pp. 375, 376.

4-2

52 TORT AND CONTRACT

which the defendant was liable had been abolished in
1694.[1] If any one could have rationalized the law it
would have been Lord Mansfield, but that was the best
he could do here. He saw the crying injustice which
must ensue if a man wrongfully appropriated the goods
of another and if, on the death of the wrongdoer, the
injured party had no remedy against the personal representative; and what influenced him in his ultimate
opinion was not the theoretical classification of trover
in tort or in contract, but the fact that the plaintiff,
though he could not sue in trover, could have recovered
in an action for money had and received.

Two other points deserve notice. It was decided
much later that not all actions on contract will survive
where the person to be sued has died; e.g. an action for
breach of promise of marriage where no special damage
is alleged.[2] And if property, or the proceeds or value
of property, have been wrongfully added by the deceased to his estate, the person wronged can sue the
personal representative;[3] but the action certainly is not
one of tort but is for money had and received. There
can be no claim in it for unliquidated damages, and if
anything solid can be grasped in the shadows that
obscure a definition of tort, it is that an action for unliquidated damages is always one remedy for it.

(ii) What causes of action survive to the executors of
a deceased person?

At Common Law, no action of trespass survived.
Why this should have been so is not clear, but perhaps
the rule that death ended an appeal, whether of the
appellor or appellee, infected the law about trespass.[4]

[1] 5 & 6 W. & M. c. 12. Pollock, *Law of Torts* (13th ed.), App. A,
p. 590.
[2] *Finlay* v. *Chirney* (1887) 20 Q.B.D. 494.
[3] *Sherrington's Case* (*temp.* Elizabeth) Sav. 40. *Phillips* v. *Homfray*
(1883) 24 Ch.D. 439, 454.
[4] 29 *Columbia Law Review* (1929), 242.

TORT AND CONTRACT 53

Legislation as early as 1267 and 1292 made some niggling exceptions to the rule, but it was not till 1330 that executors were enabled to sue for trespass done to their testators by carrying away their goods and chattels.[1] There was a good deal of litigation on the interpretation of this statute, but we can pass it by until *Mason* v. *Dixon*, which was decided in 1626 and reported under various names.[2] Dixon had allowed one who was in his custody for debt to J.S. to escape. J.S. died. Mason, his executor, sued Dixon. The court was evenly divided as to whether the action survived, but the case does not concern us except for a classification of actions by Doderidge J. which is the more interesting because this judge wrote several legal treatises, one of which was an attempt to handle law on the theoretical side.[3] Actions, he said, were (*a*) *ex contractu*; (*b*) *quasi ex contractu*; (*c*) *ex maleficio*. The first he exemplified by debt and covenant. The second were related to contract, as in the case before him, where the original indenture created a contract (debt), and where the secondary cause was the escape. The third kind he illustrated by trespass *vi et armis* and battery.[4] Yet no one seems to have attached any importance to his classification, and only one of four reporters gives it. It is the more curious because English law of that period strikes a modern student as saturated with legal relations explicable far more easily on a theory of quasi-contract than on the mere bifurcation, contract-tort.

The result is that death of a wrongdoer or of the party wronged will teach us nothing of value for distinguishing positively tort from contract, and the comparatively modern cases shew a greater tendency than the older

---

[1] 29 *Columbia Law Review* (1929), 242–243.
[2] W. Jones, 173. Latch, 167. Popham, 189. Noy, 87.
[3] *The Lawyers Light, or a due direction for the study of the law.* I.D. 1629. [4] W. Jones, 173.

54 TORT AND CONTRACT

ones to ignore this division and to concentrate attention on the question whether the action is "personal" or not.[1] It is worth while adding that much the same applies to transmissibility of claims from a debtor to his trustee in bankruptcy. The line is drawn, not between contract on the one side and tort on the other, but between personal contracts and torts (claims on which remain with the bankrupt) and other contracts and torts (claims on which pass to the trustee).[2]

(3) *Joint parties.* Here the path of investigation indicated by Maitland can be made wider by including not only the liability of co-defendants but also the capacity of several plaintiffs to join in one action. Under this head the difference between contract and tort was, and still is, of some importance, and as the history of the rules themselves does not seem to have been traced elsewhere, that must be an excuse for giving it in some detail here. Until the seventeenth century the reports are silent about the difference, at any rate under the words "contract", "tort". Maitland regarded Brooke's *Abridgment* as the earliest authority for setting up the distinction on somewhat different and more procedural lines—between *praecipe quod reddat* and debt on the one hand and "trespass et hujusmodi" on the other.[3] It is interesting to note another example of the implied use of the procedural division, *praecipe quod reddat—si fecerit te securum* to which reference has already been made. However, cases of the seventeenth century shew that the line of cleavage is roughly between contract and tort, and that, while non-joinder or misjoinder of parties was likely to be prejudicial, if not fatal, to claims on contract, it had much less effect in actions for tort.

---

[1] E.g. *Chamberlain* v. *Williamson* (1814) 2 M. & S. 408. *Finlay* v. *Chirney* (1887) 20 Q.B.D. 494.

[2] Wace, *Bankruptcy* (1904 ed.), 201.

[3] Brooke, *Abr.* Responder 54. Brooke's reference to 46 Lib. Ass. pl. 13, is but a slender prop for his statement.

TORT AND CONTRACT 55

The rules were not quite the same for joint plaintiffs as for joint defendants, and we must take them separately, first under tort and then under contract.

(i) In tort, the rule was that, if one of two parties who had been jointly injured improperly sued alone, the non-joinder might be pleaded in abatement by the defendant. Why this was so is a mystery. Generally, in this connection, the last thing that can be found in any of the books is a rational explanation of why the law was so.[1] Possibly the reason was to discourage multiplicity of actions by different parties having the same grievance. In any event, the consequences of non-joinder, though unpleasant, were not irremediable; for a plea in abatement, if successful, merely put an end to the action to which it was set up as a defence, but it did not prevent the suing of another.

Liability in tort, being joint as well as several, made it needless to join all tortfeasors as co-defendants. This was no injustice to the particular defendant (or defendants) selected, for the wrong committed was just as much wholly attributable to him as to each or all of the others.[2] In fact, matters here went so far in favour of the plaintiff that, even if he included among the defendants persons who had not committed the wrong, he incurred no risk, for the acquitted defendants had no remedy for their costs. This led to reckless and unwarrantable joinder of persons on the remote possibility of their being concerned in the wrong which was the subject of the action, or for the tactical purpose of preventing them from giving evidence for other defendants,

---

[1] For the rule see Comyns, *Digest* (1822 ed.), i, 54; *Child* v. *Sands* (1692) 1 Salk. 31; 3 Lev. 351; *dictum* in *Leglise* v. *Champante* (1728) 2 Stra. 829; 1 Williams' Saund. (1871 ed.), 478. The explanation in Comyns, *Dig.* i, 45, may do for misjoinder, but will not cover non-joinder: "Why sue in the name of one who is to derive no benefit from the event?"

[2] Comyns, *Dig.* i, 76.

56 TORT AND CONTRACT

and this abuse was wiped out by 8 & 9 Will. III, c. 11, as to trespass and by 3 & 4 Will. IV, c. 42, s. 32, as to all personal actions. Thereafter, acquitted defendants got their costs.[1] Another practical check on this speculative testing of liability was the likelihood of prejudice on the part of the jury against a plaintiff who could adduce no evidence against a particular defendant, and of a direction of his acquittal by the judge directly the plaintiff's case closed, so as to enable him to give evidence for the other defendants.[2]

(ii) In contract, non-joinder of co-contractors as plaintiffs was a good defence. The mode in which the defendant must take advantage of it was by plea of *non assumpsit* in an action on a simple contract, whether parol or written. If the contract were under seal, there was a dispute as to the correct procedure into which it is unnecessary to enter here.[3] The reason why mistakes about joinder of plaintiffs in contract were material was that only those who had made the agreement could enforce it.[4]

As to co-contractors who were defendants, all must be joined, otherwise the plaintiff might be met by a plea in abatement.[5] For this rule, which is in sharp contrast with that as to defendant tortfeasors, various reasons were suggested. It was said to be based on the entirety of contract,[6] or on the convenience of getting one judgment against all who were liable to the plaintiff's demand.[7] Lord Mansfield, in 1770, scouted this latter reason, and said that experience shewed that it was both inconvenient and unjust. The action before him was against one of two partners on a partnership account,

[1] Chitty, *Practice of the Law* (2nd ed. 1834), ii, 51.
[2] *Ibid.* iii, 127.
[3] 1 Williams' Saund. 477–478.
[4] Comyns, *Dig.* i, 45–46.   [5] *Ibid.* 72.
[6] Lord Kenyon C.J. in *Sheppard* v. *Baillie* (1795) 6 T.R. 327, 329.
[7] Lord Mansfield in *Rice* v. *Shute* (1770) 5 Burr. 2611, 2613.

TORT AND CONTRACT 57

and the plaintiff was non-suited because he had not joined the other. The Court of King's Bench made absolute a rule for a new trial. It was pointed out that a creditor might be non-suited twenty times or driven to a suit in Equity for discovery before he could ascertain who all the members of a partnership were; and that, if the defendant wanted to avail himself of the non-joinder, he ought to have done so by plea in abatement. He had not done so, and had therefore waived his objection.[1] This decision was taken to be applicable to actions on contract in general, though in terms it refers to a partnership action. The substitution of a plea in abatement for non-suit may not impress a modern reader as much in the way of reform, especially from a judge like Mansfield, who was "ashamed to see either hitch or hang upon pins or particles, contrary to the true manifest meaning of the contract";[2] but, more closely considered, his decision not only effected a great improvement in the law, but also surprised his contemporaries by its boldness. If a defendant pleaded in abatement that someone else ought to have been joined with him, he was driven to disclose who the other party was.[3] It took two generations and the pungent criticisms of the Common Law Commissioners to make Mansfield's reform more extensive and to prick the legislature into more drastic amendment of the law. The worst consequence of it occurred where a joint contractor resided abroad, for it compelled a plaintiff, who wished to sue him, to resort to the cruel expense and delay of outlawry.[4] The Civil Procedure Act, 1833, remedied this,[5] and the Common Law Procedure Act gave relief in

[1] *Rice* v. *Shute, supra,*
[2] In *Rees* v. *Abbott* (1778) 2 Cowp. 832.
[3] *Rice* v. *Shute* (1770) 5 Burr. at p. 2613.
[4] H. J. Stephen, *Treatise on the Principles of Pleading in Civil Actions* (5th ed. 1843), Note 18, pp. xxviii–xxix.
[5] 3 & 4 Will. IV, c. 42, s. 8.

58 TORT AND CONTRACT

misjoinder,[1] but neither enactment made non-joinder or misjoinder of defendant co-contractors entirely innocuous;[2] nor, indeed does existing law do so. Intermediate reforms can be noticed very briefly before we proceed to state it. The Common Law Procedure Act, 1852, enabled amendment of misjoinder or non-joinder of plaintiffs in any action (including, of course, one on tort as well as one on contract) to be made before trial.[3] Pleas in abatement were abolished in 1875, and the present law is to be found in the Rules of the Supreme Court founded upon the Judicature Acts of that period. The misjoinder or non-joinder of parties cannot defeat any cause or matter.[4] The utmost they can do is to cause delay and expense, for the other party, if he wishes to object, can do so by taking out a summons or making a motion before the trial to stay the action until the mistake is corrected; or he can make a summary application at the trial of the action. The offending party must, as a general rule, pay the costs thrown away by his error.[5] There is no difference here between actions in tort and actions for breach of contract,[6] subject to one qualification. Nothing has altered the substantial difference between tort and breach of contract that all co-contractors must be sued (subject to a few exceptions),[7] but that all joint tortfeasors need not be sued. A co-contractor still has a legal grievance if all his co-contractors are not made joint defendants with him. A joint tortfeasor in similar circumstances has none, and that was recognized as law long ago.[8] Perhaps this was

[1] S. 37.
[2] Chitty, *Practice of the Law* (2nd ed. 1836), iii, 126.
[3] S. 34.   [4] Order 16, r. 11.
[5] *Ibid.* r. 12.
[6] *Annual Practice.* Notes to Order 16, r. 1.
[7] *Ibid.* Order 16, r. 11. Note "Joint contractors".
[8] Y.B. Hil. 14 Hen. IV, f. 21, pl. 27, where Serjeant Cheyne's proposition, "if two commit a trespass against me, and I bring my action

TORT AND CONTRACT 59

owing to the penal nature of trespass in early times. Given the principle that trespass was a crime as well as a civil wrong, it is easy to see that there is no substance in the argument, "If I did the trespass, so did other people, and you cannot sue me unless you sue them".

There is a fair number of cases on the joinder of parties in contract or in tort from the seventeenth century down to the statutes which made pleaders' errors in this matter much less serious in consequences. In none of them, however, is there any scientific assessment of the difference between contract and tort. Yet the land is not so barren as might appear. The judges were forced to consider what was to be done with an action based upon a failure by the defendant to do competently something which his mere profession of a particular trade or calling bound him to do competently. A man who professed a "common calling", like that of a smith, a farrier, an attorney, a surgeon, an innkeeper, a common carrier, was liable for negligence in its performance; for "it is the duty of every artificer to exercise his art rightly and truly as he ought".[1] So wrote Fitzherbert four hundred years ago, and the rule is just as much law now as it was then. Such an obligation was a puzzling thing to classify. The duty of competence arose quite independently of contract between the parties, though it is obvious that in most instances of it there would be a co-existent contract. We put aside deliberately for later consideration the case of one who, though he professes a common calling, refuses to exercise it at all when another person demands his services, for it is one of peculiar difficulty; and we limit discussion to examples where the defendant has actually entered upon

---

against one only, it will be no plea for him to say that he committed the trespass with another", seems to have been the more acceptable opinion; see Hankford J. at ff. 22*a*–22*b*; also Serjeant Frowyk in Y.B. 11 Hen. VII, f. 6, pl. 23.   [1] F.N.B. 94 D.

60   TORT AND CONTRACT

the discharge of his duty and has injured the plaintiff
by his lack of care. The courts had to consider whether
the duty was contractual or delictal in several connec-
tions and, in particular, as an incident to deciding what
rules were to be applied where there were joint plaintiffs
or joint defendants. They forced such cases under the
dichotomy of "tort or contract", and for some time they
could not make up their minds upon which branch of
the dichotomy the relation ought to be grafted. Occasionally they selected one or the other, but they usually
passed through a period of hesitation and finally held
that in most of the "common calling" cases the plaintiff
could sue either in tort or on contract. No better illustration of their vacillation can be chosen than negligence
on the part of a common carrier. We begin with seventeenth-century decisions because that is where the
"joinder of parties" cases on contract and tort begin.
In outline what happened was this. A common carrier
was liable to an action for negligence "on the custom of
the realm", a remedy of very ancient origin and far
earlier than the development of *assumpsit*. But, as *assumpsit* grew, a convenient application of it was to this
class of cases, and it was just at the moment that this
practice was in vogue that the seventeenth-century litigation on joinder of parties in "tort" and in "contract"
begin. There was a decision in 1689 that the action
against a common carrier was "*quasi ex contractu*", or
"founded *quasi ex contractu* by implication of law",[1] and
down to the early years of the nineteenth century there
were other decisions to the like effect.[2] Sometimes it
was held to be *ex contractu*, for that might be inferred

---

[1] *Boson* v. *Sandford* 3 Salk. 203; Carth. 58, 62.

[2] *Buddle* v. *Wilson* (1795) 6 T.R. 369 (the court citing C. J. Holt
that the liability was *quasi ex contractu*). *Powell* v. *Layton* (1806)
2 B. & P. (N.R.) 365 ("founded on contract"). *Max* v. *Roberts* (1807)
2 B. & P. (N.R.) 454 ("founded on contract"; the decision was reversed on other grounds; 12 East, 89).

TORT AND CONTRACT 61

from the allegation in the old forms that the defendant "undertook" the duty.[1] At other times it was based on tort. Wilmot L.C.J. in 1766 regarded it as *ex delicto*,[2] and in 1802 Lord Ellenborough followed this.[3] After that, the current of opinion set steadily in favour of holding the liability to be delictal still (as it was assumed to be in origin), but nevertheless to give rise to an alternative action on contract. Sir James Mansfield C.J. professed himself unable to understand how it ever came to be tortious in nature, but he admitted that it was so,[4] and in 1817 Lord Ellenborough C.J. said that since *Dale* v. *Hall* (1750)[5], it had been usual to declare against a common carrier in contract, and not upon the custom of the realm; "yet the modern use does not supersede, although it has supplanted, the former procedure of declaring in tort".[6] This doctrine was driven home by the Court of Exchequer Chamber in *Bretherton* v. *Wood*.[7] In a declaration upon the case against a common carrier for negligent injury to a passenger, the first count alleged breach of a duty undertaken for hire and reward, the second, breach of a duty after receiving the plaintiff as a passenger. It was held that the action was founded on misfeasance, that the duty of safe carriage by a common carrier was imposed by law and needed no contract to support it, and that it was immaterial that *assumpsit* might have lain; *assumpsit* as applied to these cases was of modern use, but the action on the case was as early as the custom or Common Law

---

[1] *Dale* v. *Hall* (1750) 1 Wils. 281. So too, Buller J. in *Brown* v. *Dixon* (1786) 1 T.R. 274.

[2] *Dickon* v. *Clifton* (1766) 2 Wils. 319.

[3] *Govett* v. *Radnidge* 3 East, 62. The actual case does not seem to have been one of common carriage.

[4] *Powell* v. *Layton* (1806) 2 B. & P. (N.R.) 365.

[5] 1 Wils. 281.

[6] *Ansell* v. *Waterhouse* (1817) 6 M. & S. 385.

[7] 3 B. & B. 54.

62 TORT AND CONTRACT

as to carriers. Later decisions are little more than illustrations of these principles.[1]

We have still to state the rule governing joinder of parties where these alternative claims in contract or tort are feasible. In 1871, the editor of *Williams' Saunders* laid down the following principle. Where the action is maintainable for the tort simply, without reference to any contract, joinder of too many or too few defendants is immaterial; e.g. actions against common carriers grounded on the common custom of the realm. But where the action is not maintainable without reference to a contract between the parties and laying a previous ground for it by showing such contract, there, although the plaintiff shapes his case in tort, he shall be liable to a plea in abatement if he omit any defendant, or to nonsuit if he join too many; for he shall not, by adopting a particular form of action, alter the situation of the defendant.[2] Presumably this principle applies at the present day, except that talk about "plea in abatement" and (in this context) "non-suit" is out of date, and that a dissatisfied defendant can do no more than apply to stay the action or take the other course already indicated. Of course if X is suing one or more persons and is not sure whether his claim is in tort or on contract, he can frame it alternatively, but the only course which will free him from all risk of argument about the nature of the action is, in case of doubt, to join all parties as defendants, that is, all parties whom he has reasonable grounds for believing to be liable.

Finally, it must be noticed how soon the talk about quasi-contract died down in the cases to which we have referred and how little analysis of this idea there was in

---

[1] *Pozzi* v. *Shipton* (1838) 8 A. & E. 963. *Marshall* v. *York, Newcastle & Berwick R. Co.* (1851) 11 C.B. 655. *Tattan* v. *G.W.R. Co.* (1860) 2 E. & E. 844.

[2] Vol. i, pp. 471–472. Note to *Cabell* v. *Vaughan*.

TORT AND CONTRACT 63

even the earlier decisions. Scientifically, there was no need to pray in aid quasi-contract at all; for, as will appear later, the liability of the person who exercises a "common calling" is neatly reducible to either contract or tort or both, without any recourse to quasi-contract. This is far from denying that there are many instances of genuine quasi-contract in our system, which is all the poorer for an inbred reluctance either to adopt the term or to recognize it as a necessary and separate department of the law.

We are now in a position to bring down to modern times the concurrence of tort with breach of contract and to state generally the existing rules. Those relating to joinder of parties have already been noticed. Several influences have been at work in a tolerably rapid settlement of the law during the last century. First, there has been the speedy development of negligence as an independent tort. We have pointed out elsewhere that from the first quarter of the nineteenth century onwards the action of negligence was greatly stimulated by the progress of mechanical invention and especially of railways.[1] Now there is no tort more likely to co-exist with breach of contract than negligence. In a great number of instances a contractor fails in what he has promised because he has acted incompetently. Lawyers were thoroughly familiar with negligence as one mode of bungling a contract or a bailment long before it became an independent tort. Nor has it ever ceased to retain this earlier signification, though it has acquired the later one. Here then was one fruitful source of coincidence of contract with liability in tort, and it shews no sign of exhaustion at the present day.

Secondly, quasi-contractual liability has, to a small extent, reacted on the distinction between tort and contract, but not so much upon its genuine merits as upon

[1] 42 *Law Quarterly Review*, 195.

64   TORT AND CONTRACT

a tendency to confuse contract with quasi-contract and to set this pseudo-quasi-contract in contrast with tort. It was inevitable that this should happen, because no clear idea of the province of quasi-contract has ever been formed. Much more important has been the waiver of a tort in order to sue upon a true quasi-contract, and of that we must speak in its proper place.

Thirdly, the County Court Acts have thrust upon us the distinction between actions "founded upon tort" and actions "founded upon contract". This Parliamentary effort of jurisprudence, whatever its practical value, has been a scientific failure. We can see at once that it deliberately ignores our legal history, and we shall see later that it has tied the hands of the judges perhaps more than they themselves suspect.

Fourthly, the almost complete abolition of forms of action during the eighteenth century cleared away the opaque screen of procedure which had made it impossible for men like Finch, and extremely difficult even for a lucid expositor like Blackstone, to reduce our substantive law to coherent shape. If we mention this influence last, it is not because we underrate it, but because its effect was general, and not peculiar to contract and tort.

So far as a definition of tort is concerned, not one of these four influences gives us anything better than the older law. There is the same ingenuity spent in differentiating contract from tort, but it is always taken for granted that those terms are understood too well to need individual explanation. We are not in the same secure position, and have already committed ourselves to a definition of tort. The distinction between tort and contract, according to that, lies in the fact that in tort the duty is fixed primarily by the law itself irrespective of the consent of the parties; in contract it is fixed primarily by the parties who either express their agreement or

TORT AND CONTRACT 65

have it implied to them by the law's interpretation of their conduct.

So much for the causes at work during the last century. In working out details, we can take as a starting-point the House of Lords decision, *Brown* v. *Boorman*, in 1844.[1] The principle there laid down was that wherever there is a contract and something to be done in the course of the employment which is the subject of that contract, if there is a breach of duty in the course of that employment, the plaintiff may recover either in tort or in contract. But this principle is only an application of a wider one which may be gathered from the judgment of the Court of Exchequer Chamber against whose decision the appeal was brought.[2] It was pointed out that there is a large class of cases in which the foundation of the action springs out of privity of contract between the parties, but in which nevertheless the remedy is alternatively in contract or in tort. Such are actions against attornies, surgeons, and other professional men for lack of skill; against common carriers; against ship-owners on bills of lading; against bailees of different descriptions, and numerous other instances. The basis of them all is that the contract creates a duty, and the neglect to perform that duty, whether a misfeasance or a non-feasance, is a tort. This, of course, does not mean that every neglect in performing or not performing any contract is a tort. Some idea seems to have prevailed before *Brown* v. *Boorman* that the violation of a bare promise, without the establishment of any breach of a general duty such as is requisite to general liability in tort, might give rise to an action in tort; and after *Brown* v. *Boorman* an unsuccessful attempt was made to use that case in support of this idea. In effect, it would have obliterated the line between contract and tort.[3] The

[1] 11 Cl. & F. 1, 44. [2] 3 Q.B. at pp. 525–526.
[3] *Courtenay* v. *Earle* (1850) 10 C.B. 73, 83.

W P   5

66 TORT AND CONTRACT

principle must refer to contracts *ejusdem generis* as those enumerated by the Court of Exchequer Chamber, and what they are the courts themselves must settle. In *Brown* v. *Boorman* itself, an agent who fell within none of the specific descriptions put by the Exchequer Chamber was included in them. A later extension took in a jobmaster who let out a defective vehicle.[1] On the other hand, an architect has been ruled out, and his duty, at any rate for the purpose of the County Courts Act, 1888, was founded on contract and on nothing else.[2]

It is certain, then, that the Exchequer Chamber in *Brown* v. *Boorman* contemplated the possibility of other instances besides those which they named. One of some historical interest is the liability arising from breach of an express warranty on a sale of goods. Very early in our law, there was an action of trespass on the case against one who had sold goods with an express warranty of their quality which proved to be untrue.[3] Later, the action was described as one of deceit.[4] But it was sharply distinguished from covenant, or, to put the matter in modern phraseology, it was an action in tort, not an action on contract. It had come into being long before any idea existed of making *assumpsit* the common remedy for breach of contract.[5] But when *assumpsit* had been thus established, pleaders tried to apply it to redress a breach of express warranty because that would give them the advantage of employing "common counts". These enabled the plaintiff to make his declaration much more elastic. Instead of narrating his claim with meticulous accuracy of detail as to the quantity of goods sold, their price, and so forth, he could merely

[1] *Hyman* v. *Nye* (1881) 6 Q.B.D. 685, 689.
[2] *Steljes* v. *Ingram* (1903) 19 T.L.R. 534. But it is submitted that the architect ought to be in the same category as the solicitor or surgeon.
[3] Fitz, *Abr.* Monstrans de faits, 160 (A.D. 1383).
[4] Y.B. Trin. 11 Ed. IV, f. 6, pl. 10.
[5] Ames, *Lectures on Legal History* (1913), 136–137.

TORT AND CONTRACT 67

state the general nature of the defendant's indebtedness to him.[1] In 1778, it was held that *assumpsit* was a proper form of action where an express warranty had been broken. The defendant vendor had fraudulently alleged that a wind-galled horse was sound.[2] Even before this decision, the practice of suing *assumpsit* in such circumstances had been in vogue for some sixteen years. There was nothing, however, to prevent the plaintiff, if he found it more convenient, from suing the old action in tort for breach of warranty. It might be more advantageous for him to take that course, for he need prove only the warranty and the breach of it. There was no need to allege fraud therein, or, if he did allege it, he need not prove it.[3] Breach of express warranty might therefore give rise to alternative causes of action, or, more exactly, to one remedy in alternative forms.[4] One thing, however, the plaintiff could not do. He could not by his choice of remedy put the defendant in a worse position either as a matter of procedure or in point of substantive law, if there were independent legal rules which forbade him to do so. Thus, it will be recollected that joint contractors must all be joined as defendants and that misjoinder might prejudice the plaintiff; but that tortfeasors need not be joined. So in *Weall* v. *King*,[5] where the plaintiff sued the defendants in case, alleging false and fraudulent warranty on a contract which every one of his counts averred to be joint, he lost his action because he could prove his claim against one defendant only. He was not allowed to evade the procedural rule by contending that his action was founded on tort. That was a decision of the King's Bench, and

[1] Ames, *op. cit.* 153–154. Chitty, *Precedents in Pleading* (3rd ed. 1867), i, 30.
[2] *Stuart* v. *Wilkins* 1 Dougl. 19.
[3] *Williamson* v. *Allison* (1802) 2 East, 446.
[4] Pollock, *Torts* (13th ed.), 558.
[5] (1810) 12 East, 452.

5-2

68 TORT AND CONTRACT

a few years later the Court of Common Pleas refused to allow a plaintiff to make a minor liable for breach of an express warranty upon an exchange of goods, by urging that his cause of action was in tort, and not upon a contract.[1] Nowadays, the law as to warranties on sales of goods is to be found in the Sale of Goods Act, 1893. Actions upon them are actions upon contract, and the seller may, of course, be liable whether he makes a fraudulent statement in an express warranty, or acts merely in mistake. If he is fraudulent, then he has committed the tort of deceit and can be sued for that, or alternatively upon contract or tort. But the facts upon which each such alternative is based must be separately and distinctly stated.[2]

Other kinds of liability in tort, besides deceit, may co-exist with the contractual liability on a warranty. The seller of dangerous goods may be liable for injury which they inflict on the buyer, if no warning of their nature is given. Such liability may be based on a breach of warranty, but it is equally well founded on a duty, entirely independent of contract, to take reasonable precautions for putting the buyer on his guard.[3]

Some practical guide is needed for ascertaining whether an alternative claim does exist or not. One is that the action is founded on contract, and on contract only, if, supposing its allegation were struck out of the pleadings, no ground of action would remain.[4] This was a decision before the Judicature Act, 1873, but, so far as it goes, it would appear to hold now.

The rule of law...is that, if, in order to make out a cause of action it is not necessary for the plaintiff to rely on a contract, the

---

[1] *Green* v. *Greenbank* (1816) 2 Marshall, 485.
[2] Bullen & Leake, *Precedents of Pleading* (8th ed. 1924), 397 note (*b*); cf. 323.
[3] *Clarke* v. *A. & N.C.S.* [1903] 1 K.B. 155, 164–165.
[4] *Legge* v. *Tucker* (1856) 1 H. & N. 500.

TORT AND CONTRACT 69

action is one founded on tort; but, on the other hand, if, in order successfully to maintain his action, it is necessary for him to rely upon and prove a contract, the action is one founded upon contract.[1] The particular form of action alleged is not the determinant factor; the vital question is the substantiality of the claim.[2] This test, however, will not assist any plaintiff in anticipating whether the courts will hold in a case *primae impressionis* that the defendant was under a duty to take care, independently of any co-existing contractual obligations, so as to make him alternatively liable for the tort of negligence. But to this we must recur later.

Where there is a substantial claim in tort, the plaintiff need not allege the existence of a contract, though it is probable that one was made setting up the same kind of obligation. An infant who is injured by the unskilfulness of a surgeon employed to cure her can recover *ex delicto*. The defendant's duty to take due care is the same whether he is called in by the infant, its parent, or any third person. If he undertakes the cure of the patient, it does not matter by whom he is retained.[3] Much less can a defendant, whose substantial liability is in tort, force upon the plaintiff a contract which he has never alleged.[4]

If there are substantial claims in both tort and contract, the plaintiff can recover on either, subject to the provisions of the County Court Acts of which we shall speak shortly. In *Denton* v. *G.N.R. Co.*,[5] the defendants published a time-table indicating that a train would

[1] *Per* A. L. Smith L.J. in *Turner* v. *Stallibrass* [1898] 1 Q.B. 56,58.
[2] *Turner* v. *Stallibrass* (*supra*); and Bramwell L.J. in *Bryant* v. *Herbert* (1878) 3 C.P.D. 389.
[3] *Gladwell* v. *Steggall* (1839) 5 Bing. N.C. 733. *Pippin* v. *Sheppard* (1822) 11 Price, 400. *De Freville* v. *Dill* (1927) 96 L.J.K.B. 1056.
[4] *Edwards* v. *Mallan* [1908] 1 K.B. 1002 (unskilful extraction of tooth by dentist).
[5] (1856) 5 E. & B. 860.

70 TORT AND CONTRACT

start at a particular time. The plaintiff, on proffering the money for a ticket at the booking-office, was told that the service had been cancelled. The defendants were held liable by the whole court for deceit, and by a majority of the court alternatively for breach of contract; and one judge, Crompton J., suggested yet another possible ground—that the defendants had committed a breach of their duties as public carriers in not accepting the plaintiff as a passenger. The case is still an authority for the principle stated above, though the ground of deceit can scarcely hold good since *Derry* v. *Peek*.[1] It shews that there may be some difficulty in particular cases in deciding whether both claims are substantial.[2] *Austin* v. *G.W.R. Co.*[3] is another example of this. A woman and her child were travelling in the defendants' train, and the child was injured through the defendants' negligence. The mother had bought a ticket for herself, but none for the child. She apparently acted in the honest belief that none was necessary, although the child was just over the age which would have entitled it to a free pass. The child sued for damages. Cockburn C.J., Shee and Lush JJ., held that there was a contract to carry the mother and the plaintiff, even though no ticket had been procured for the child. Cockburn C.J. went further, and said that the plaintiff could still have recovered for negligence, even if the mother had made a misrepresentation which would have rendered her liable for the residue of the fare and to a penalty under a by-law of the defendants. Blackburn J.[4]

---

[1] (1889) 14 App. Cas. 337. See the criticisms of *Denton* v. *G.N.R. Co.* in Pollock, *Torts* (13th ed.), 305, 561.

[2] Crompton J. doubted whether there was a contract. *Hayn* v. *Culliford* (1879) 4 C.P.D. 182 is an instance in which there was some doubt as to the existence of a contract, but none at all as to the existence of a tort.

[3] (1867) 8 B. & S. 327.

[4] Following Jervis C.J. in *Marshall* v. *York, etc. R. Co.* (1851) 11 C.B. 655.

TORT AND CONTRACT 71

took what appears to be a much more persuasive view than either of those adopted by his judicial brethren. He held that the ground of the action was not contract, but the duty to carry the plaintiff safely; and that no such duty would have arisen if the plaintiff had been taken into the train without the authority of the defendants, or if there had been fraud on the mother's part. A later decision, in which the earlier authorities were reviewed, adopted the same reasoning and laid it down that, whether there is a co-existent contract or not, the duty extends to anyone whom a railway company invites, or knowingly permits, to enter their train.[1] This is a more felicitous explanation of their liability than unduly straining the law of contract as the majority of the judges did in *Austin* v. *G.W.R. Co.*, or bringing it into collision with the law of deceit, as Cockburn C.J. did. The duty extends to the passenger's luggage as well as to his person.[2] The law, past and present, was clearly put by Lord Esher in *Kelly* v. *Metropolitan R. Co.*[3]

In old times the question of injury to a passenger through something done by the servants of a railway company gave rise to a dispute whether such an action was an action of contract or one of tort, and it was ultimately settled that the plaintiff might maintain an action either in contract or in tort. In the former case he might allege a contract by the railway company to carry him with reasonable care and skill, and a breach of that contract; and on the other hand, he might allege that he was being carried by the railway company to the knowledge of their servants, who were bound not to injure him by any negligence on their part, and if they were negligent that was a matter on which an action of tort could be brought. At the present time a plaintiff may frame his claim in either way, but he is not bound by the pleadings, and if he puts his claim on one ground and proves it on

---

[1] *Foulkes* v. *Metrop. Dist. R. Co.* (1879) 4 C.P.D. 267, 5 C.P.D. 157.
[2] *Marshall* v. *York, etc. R. Co.* (1851) 11 C.B. 655.
[3] [1895] 1 Q.B. 944, 946.

72   TORT AND CONTRACT

another he is not now embarrassed by any rules as to departure. The question to be tried is the same in either case. The plaintiff must rely on and prove negligence, and whether that negligence is active or passive seems to me to be immaterial.

The principle is not limited to railway companies. In *Dalyell* v. *Tyrer*,[1] a passenger who had a season ticket with X, a ferryman, was negligently injured while being ferried by Y on Y's boat, which X had hired in order to deal with extra traffic. The passenger sued Y successfully. Erle J. regarded him as a passenger for hire because he had hired X, who in turn had hired Y; but both Erle J. and the other judge, Hill J., thought it immaterial whether there were hire of Y, or not, by the plaintiff; it was enough that the plaintiff was on board Y's ship with Y's consent.

If the wrong alleged amounts to neither breach of contract nor to tort, no action will lie. This axiom would not be worth stating but for the fact that attempts have been made to set it at naught. No amount of ingenuity in pleading will enable a plaintiff to succeed in alternative claims on contract or in tort where the contract is not with the defendant and where the ingredients of the tort alleged are not all present.[2]

Up to this point, discussion has been confined to alternative claims against the same party, though in some of the cases cited it is apparent that a claim might have existed against another person. We have now to consider more closely variations of facts of this sort. The circumstance that a plaintiff, who is suing John in tort, may also have an alternative remedy in contract against Peter, will not prevent him from succeeding in the action against John. There can be no doubt that if the plaintiff in *Dalyell* v. *Tyrer* had preferred to sue the

---

[1] (1858) E.B. & E. 899.
[2] *Tollit* v. *Sherstone* (1839) 5 M. & W. 283. *Howard* v. *Shepherd* (1850) 9 C.B. 297.

TORT AND CONTRACT 73

person with whom he had originally contracted he would have been perfectly entitled to do so. And there is later actual authority which supports this. A master paid for his servant's railway ticket, and the servant's luggage was negligently injured by the railway company's employees. The company were held liable to the servant, for their duty arose, not from any contract, but by reason of a duty implied by law to carry the plaintiff safely.[1] So too where the plaintiff was injured by the negligence of the *A* railway company, he recovered damages in tort against them, although his ticket was issued by the *B* railway company; for there was an arrangement between the companies under which one made use of the station and platform belonging to the other.[2] Naturally the plaintiff cannot get damages twice over, but some of the arguments in this last case went the length of urging that he could not recover any at all.[3]

The like law applies where, on the same facts, one wrongdoer has exposed himself to separate actions by *A* for breach of contract and by *B* for tort. The absence of any such contract would not release him from liability in tort. The presence of it is equally irrelevant on that point.[4]

So far there is little difficulty, but a clear rule has been somewhat obscured by unwarrantable attempts to press the doctrine of privity of contract beyond its true limits. It is a trite saying in our law that, in general, no one except the parties to a contract can sue for a breach of it. But it is equally true that a stranger to a contract

[1] *Marshall* v. *York, etc. R. Co.* (1851) 11 C.B. 655.
[2] *Foulkes* v. *Metrop. Dist. R. Co.* (1879) 4 C.P.D. 267. 5 C.P.D. 157.
[3] *Ibid.* See too Bramwell B. in *Martin* v. *G.I.P.R. Co.* (1867) L.R. 3 C.P. 9, 14.
[4] *Meux* v. *G.E.R. Co.* [1895] 2 Q.B. 387 (negligent injury to livery of plaintiff's servant, the contract of carriage being with the servant).

74   TORT AND CONTRACT

may have a good cause of action against one of the
parties to a contract, not because that party happens to
be a contractor, but because he has committed an independent tort by conduct which happens also to be
the misperformance of his contract. In other words, the
existence of a contract between A and B is entirely irrelevant to the determination of A's liability in tort to C.
It cannot help C, but it cannot hinder him. The second
limb of this proposition is apt to be overlooked. In the
oft-cited case of *Winterbottom* v. *Wright*,[1] A contracted
with the Postmaster-General to provide a coach for
carriage of mail-bags along a certain road. B contracted
to horse the coach along the same road, and hired C to
drive the coach. It was held by the Court of Exchequer
that C could not maintain an action against A for an
injury sustained by him while driving the coach, owing
to its breakdown from latent defects in its construction.
A could not be liable to C on a contract made between
A and the Postmaster-General. That decision was
correct and it has been repeatedly followed, but some
of the expressions used in it, especially by Lord Abinger C.B., are likely to be misconstrued. They shew such
strong concentration on the sacredness of privity of
contract that they seem to ignore the possibility of
further development of the law of tort, and especially
of the law of negligence. The sphere of that has steadily
broadened since *Winterbottom* v. *Wright*, and the fixing
of new duties which raise liability for it has given a
remedy in tort to many a plaintiff who would have gone
away empty-handed a century ago. Lord Abinger's
judgment represents the law as more static than it was
in this respect even in his own time, and *Winterbottom* v.
Wright induced in some quarters a hypnotic gaze on
privity of contract which has gone perilously near to the
argument that *because* there is a contract between A and

[1] (1842) 10 M. & W. 109.

TORT AND CONTRACT 75

B, *C* cannot recover in tort against *A* on facts which constitute also a breach of that contract. This fallacy appears in *Alton* v. *M.R. Co.*[1] The decision was that an action will not lie against a railway company as carriers of passengers for hire, at the suit of a master for negligent injury to his servant causing loss of his services; for the contract to carry safely was between the company and the servant. The case has met with acute criticism and cannot now be regarded as law.[2] Even Willes J., who was one of the four judges, seems to have confused two different propositions: (*a*) No stranger to a contract can, in general, sue on it. (*b*) A master can sue a person in tort for an injury done to his servant which deprives him of the latter's services. These rules are quite independent of each other and quite consistent with each other.[3]

A less mischievous, though still objectionable, way of applying *Winterbottom* v. *Wright* is in connection with ulterior liability arising from the sale of a dangerous chattel. If *A* sells such a thing to *B*, who resells it to *C* and *C* is injured thereby, has *C* a remedy in tort against *A*? One line of approaching this problem is to say that *C* cannot sue *A* on a contract made between *A* and *B* except in certain cases, then to enumerate those cases, and finally to ascertain whether *C*'s claim comes within them.[4] But a more accurate way of considering *A*'s liability to *C* is entirely to ignore the existence of the contract between *A* and *B*, and to apply the law of tort only, bearing in mind that it is still growing and that it

---

[1] (1865) 19 C.B.N.S. 213.

[2] E.g. 1 Williams' Saund. (ed. 1871), 473–474. Pollock, *Torts* (13th ed.), 568–570.

[3] This is not the only misadventure which rule (*b*) has undeservedly encountered in the courts. *Osborn* v. *Gillett* (1873) L.R. 8 Ex. 88; *Clark* v. *L.G.O. Co.* [1906] 2 K.B. 648.

[4] Lush J. in *Blacker* v. *Lake & Elliot, Ld.* (1912) 106 L.T. 533, 540–541.

76   TORT AND CONTRACT

is capable of creating new duties in no way derogatory to privity of contract and quite separate from it.

Contract is a province of the law in which conceptions are much more settled than in the law of tort, and there is a danger of giving undue precedence to fixed ideas in the former when they come in contact with the latter. In negligence, for example, it is impossible to render a person liable in tort unless there is a preceding duty to take care. That is a question of law. Judges must decide in each case whether such a duty exists, and they have not always appreciated that this is their province. Such expressions as "There is nothing to shew how any liability or duty to the plaintiff could arise"[1] mask the fact that the plaintiff may well be, and often has been, successful, not because he has been able to prove the existence of duty by citing any previous case but simply because the court there and then is minded to hold that one exists.

Incidentally, it is interesting to notice that the idea of privity of contract as the perfect sphere which must be marred by neither indentation nor protuberance has met with less respect in current American law than on the English side of the Atlantic. We cannot say more of it here, for it is appropriate to the borderland between contract and trust, not to that between contract and tort.[2]

The influence of the County Court Acts on the division between contract and tort, whatever its practical success, has been unfortunate as a matter of science. We have noted that for certain purposes those Acts classify actions as either "founded upon contract", or

---

[1] Bovill C.J. in *Collis* v. *Selden* (1868) L.R. 3 C.P. 95.

[2] *Restatement of the Law of Contracts* (Official draft, 1928), chap. 6. See too Professor A. L. Corbin in 46 *Law Quarterly Review* (1930), 12–45, and the author in 11 *Journal of Comparative Legislation* (1929), 187–188.

TORT AND CONTRACT 77

"founded upon tort".[1] Now this takes no account of the existence of quasi-contract, and it sets up a statutory exception to the rule that a plaintiff can allege in the same action two different causes of action and that he will have the benefit of whichever he proves. According to the County Court Acts, the claim must be either in tort or on contract; it cannot be both. The High Court judges have loyally done their best to apply this legislation, but the task has been an unpalatable one for some of them. Lindley L.J. (as he then was) said in 1895:

We no longer have to consider forms of actions, but are compelled by the legislature to put every action which can be brought in the County Court, but is brought in the High Court, into one or the other of these two categories. Every one who has studied the English law will know perfectly well that there is a debateable ground between torts and contracts. There are what are called quasi-contracts and quasi-torts; and it is sometimes not easy to say whether a cause is founded on contract or on tort. Very often a cause of action may be treated either as a breach of contract or as a tort. But here we are compelled to draw the line hard and fast and put every one of the actions into one class or the other.[2]

This compulsory dichotomy has in one direction forced the courts to attach more weight to what is embodied in the declaration (or, as it now is, the statement of claim) than to the substance of the claim. True, "it has been repeatedly laid down that this question of costs does not depend on the technical form of the pleadings, but that the substance of the matter must be looked at".[3] True, again, this principle is applicable with ease where the facts shew clearly that there is exclusively a tort and

---

[1] *Ante*, p. 64.

[2] *Taylor* v. *M.S. & L.R. Co.* [1895] 1 Q.B. 134, 138. So too Collins M.R. in *Sachs* v. *Henderson* [1902] 1 K.B. 612, 616.

[3] Collins M.R. in *Sachs* v. *Henderson* [1902] 1 K.B. 612, 615. Bramwell L.J. in *Bryant* v. *Herbert* (1878) 3 C.P.D. 389, 390. *Turner* v. *Stallibrass* [1898] 1 Q.B. 56. *Steljes* v. *Ingram* (1903) 19 T.L.R. 534.

78 TORT AND CONTRACT

nothing else, or exclusively a breach of contract and nothing else. But it breaks down where the plaintiff shews on the same facts both a substantial cause of action in tort and a substantial cause of action for breach of contract. The County Court Acts have deprived the judicature of the power to pronounce that the plaintiff may (in the matter of costs) have a good claim in either contract or tort. The awkwardness of this Procrustean treatment of the law was exemplified in *Pontifex* v. *M.R. Co.*[1] It was held that where a seller directs a common carrier not to deliver goods to an insolvent buyer, and the carrier nevertheless delivers the goods, the action against him is founded on tort and not on contract, within the County Courts Act, 1867. The court regarded the contract of carriage as terminated by the demand for the return of the goods. From that moment the defendant's retention of, and dealing with, them became tortious. But it would have been more natural for the court to hold (if the legislature had not deprived it of the power to do so) that the claim was as substantially a breach of contract as a tort.

Moreover, some of the decisions on the statutory distinction are not easily reconcilable.[2] But odd results must be expected when Parliament lays violent hands upon legal history.

Next, as to the measure of damages when the plaintiff alleges facts which may alternatively constitute a tort or a breach of contract. It has been noticed already that vindictive damages are possible in tort but only

---

[1] (1877) 3 Q.B.D. 23.

[2] *Fleming* v. *M.S. & L.R. Co.* (1878) 4 Q.B.D. 81 is consistent with *Tattan* v. *G.W.R. Co.* (1860) 2 E. & E. 844, only if it is taken as a decision on an earlier Act. Even so, the C.A. regarded *Tattan's Case* as unsatisfactory. *Baylis* v. *Lintott* (1873) L.R. 8 C.P. is not so much a reflection on the County Court Acts as upon the conservatism of the court in declining to hold that there was a duty to take care, independently of contract.

TORT AND CONTRACT 79

very exceptionally for breach of contract. Again, a claim in conversion may entitle the plaintiff to the full value of the goods converted, while a claim on a co-existent contract will give him no more than compensation for the loss of his bargain. Where there are differences of this sort in his favour, is he to be deprived of the higher award of damages simply because he has alleged alternatively in his action a breach of contract? The common-sense answer is, "No, if he has really established a tort". Why should he be the worse off because he has joined two causes of action and has proved one only, if that one puts him in a position to ask for a larger amount of damages? Or, to vary the question, why should a defendant profit by the fact that he has presumptively committed two wrongs instead of one?

The law seems to follow the common-sense argument here.

"During many years when I was a junior at the Bar", said Lord James of Hereford, "when I was drawing pleadings, I often strove to convert a breach of contract into a tort in order to recover a higher scale of damages, it having been then as it is now, I believe, the general impression of the profession that such damages cannot be recovered in an action of contract as distinguished from tort....That view, which I was taught early to understand was the law in olden days, remains true to this day."[1]

Marzetti v. *Williams*[2] is a case in point. A banker, who had funds belonging to a customer sufficient to meet the customer's cheque, nevertheless dishonoured it. The customer sued the banker in tort. He could prove no actual damage. The Court of King's Bench unanimously held that he was entitled to nominal damages as for breach of contract. The action was in fact founded on contract, for a banker does contract with his

[1] *Addis* v. *Gramophone Co. Ld.* [1909] A.C. 488, 492.
[2] (1830) 1 B. & Ad. 415.

80   TORT AND CONTRACT

customer that he will pay cheques drawn by him, provided he has money in his hands belonging to that customer. The plaintiff might therefore have declared in *assumpsit*. But it was immaterial whether he cast his claim in that form or in tort.[1] It was substantially founded on contract and that was enough to give him nominal damages. A plaintiff cannot, however, evade a substantive rule of law by framing his claim alternatively, whether for the purpose of swelling the amount of damages or in order to secure any other end. No minor can be made liable in contract merely by suing him in tort.[2] But this is only another way of saying that the claim in tort has no substance at all.[3]

Chinery v. *Viall*[4] is a decision not easy to reconcile with principle. *A* sold some sheep to *B*, *B* thereby acquiring ownership of them. *A* remained in possession of the sheep as *B*'s agent and resold them to *C*. *B* sued *A*, and in his declaration counted, first, upon breach of contract, secondly, upon trover. It was held that the resale was a conversion of the sheep by *A*, but that the measure of damages was not the sheep (about £119) but £5 which was the loss sustained by *B*. This was a strong case, for the court had no doubt that trover had been proved, but they regarded the principle as established that "a man cannot by merely changing the form of action entitle himself to recover damages greater than the amount to which he is in law entitled, according to the true facts of the case and the real nature of the transaction".[5] This seems to be a sound statement of principle, but a misapplication of it to the facts in hand. If the plaintiff has not made out a substantial claim, be it

[1] It could scarcely come within any current definition of tort. Cf. Salmond, *Torts* (7th ed.), pp. 5–6.
[2] *Green* v. *Greenbank* (1816) 2 Marshall, 485.
[3] See *Clark* v. *Urquhart* [1930] A.C 28, at p. 50.
[4] (1860) 5 H. & N. 288.
[5] At p. 295.

TORT AND CONTRACT 81

in contract or in tort, he can recover nothing. If he has established a substantial claim in one, but not in the other, his damages must be awarded on the scale appropriate to that one. If both claims are substantial, then he ought to have the benefit of the higher scale. The facts in *Chinery* v. *Viall* fell under this third head. Yet the court seems to have penalized the plaintiff because he had two good claims instead of one. Perhaps, however, a better way of looking at the decision is to regard it as a limitation on the general rule that in trover the measure of damages is the full value of the goods. Unqualified application of that rule would have been unfair to the defendant in *Chinery* v. *Viall*.[1]

Whatever may be the explanation of this case, it seems correct to say that, both anciently and at the present day, a plaintiff may sue alternatively where he has alternative claims and may reap the benefit of whichever claim he establishes to be the substantial one, and that if both prove to be substantial, he gets the advantages attendant upon the superior claim, but that he is not allowed to turn a substantial claim into what is really an unsubstantial one in order to profit by the latter. Thus in *Columbus Co. Ld.* v. *Clowes*[2] the plaintiffs claimed alternatively (*a*) return of money by the defendant on a total failure of consideration; (*b*) damages for the defendant's negligence. The first claim failed because the failure of consideration was not total, and, though the second was good, still only nominal damages were recoverable, because the plaintiffs had suffered no loss.[3]

There are other points of contact between tort and contract, besides the common ground of alternative claims.

---

[1] But see Clerk & Lindsell, *Torts* (8th ed. 1929), 242 note *o*.
[2] [1903] 1 K.B. 244.
[3] Acceptance by the plaintiff of money paid into court by the defendant may extinguish all alternative claims. *Clark* v. *Urquhart* [1930] A.C. 28.

W P

82 TORT AND CONTRACT

Of the torts of wilful inducement of breach of contract and of unlawful interference with freedom of contract, nothing can usefully be said that is not accessible in any textbook on tort. And for the same reason we can pass by such familiar rules as that minors or married women cannot be made liable on a pure contract by suing them in tort.

But the relation of contract to the maxim, *Volenti non fit injuria*, deserves more attention. The Latin maxim epitomizes the general rule that harm suffered in a lawful sport, operation, or other process, cannot be made the subject of an action in tort by one who has consented to such harm, or (what is more usual) to the risks normally incident to such matters. The maxim is commonly cited in connection with injuries to the person, but it extends to injuries to property as well,[1] though the principle in its application to them is generally to be found under the rubric, "leave and licence", or "licence". Many examples of it have nothing whatever to do with contract, e.g. harm sustained in games like cricket and football; and they are outside the scope of our present inquiry. On the other hand, it is easy to suggest illustrations of assent to the injury, or to the chance of it, being based on contract. A surgeon usually operates under a contract to do so. It seems to be difficult to get modern pugilists into the ring without a preliminary contract between them in which the consideration is substantial. So too contracts for performances, to which bodily perils are incidental, are commonly undertaken by cinematograph actors. Suppose that in any of these contracts the

---

[1] Bracton, f. 413 *b*, uses it without its later technicality, but certainly with no limitation of it to injuries to the person. It occurs in argument in a property case in Y.B. 33 Ed. I (R.S.), pp. 8–9. It is used generally by Manwood J. in *Grendon* v. *Bishop of Lincoln* (18 & 19 Eliz.) Plowden, ff. 493, 500 *b*. In *Horne* v. *Widlake* (6 Jac. I) Yelv. 141, it was the basis of a decision in a property case (trespass *quare clausum fregit*). Addison, *Torts*, seems to prefer "licence" to *volenti non fit injuria*.

TORT AND CONTRACT 83

dangers go beyond what the law allows any person voluntarily to encounter, and he is injured, what is his legal position? The surgeon may have contracted for the performance of a merely experimental operation perilous to the life of one who consents to undergo it in what both consider to be the interests of science, though it has no bearing on the extirpation of disease. Pugilists may have agreed to fight with gloves of less than the regulation weight. The cinematograph actor may have undertaken, indeed often does undertake in America, risks of the most foolhardy kind.

These cases must be considered in three separate aspects of the law.

(*a*) *Criminal law*. A contract to commit a crime is, in general, unlawful. Not only does it not salve whatever crime may be the subject of the contract, but it constitutes the substantive crime of conspiracy. The parties to it are punishable accordingly. Two of the three hypothetical cases which we have suggested are contracts to commit crime; in the first two instances there are bargains for assault and battery; but the third is doubtful. Sir James Stephen was not sure whether any of the parties would be guilty of manslaughter where *A*, with *B's* consent, wheels *B* in a barrow along a tight-rope at a great height from the ground, and spectators pay money to watch this performance, and *B* is killed. On the analogy of prize fights, he was inclined to regard such an exhibition as illegal, and also as a public nuisance in some circumstances.[1] It may also be suggested that, with the modern extension of conspiracy, it might fall under that crime. So far as children are concerned, the legislature has made specific provision for bodily harm sustained by them while taking part in a public ex-

[1] *Digest of Criminal Law* (7th ed. 1926), art. 293. Stephen had no doubt that consent cannot negative criminal liability where death or maim is inflicted for any purpose injurious to the public. *Ibid.* art. 291.

84 TORT AND CONTRACT

hibition dangerous to life.[1] It does not, however, follow that every agreement which may result in the commission of a crime is unlawful. Probably not every contract which leads to a breach of the peace is against the law.[2]

(*b*) *Law of contract.* Contracts of the type to which we have referred are unlawful, and nothing is recoverable under them. But the grounds on which they are unlawful have not always been properly appreciated. It may be said that a contract to commit a tort is forbidden by the law and that this is a sufficient reason. But this bald proposition needs a good deal of qualification. As a general rule, a contract between Smith and Jones to commit a tort on Brown is unlawful, as where Smith hires Jones to beat Brown; but the decided cases go no farther than that.[3] Nor is it always unlawful even then. Thus, if several people agree to trespass on *A*'s land, in order to decide a dispute as to a right of way, it may turn out that what they do is a trespass, but, assuming that they have acted in good faith, each has a right of contribution against the others.

Where the contract provides for the commission of a tort on one of the contracting parties, it may be lawful. It is doubtful whether an express term that fraud shall not vitiate a contract would be bad in law.[4] Again many acts done upon the land of another would be trespass but for a contract which expressly or implicitly permits them. If there be a covenant for re-entry by a lessor on

[1] Children's Dangerous Performances Act, 1879, s. 3. The employer is indictable for assault and, if convicted, may be ordered to award compensation up to £20.

[2] Cf. Phillimore J. in *Dann* v. *Curzon* (1910) 104 L.T. 66, 68, with *Woodward* v. *Mayor, etc. of Battersea* (1911) 104 L.T. 51, and Hawkins J. in *R.* v. *Coney* (1882) 8 Q.B.D. 534, 553.

[3] They are collected in Pollock, *Contract* (9th ed. 1921), 342 *seq.* American law is to the like effect; Williston, *Contracts* (1920), § 1738.

[4] Lord James of Hereford in *S. Pearson, Ld.* v. *Dublin Corporation* [1907] A.C. 351, 362. Cf. *Redmond* v. *Wynne* (1892) 13 N.S.W.L.R. 39.

TORT AND CONTRACT

non-payment of rent by the lessee, that will justify trespass to the land and possibly assault also.[1] So too a private nuisance may be authorized by contract. It may be urged that in all these instances there is no tort from the very beginning, because one of the essentials of such liability is absent. But whether we take this view or the one that there is presumptively tortious liability which the law allows to be negatived by the consent of the parties, such consent being a plea of justification, is immaterial. In either event the question remains, "In what circumstances is a contract unlawful if its purpose is a negation of tortious liability?" The answer seems to be that where the conduct contemplated is likely to menace public morality or safety, or, more broadly, is contrary to public policy, any contract to pursue such conduct is unlawful, and nothing is recoverable. *Ex turpi causa non oritur actio.* All three contracts which were put as examples above, seem to be vitiated on this ground. There is no fixed line for determining what is public policy. At any given time it is the sense of the community as interpreted by the courts.[2]

A curious illustration of the test which we have suggested is *Dann* v. *Curzon.*[3] In order to advertise the theatre of the defendant who was lessee of it, the plaintiffs contracted with him to occupy stalls in which they would wear large hats calculated to obstruct the view of other spectators. It was arranged that they should be requested to remove their hats, and, on refusing to do so, that they should be formally arrested, and that they should then summon the defendant for assault. His defence was to be that he was protecting the convenience of the audience. The scheme was carried out. The

---

[1] *Kavanagh* v. *Gudge* (1844) 7 M. & G. 316.

[2] 42 *Harvard Law Review*, 96–100. For an apparent coincidence of tort and contract see Salmond & Winfield, *Contracts*, pp. 150–152.

[3] (1910) 104 L.T. 66.

86   TORT AND CONTRACT

magistrate dismissed the summons. The plaintiffs sued the defendant for the reward promised to them. The Divisional Court held that it was irrecoverable, because the agreements were against public policy and were therefore illegal and unenforceable. Each side was left to pay its own costs. There was no assault, because the agreement negatived it, but the contract was in the nature of a fraud upon the administration of justice, for it was to procure an adjudication upon something which, to the knowledge of the parties, had never happened. "It was an agreement to make a plaything of the administration of justice for the purpose of advertising a theatre."[1]

The basis of the decision was, therefore, not the narrow one of agreement to commit a crime or a tort, but the broad one of public policy.

(c) *Law of tort.* It is admitted that *volenti non fit injuria* does not apply to unlawful sports, operations, or processes, or to unlawful incidents in sports, etc., which are lawful. Logically, therefore, the plaintiff ought to be able to sue for any injury which he has sustained in such circumstances; and whether there has been a contract or not ought to make no difference. But the textbooks are not in agreement as to whether this is the law.[2] The reported cases and *dicta* are scanty.

---

[1] Horridge J. at p. 69.

[2] Pollock, *Torts*, 164, holds it to be the better opinion that a man who licenses another to beat him is not deprived of his right of action. Salmond, *Torts*, § 13 (2), says that if two men injure each other in a prize fight, it is difficult to suppose that either of them has a good cause of action against the other. Note (*o*) on p. 59, deals rather too summarily with the matter; *Christopherson* v. *Bare* (1848) 11 Q.B. 473, 477, does not support the statement for which it is cited. Clerk & Lindsell, 174, concentrate attention more on the criminal aspect of the conduct than on its tortious side, and it is difficult to say what is the opinion of the learned authors. They cite without comment *Boulter* v. *Clark* (1747) Buller N.P. 16 (*post*, p. 87). Addison, *Torts* (8th ed. 1906), 70, expresses no opinion.

TORT AND CONTRACT

In *Clark's Case* (1596),[1] the plea to an action for false imprisonment was that the plaintiff was a burgess in the St Alban's Corporation and had consented to a by-law which justified his imprisonment. The plea was held bad, and the plaintiff had judgment. "The plaintiff's assent cannot alter the law in such case." This is not to say that restraint of the person can never be justified by agreement or contract; e.g. a patient in a nursing home.

Matthew v. *Ollerton* (1694)[2] contains an *obiter dictum* of the King's Bench that "licence to beat me is void, because 'tis against the Peace".

In *Boulter* v. *Clark* (1747),[3] counsel for the defence in an action for assault and battery wished to bring evidence to shew that the parties fought by consent and that this would bar the action, for *volenti non fit injuria*. But Parker C.B. denied it, and said that, fighting being unlawful, the consent of the plaintiff to fight (if proved) would be no bar to his action, and that he was entitled to a verdict for the injury done to him.[4]

There are several *dicta* in criminal cases which need not be reproduced here, as their context makes it doubtful whether they are to be regarded as applying to the possibility of an action in tort. One exception is an opinion of Hawkins J. in *R.* v. *Coney*.[5]

It may be that consent can in all cases be given so as to operate as a bar to a civil action; upon the ground that no man can claim damages for an act to which he himself was an assenting party.... It is not necessary, however, upon the present occasion to express any decided opinion upon the point.

These cases and opinions are not of much assistance

[1] 5 Rep. 64*a*. [2] Comb. 218.
[3] Buller N.P. 16. Cited by Cave J. in *R.* v. *Coney* (1882) 8 Q.B.D. 534, 538.
[4] *Christopherson* v. *Bare* (1848) 11 Q.B. 473, proceeded upon a point in pleading.
[5] (1882) 8 Q.B.D. 534, 553.

88 TORT AND CONTRACT

for they are either confined to some particular tort or are obviously unconsidered generalities.

Perhaps the true principle is that which we have suggested in the law of contract. There is no sweeping rule either that the plaintiff, where *volenti non fit injuria* has no application, can always maintain an action in tort, or that he can never maintain one. Either way unjust results would ensue, and neither view is supported by authority. A more acceptable rule is that the plaintiff can sue and recover damages, unless allowing him to do so would be against public policy in general, or would be the condonation of a breach of public morals or public safety in particular. Thus, in a boxing match, the plaintiff may have committed a breach of the rules, and this may have provoked an assault upon him by the defendant. The facts fall outside *volenti non fit injuria*, but there can be no doubt that the plaintiff may recover at least nominal damages for assault. There is nothing contrary to public policy in allowing him to do so. On the other hand, if the whole contest be illegal, like a fight with bare fists, it would appear to be against public policy to allow either combatant to bring an action for assault against the other. Useful arguments here may be adopted from the attitude of criminal law towards such fighting, and especially from some of the *dicta* in *R.* v. *Coney.*[1] The court had not the least doubt about the illegality of a fight (apparently with bare fists) between two trained pugilists; and the reason for this was clearly put by Stephen J.[2] "The injuries given and received in prize-fights are injurious to the public, both because it is against the public interest that the lives and the health of the combatants should be endangered by blows, and because prize-fights are disorderly exhibitions, mischievous on many obvious grounds." This reasoning

[1] (1882) 8 Q.B.D. 534.
[2] *Ibid.* 549. See too Mathew J. at p. 544.

TORT AND CONTRACT

seems to be equally applicable to preventing either combatant from suing the other for any injuries received. The law ought to forbid him from bringing such an action, for though his consent, or contract, to endure such assaults and batteries was futile, yet it would be against public policy that he should get any private redress in the matter. If this is not a genuine example of the working of *ex turpi causa non oritur actio*, what is? If, however, one combatant killed the other, ought the relatives of the dead man to be allowed to maintain an action under Lord Campbell's Act, 1846? Yes, both on the principle stated and on the construction of the Act, section 1 of which provides that the action conferred by the Statute shall be maintainable, although the death in respect of which it is brought shall have been caused by a felony.

It appears, then, that different conclusions are quite possible even with respect to the same tort, and this must necessarily be so wherever public policy is in question. Much more will there be variant solutions throughout the range of torts in general. Where leave and licence are abused in connection with interference with property, it is difficult to imagine cases in which the injured party would be disentitled from suing. He might lose his action on other grounds,[1] but not because the mere bringing of it would be obnoxious to public policy, unless indeed it were a sham tort of the kind alleged in *Dann* v. *Curzon*.[2]

Another example that neatly illustrates the principle is a contract which authorizes the commission, within limits, of a nuisance. If such limits are exceeded, the injured party would be able to sue in tort; but no agreement between parties will make a public nuisance non-criminal.

---

[1] E.g. *Six Carpenters' Case* (1610) 8 Rep. 146*a*.
[2] (1910) 104 L.T. 66, *ante*, p. 85.

90 TORT AND CONTRACT

Some difficulty has been felt about the hypothetical case of two men who have been guilty of indecent conduct towards each other bringing cross-actions for assault. It is said that it would seem strange to allow such actions, and this incongruity is made the starting-point of an argument against permitting an action of any sort where the harm is such as the law does not countenance.[1] It might be urged that the strangeness would consist, not in allowing the actions, but in imagining the effrontery of any persons in instituting them; but more impudent litigation than that has been promoted in our law courts.[2] The real solution of the difficulty is once again the application of public policy, which would almost certainly deny the use of legal procedure for such a scandalous purpose.[3]

Public policy of this sort is occasionally embodied in an Act of Parliament. The Workmen's Compensation Acts within the last generation have in effect insured most workmen against the risks of their employment. Contracting out of the operation of this legislation is permissible only on stringent conditions. It can only take the form of the substitution of a benefit scheme between the workman and the employer, which is approved by the Registrar of Friendly Societies, and it must be at least as beneficial to the workman as his

[1] Clerk & Lindsell (8th ed.), 174.
[2] In *Everet* v. *Williams* (1725) 9 *Law Quarterly Review*, 197, one highwayman sued another for a partnership account of the proceeds of their robberies. The action was dismissed. The plaintiff and the defendant were hanged.
[3] In *Hegarty* v. *Shine* (1878) 14 Cox C.C. 145, the Irish C.A. held, in a civil action for assault by a woman who had been infected with venereal disease by the defendant with whom she was cohabiting, and who concealed the fact that he was infected, that the action was not maintainable, first, because the plaintiff's consent to the intercourse negatived the allegation of assault; secondly, because the action was based on immorality.

TORT AND CONTRACT 91

statutory rights.[1] Unless these requirements are satisfied, the workman can sue for injury from negligence and other accidental harm, despite his contract.

This completes our examination of tort in relation to contract. Matters of wider application, like the Statutes of Limitations are dealt with in a later lecture.[2]

[1] Workmen's Compensation Act, 1925, ss. 1 (3), 31 (1).
[2] *Post*, chap. XI.

Chapter V

TORT AND BAILMENT[1]

THE relation of tort to breach of bailment and of bailment to contract is necessarily affected by the very early appearance of the idea of bailment in our law as covering any delivery of the possession of goods to another for any purpose. Moreover, all the forms of bailment which we know at the present day were recognized in Bracton's time.[2] This is one of the notably Romanesque parts of his book, and centuries later Chief Justice Holt, in founding the modern law of bailment, acted under similar influence. In Bracton's time, the relations of bailor to bailee are described simply enough. The bailee was strictly, perhaps absolutely, liable to the bailor for loss of, or injury to, the article bailed. That is what Glanvill says of the *commodatarius*,[3] and there is reason to think that it applied to other bailees.[4] Bracton, influenced by Roman law, was willing to mitigate this severe rule, which, incidentally, seems to be one of the very few genuine examples of "absolute" liability;[5] but his attempt was premature.[6] That is Maitland's view, but Britton does excuse the borrower for accident by fire, water, robbery or larceny, or accidents other than those due to negligence.[7] Professor Holdsworth

---

[1] For the history of bailment, see Street, *Foundations of Liability* (1906), ii, 251–307; Holdsworth, *History of English Law*, iii, 336–349; vii, 448–455; Ames, *Lectures on Legal History*, Index, "Bailment".

[2] Pollock & Maitland, ii, 169, 170.

[3] x, 13.

[4] Pollock & Maitland, ii, 171. Holdsworth, *op. cit.* iii, 338–339.

[5] 42 *Law Quarterly Review*, 37–51.

[6] Pollock & Maitland, ii, 171.

[7] Ed. Nichols, i, 157.

TORT AND BAILMENT 93

also admits that in the Year Books there are some indications of a tendency to modify the bailee's liability, though, in his opinion, these attempts were unsuccessful.[1] At any rate, where suit was possible at all, the bailee in general could sue for injury to, or loss of, the goods.

Now this right of the bailee was settled in our law before we had any real theory of contract, and therefore the relations of bailment to contract could scarcely have troubled lawyers. The bailee's right was consistently based on his possession of the chattel. Why then seek any other ground of liability at that period?

As to liability in what we should now call tort, in the fifteenth century the bailee who was guilty of negligent misfeasance in breach of his undertaking was liable to an action in tort based on his undertaking.[2] The normal remedy against the bailee was detinue. But the concurrent remedy of action on the case was needed, partly because the wager of law might be used by the defendant in detinue and might defeat the action, partly because, if the plaintiff had paid in advance for the safe custody of his property, he could by suing detinue recover, not his money, but only the value of the property.

Action upon the case first appears in this connection in 1449,[3] was impliedly recognized in 1472,[4] and was expressly upheld in 1487.[5] The action was in tort, not on contract. It was based, like the action against the surgeon or the carpenter, on an undertaking (an as-

---

[1] *Op. cit.* iii, 342–343. The learned author, however, gives examples from the Y.BB. which shew the development of the theory that if the bailee cannot sue (e.g. in damage by the King's enemies or the act of God) he is not liable to the bailor. *Ibid.* 343–344.

[2] Statham, *Abr.* Accion sur le cas (27 Hen. VI), 25, and Y.BB. Mich. 12 Ed. IV, pl. 10; Hil. 2 Hen. VII, pl. 9. Ames, *op. cit.* 132, 133.

[3] Statham, *Abr.* Accion sur le cas, 25.

[4] Y.B. Mich. 12 Ed. IV, f. 13, pl. 10.

[5] Y.B. Hil. 2 Hen. VII, f. 11, pl. 9.

94 TORT AND BAILMENT

sumpsit); and consideration was no more an essential of liability in the one case than in the other.[1] It is styled merely "action upon the case", but we may safely describe it as an action in tort. Liability of the "undertaking" type is much older than the application of *assumpsit* to make simple contracts enforceable. At first, it was necessary to allege *assumpsit* in suing this action upon the case, except against those bailees whose calling was of a quasi-public nature, such as the common carrier and innkeeper, for they were chargeable by the custom of the realm,[2] which may be taken as equivalent to the Common Law. In 1598, all four judges present in the Queen's Bench held that the action did not lie without such special *assumpsit*.[3] But in 1628, in an action against a common lighterman, the King's Bench held that the plaintiff could recover for the defendant's negligence though there had been no promise and no allegation that he was a common lighterman. The case well illustrates difficulties of classification of the action, for while the Chief Justice said that "delivery makes the contract", Whitlock J stated the action to be "*ex malefacto* not *ex contractu*".[4] However that may be, an express undertaking ceased to be necessary.[5] But meanwhile another element of confusion had insinuated itself into bailment. This was the doctrine of consideration. The seeds of this complication had been sown in Elizabethan times, and they produced a fair crop of inconsistent decisions in the course of the next century. Thus, where *A* had delivered wheat to *B*, and *B* had promised to redeliver it to *A* upon *A*'s request, there was undoubtedly a bailment, but when *A* sued *B* in an action

[1] Ames, *op. cit.* 132–133.
[2] *Ibid.* 134.
[3] *Mosley* v. *Fosset*, Moore, 543.
[4] *Symons* v. *Darknoll*, 81 Eng. Rep. 1202. Palmer, 523.
[5] Ames, *op. cit.* 135.

TORT AND BAILMENT 95

of *assumpsit*, nothing was said of bailment, but the King's Bench unanimously held the mere possession of the wheat to be "a good consideration"; but this was reversed in the Exchequer Chamber.[1] This application of consideration to bailments did not escape criticism and doubts,[2] but it was admitted by the whole court in 1608.[3] However, in 1623 the King's Bench veered round to the doctrine that, though there was no consideration in a gratuitous bailment, yet the mere detention of the thing bailed, to the detriment of the bailor, was damage to him upon which he could have his action;[4] but the report appears to put the doctrine aside altogether, and to make the bailee liable in spite of the absence of consideration.[5] Then in *Coggs* v. *Bernard*,[6] which has always been reckoned as the leading case on bailment, and the source of the modern law about it, the court swung back to the necessity of finding consideration. Holt C.J. and Gould J. discovered it in the fact that the owner had trusted the bailee with the goods,[7] and Powell J.'s view was not notably different.[8] The action itself in *Coggs* v. *Bernard* was upon the case, and alleged *assumpsit* on the defendant's part to take care, and neglect to do so.

"The truth is", says Professor Holdsworth, "that all these cases are really cases of delictual liability disguised by the form of

[1] *Riches* v. *Bridges* (1602) Cro. Eliz. 883, Yelv. 4. This is cited by Ames, *op. cit.* 134, note 3. His first citation seems to be wide of the mark. *Howlet* v. *Osborne*, Cro. Eliz. 380, was an action by a *third party* against the bailee.

[2] *Game* v. *Harvie* (1630) Yelv. 50. *Gelley* v. *Clerk* (1606) Cro. Jac. 188. Noy, 126.

[3] *Pickas* v. *Guide* Yelv. 128.

[4] *Loes Case* Palmer, 281; 81 Eng. Rep. 1083; reported as *Wheatley* v. *Low* Cro. Jac. 668. Ames pointed out the great strain which this put on the doctrine of consideration; *op. cit.* 134.

[5] Cf. Holdsworth, *op. cit.* iii, 449.

[6] (1703) 2 Ld Raym. 909.   [7] *Ibid.* 909, 919.

[8] *Ibid.* 911. Cf. Holdsworth, *op. cit.* iii, 449.

96 TORT AND BAILMENT

action. The whole difficulty arises from the fact that the courts allowed a cause of action founded on tort to masquerade as an action founded on contract. The parties were allowed to waive the tort and sue in contract."[1]

Another, though not necessarily dissimilar, impression left by the cases is that the courts never from the first made up their minds that the action was either in tort or on contract, partly because they never analysed "tort", partly because the peculiar origin of *assumpsit* would have puzzled any one who tried to draw a distinction between tort and contract, and partly because the position in our law of those who profess a quasi-public calling was obscure then and even at the present day is not clearly ascertained.[2]

At the beginning of the seventeenth century, the bailee was liable to the bailor:

(i) in detinue, if he did not redeliver the goods;

(ii) in trover, if he converted them;

(iii) in an action upon the case, if he damaged them by negligence, or other wrongful act falling short of conversion.[3]

During the seventeenth and succeeding centuries, the contractual element became more prominent.[4] Sir William Jones, in his final definition of bailment,[5] says that it is "a delivery of goods in trust, on a contract express or implied, that the trust shall be duly executed, and the goods redelivered, as soon as the time or use for which they were bailed shall have elapsed or be performed".

---

[1] Holdsworth, *op. cit.* iii, 449–450.

[2] Cf. O. W. Holmes, *Common Law*, 187.

[3] Holdsworth, *op. cit.* vii, 433.　　　　　[4] *Ibid.*

[5] *Law of Bailments* (1781), 117. It is not stated in his first definition (p. 1), but it is almost instantly implied in the succeeding pages. His strenuous argument that neither consideration *nor feasance* is necessary to found an action on bailment, because that is a peculiarity of bailment, cannot now be accepted. Cf. Story, *Bailments* (1839), 6.

TORT AND BAILMENT 97

We can make this our point of departure for distinguishing at the present day bailment from contract on the one hand and from obligation in tort on the other hand.

It is singular that not more has been done in the way of analyzing the position of bailment in modern law. Sir William Jones and Story were too much hampered by procedural cross-currents to set any very clear course in their time. To-day, something, but not much, might have been expected of monographs for the use of practitioners, but even that small amount is not forthcoming. In jurisprudential literature the omission is more surprising. One of the two leading English textbooks which profess to deal exhaustively with jurisprudence does not even index "Bailment"[1] and the other rests satisfied with the cut-and-dried idea that it is a species of contract.[2] Professor Terry's work, published in the United States, devotes more attention to the abstract side of the subject than it has met with here.[3]

If we adhered to the definition of bailment in most of the textbooks, we should have to place it under the law of contract. With more or less modification they take over the definition which we have just cited from Sir William Jones.[4] In two other learned works, however, it is pointed out that bailment may exist independently of contract,[5] and there is authority in support of this which, if indirect, is of respectable weight. In *R. v.*

---

[1] Salmond, *Jurisprudence* (7th ed. 1924).

[2] Holland, *Jurisprudence* (13th ed. 1924), 289 *seq.*

[3] *Leading Principles of Anglo-American Law* (1884), Index "Bailment".

[4] Story, *Bailments* (1839). Wyatt Paine, *Bailment* (1901), 2. Williams, *Personal Property* (18th ed. 1926), 57. 1 *Laws of England* (Halsbury), § 1071.

[5] Pollock & Wright, *Possession* (1888), 41 note 1, 160. Goodeve, *Personal Property* (6th ed. 1926), 25.

W P   7

98 TORT AND BAILMENT

Robson,[1] a married woman was held by the Court for Crown Cases Reserved to have been rightly convicted of larceny as a bailee under the Act of 1857.[2] It was argued in her defence that a bailment is a contract and that she could not contract (which, in fact, was the general rule then). But Martin and Pollock BB. were of opinion that she might nevertheless become a bailee within the statute. This must be taken to have overruled *R. v. Denmour*[3] where Martin B. had ruled to the contrary earlier in the same year. Again, in *R. v. McDonald*,[4] a minor over fourteen years of age was held to have been rightly convicted of larceny as a bailee of goods which he had fraudulently converted to his own use. Some doubt was raised as to the correctness of this decision and it was re-argued before thirteen judges, the majority of whom held that McDonald was properly convicted. It appears from *R. v. Ashwell*[5] that Lord Coleridge C.J. was one of the minority judges in *R. v. McDonald*, for he said as much in *R. v. Ashwell*, and adopted his opinion in the earlier case that "bailment is not a mere delivery on a contract, but is a contract itself". But his support of this amounted to no more than the citation of the older textbooks and they do not say *why* bailment must always be identified with contract. Upon the whole, though the authorities are not conclusive in the absence of a decision in a civil case, the view that bailment may exist without any contract is in accordance with the conception of it and with its actual treatment as a separate branch of the law. Writers on the law of contract do not usually deal with it as one limb of their subject. Where they have done so, they have either ignored the difficulty of co-ordinating gratuitous bail-

[1] (1861) 31 L.J.N.S. (M.C.) 22.
[2] 20 & 21 Vict. c. 54, s. 4.
[3] (1861) 8 Cox, 440.
[4] (1885) 15 Q.B.D. 323.
[5] (1885) 16 Q.B.D. 190, 223–224.

TORT AND BAILMENT 99

ments with the doctrine of consideration,[1] or have achieved reconciliation of the two by reliance on older theories of bailment.[2] Where the gratuitous bailment involves parting with the possession of goods, consideration may be found in the detriment of giving up such possession, but the theory is not without its difficulties, as Sir Frederick Pollock has noted.[3] Where it is for gratuitous services, the difficulties are still greater.[4]

Next as to tort. In two respects we can mark it off from breach of bailment.

(1) In the law of tort the duty is towards persons generally, but the duties of the parties in bailment are towards each other and do not travel beyond that.

(2) Liability in tort is primarily fixed by the law itself, irrespective of the assent of the persons bound; but in bailment it is primarily fixed by the parties themselves. When once they have entered into the relation, a good many legal consequences follow and some of them were probably never contemplated by either bailor or bailee. But just the same sort of thing occurs with many of the obligations that arise from contract, yet no one doubts that it is by the parties to it, and not by the law, that the obligations arising from contract are primarily imposed. What happens in the way of secondary duties which are annexed to bailments by the law does not here concern us. A bailee, like a contractor, may protest against some of them as harsh and not contemplated by him when he became a bailee, but that does not alter the fact that primarily it was he, and not the law, that brought into being the legal relation to which these consequences are attached. Bailment originates in an agreement, express or implied, and

[1] Chitty, *Contracts* (17th ed. 1921), 490–494.
[2] Addison, *Contracts* (11th ed. 1911).
[3] *Contract* (9th ed. 1921), 188.
[4] Anson, *Contract* (17th ed. 1929), 101–102.

7-2

100 TORT AND BAILMENT

tortious liability does not. Historically, this might be
a debatable point, for, as we have shewn, it would be
almost impossible at one period of the development of
bailment to say whether the bailee's liability sprang
from tort or from contract, but we are concerned with
the law here and now; and, though it is possible, according to the balance of opinion, to have a bailment without
a contract, it is not possible to have it without agreement.
A man cannot without his knowledge and consent be
considered as a bailee of property. So Abbott C.J. in
Lethbridge v. *Phillips*,[1] where a miniature portrait belonging to the plaintiff was handed by a third person,
with the assent of the plaintiff, but not with that of the
defendant, to the defendant's son for the purpose of
shewing it to the defendant. The son took it to his
father's house, and it was much damaged by being
placed on a mantelpiece too near a large stove. The
defendant was held not liable.[2] It is not within our
province to notice the circumstances from which agreement may be implied in cases like *Lethbridge* v. *Phillips*,
or those in which, agreement or no agreement, a re-
cipient of goods which he has not demanded may incur
liability.[3] The main rule is clear enough and indeed is a
practical necessity, unless every one is to be placed at
the mercy of pushing tradesmen who send goods that
have not been solicited.

The upshot is that bailment is more fittingly regarded
as a distinct branch of the Law of Property, under the
title Possession than as appropriate to either the law of
contract or the law of tort. This is far from saying that
remedies in contract or in tort are inapplicable to breach
of bailment. If there be a contract, as there very fre-

[1] (1819) 2 Stark. 544.
[2] So too *Howard* v. *Harris* (1884) Cab. & Ellis, 253. Paine, *Bailments* (1901), 18, 19.
[3] See 1 *Laws of England* (Halsbury), § 1078.

TORT AND BAILMENT   101

quently is, in a bailment, then an action on contract is one of the remedies. If, again, the bailee has committed negligence, or any other tort in connection with the property bailed, then he is liable in tort. Here the analysis is apt to be obscured by the fact that at the time of Holt's judgment in *Coggs* v. *Bernard* negligence was not an independent tort, but rather a mode in which certain wrongs could be committed. Nowadays, it is clearly an independent tort as well as a mode of unlawful conduct, and it is not by any means the only tort for which a bailee or bailor may be reciprocally liable with respect to the thing bailed. But to treat bailment purely as a matter of contract or of tort is not an adequate explanation of its position in the legal system. It is true that books of pleading appear to thrust this dichotomy upon it. One would infer from Bullen and Leake's *Precedents of Pleadings* that the action is either on contract[1] or in tort,[2] but not for breach of "bailment". At any rate no mention of bailment is to be found in their precedents of statements of claim. It may well be that this is because nearly every action against the bailee can be reduced to either contract or tort, but there seems to be no inherent reason why a statement of claim in an action between bailor and bailee should not allege breach of bailment as the sole ground of the action. It is true, also, that for the purposes of the County Court Acts, an action founded upon the Common Law liability of a bailee is founded on tort,[3] but in trying to arrange the legal system we need not be terrified by legislative insistence upon "contract or tort, and nothing else" in a limited class of cases.

The salient feature of bailment is, as we have said, the element of possession. Bailment is not only one of the modes of transferring possession, but while the

---

[1] 8th ed. (1924), 104–106.   [2] *Ibid.* 341–345.
[3] *Turner* v. *Stallibrass* [1898] 1 Q.B. 56.

TORT AND BAILMENT

bailment lasts it connotes possession. As between bailor and bailee that was recognized very early in our law. As between the bailee and a third party, it was very late in our history that this was settled. The older view was that he could sue the third party who interfered with the property bailed only if he (the bailee) were liable over to the bailor. But in *The Winkfield*[1] it was decided that the reason why he can sue a third party who negligently injures the goods is simply because he has possession. It has been admirably shewn elsewhere why this decision was historically correct, and why its arrival lagged until the early twentieth century.[2]

This conspicuous element of possession is a justification for separating bailment from both contract and tort. As to contract, putting aside gratuitous bailments for the moment, the tendency in books of practice, as well as in books of jurisprudence, is to treat contracts which transfer rights *in rem* on a basis different from that of other contracts. They are considered, and quite rightly so, just like other contracts in so far as they are mere vehicles for carrying the right *in rem* from one person to another. But when once the transfer is accomplished, a host of rights and duties arises which take in persons generally as well as the contracting parties. They are all incidental to property, and have no necessary connection whatever with the contract, the vehicle which transferred them. Any other vehicle recognized by the law would have done as well, e.g. gift. Such contracts are therefore usually isolated and treated as separate topics so far as their effects are concerned, and, as it is difficult to expound their effects without describing their origin, the contract *and* its effects are examined together. It may look like a confusion of rights *in personam* with rights *in rem*, or, if the phrases be preferred,

[1] [1902] P. 42.
[2] Holdsworth, *op. cit.* vii, 451–455; also iii, 336–350.

TORT AND BAILMENT 103

of obligation with property; but it is justifiable on the score of convenience, and indeed of practical necessity. A practitioner prefers to consult one book instead of two. Examples of topics of the "contract-conveyance" type (if we may coin the phrase), which have been successfully isolated in this way are sales and leases. Even if bailments were always based on contracts, there would be quite as much reason for isolating them from contracts in general, because, by giving the bailee possession of the goods, they force upon us a consideration of that esoteric right *in rem*. But the argument in favour of this separation becomes overwhelming if, as appears to be the better view, it is possible to have bailments which are independent of contract altogether.

As to tort, reasons have already been put forward for regarding breach of bailment as not necessarily co-incident with liability in tort. It is true that the bailee, having possession, can, of course, sue any third person for infringement of it and that this action is unquestionably in tort, and, in proper circumstances, will lie against the bailor also. It is equally true that the bailor can also sue a third person for injury to his outstanding right of ownership, while the chattel is in the bailee's hands; and that, if the bailee has wrongfully determined the bailment, the bailor can sue not only him, but also third persons who deal in any way with the chattel.[1] But these actions in tort are remedies, not upon bailment *per se*, but for injuries to possession. Such remedies would be the same, however possession arose, whether by bailment or in any other way; they are inadequate to explain what may be called the static side of bailment, i.e. its mode of creation and its varieties, and they do not exhaust its dynamic side, i.e. the remedies incidental to it.

---

[1] 1 *Laws of England* (Halsbury), § 1142.

Chapter VI

TORT AND BREACH OF TRUST

THE distinction between tort and breach of trust might be dismissed in a very few sentences if every one regarded trusts as a portion of the law so self-contained as to be easily detachable from the rest of the legal system. That is the view which is adopted at the end of this chapter. It has the great advantage of coinciding with the opinion of practitioners, and that ought to be the aim of every writer on jurisprudence if by any reasonable intendment it can be reconciled with scientific analysis. The execution of trusts, private or charitable, is assigned to the Chancery Division of the High Court of Justice, and the Common Law practitioner is rarely concerned with them. How can it be otherwise when a young man must decide almost at the outset of his career at the Bar whether he will go on the Chancery side or on the Common Law side? Arguing along these lines, we might take advantage of the jurisdictional *enclave* in which trusts are administered, and pass it by without examining very closely its contents. But this would be unfair treatment of several controversies that have arisen in connection with the essential nature of trusts.

In the first place, courts other than the Chancery Division are not in the least absolved from incidental consideration of the question whether a trust does, or does not, exist, merely because the problems relating to their direct execution are appropriate to that Division. Thus, it has been found that the same set of facts may involve both a breach of contract and a breach of trust, and it is hardly necessary to say that the former falls

TORT AND BREACH OF TRUST 105

within Common Law jurisdiction. A recent case before the Judicial Committee of the Privy Council illustrates this point. In *Lord Strathcona S.S. Co.* v. *Dominion Coal Co.*[1] the Dominion Co. held on a long term charter-party a ship owned by the *X* Co. The *X* Co. sold this ship to the Strathcona Co., who took with notice of the charter-party, but who contended that it was not binding on them, because there was no privity of contract between them and the Dominion Co. The action which the Dominion Co. brought against them was, in origin, nothing like one for breach of trust. It was for a declaration that the Strathcona Co. were bound to carry out the charter-party and for an injunction against their using the ship in any way inconsistent with the charter-party. The Judicial Committee gave judgment for the Dominion Co.

If a man acquires from another rights in a ship which is already under charter, with notice of rights which required the ship to be used for a particular purpose and not inconsistently with it, then he appears to be plainly in the position of a constructive trustee with obligations which a Court of equity will not permit him to violate.[2]

And they followed a *dictum* of Knight Bruce L.J. in *De Mattos* v. *Gibson*:[3]

Reason and justice seem to prescribe that, at least as a general rule, where a man, by gift or purchase, acquires property from another, with knowledge of a previous contract, lawfully and for valuable consideration made by him with a third person, to use and employ the property for a particular purpose in a specified manner, the acquirer shall not, to the material damage of the third person, in opposition to the contract and inconsistently with it, use and employ the property in a manner not allowable to the giver or seller.

---

[1] [1926] A.C. 108. [2] *Ibid.* 125.
[3] (1859) 4 De G. & J. 276.

106   TORT AND BREACH OF TRUST

Now Knight Bruce L.J.'s *dictum* looks like an exception to the rule about privity of contract, and the quotation which has been made from the *Strathcona Case* looks like a skilful evasion of privity by means of a trust. This is not said by way of adverse criticism on the decision which is reasonable enough, but where exactly is this doctrine of constructive trust to end? Its limits are that it applies only to *user* of the article transferred and that an interest in it must remain with the person who seeks to enforce the injunction. These are stated in the *Strathcona Case* itself, and the learned editors of the current edition of Anson's *Law of Contract*[1] mark the distinction thus set up between that case and decisions like those in *McGruther* v. *Pitcher*,[2] where it was held that it is futile for *A*, the seller of an article (unless he is the patentee of it), to attempt to impose conditions on its resale by *B* to third parties. Other writers are not so sure about the lengths to which the *Strathcona* doctrine may take us. Would the law allow the hirer of a motor car to get an injunction against the purchaser of the car, if he buys with knowledge that the garage proprietor had let out the car on hire? That is a question which the poser of it thinks must be answered "No", at present, though he considers that there would be nothing unreasonable in "Yes";[3] and, on further reflection, he has pointed out that the doctrine of privity of contract has done little more than fog the issue as to whether restrictions on user of chattels ought to be enforced when they reach the hands of third parties who take with notice.[4] In America, another learned writer has not only used the *Strathcona Case* to illustrate the close relation between "equitable servitudes on chattels" and the interest created by contract to deliver a chattel, but has

[1] 17th ed. (1929), 277–278.   [2] [1904] 2 Ch. 306.
[3] 42 *Law Quarterly Review* (1926), 139–141.
[4] E. C. S. Wade, in 44 *Law Quarterly Review* (1928), 51–65.

TORT AND BREACH OF TRUST 107

also urged that such "servitudes" are both possible and reasonable, though he frankly admits his inability to find a single decision in a court of last resort which establishes such a conception.[1]

Again, a more serious attack on the severability of contract from trust has been made by Professor Arthur L. Corbin.[2] He shews that, in spite of the general rule about privity of contract which prevents a third person who is named as a beneficiary in the contract from suing upon it, it has been held nevertheless that such a beneficiary can sue if the promisor in the contract can be regarded as a trustee. Indeed, some of the decisions shew "that the device of a trust can be made equally successful by fiction in cases where the contracting parties do not expressly adopt it, use no such words as trust and trustee, and are not even conscious of the existence of such concepts".[3] And some of the English decisions of the highest authority would lead any one, except an uncompromising Equity lawyer or a fanatical devotee of privity of contract, to say that when the courts wish to enable the beneficiary to sue they make the promisor a trustee, and when they wish to prevent him from doing so they fall back on the shibboleth of privity of contract.[4] American experts in contract law are not so nervous as we are about the extension of an action upon contract to a third party beneficiary, and proof of this is to be found in their *Restatement of the Law of Contracts*.[5]

[1] Professor Z. Chafee, in 41 *Harvard Law Review* (1928), 945–1013, esp. 962–967. Professor Chafee demonstrates admirably the economic forces which have thrust forward legal questions of this kind; *ibid.* 946–954.

[2] 46 *Law Quarterly Review* (1930), 12–45.

[3] *Ibid.* 17.

[4] Cf. *Dunlop Pneumatic Tyre Co. Ld.* v. *Selfridge Co. Ld.* [1915] A.C. 847, with *Les Affréteurs, etc.* v. *Walford* [1919] A.C. 801, and the remarks on these cases by Professor Corbin in 46 *Law Quarterly Review*, 33–36, and by Professor Z. Chafee in 41 *Harvard Law Review* (1928), 951–952.

[5] (1928) ss. 133–147.

108 TORT AND BREACH OF TRUST

Being used to the idea of allowing such an action, they have a quicker eye for detecting the inconsistencies and fictions on this point in English law. Our leading textbooks on the law of trusts do not seem even to realize the difficulties which present themselves to Professor Corbin, much less to discuss them.[1]

So far we have noticed some of the obstacles against entire separation of trust from contract, and we have done this for the purpose of shewing that in some respects trusts do not form a completely insulated topic. We now pass to a question more directly relevant to the subject of these lectures, which is "What is the distinction between breach of trust and liability in tort?" In the definition of tort adopted in an earlier chapter,[2] all reference to its being a breach of a right *in rem* was avoided for reasons which will appear in the final chapter of this book. But no one definition of tort has yet been accepted, and among others that have been offered, one is that a tort is a violation of a right *in rem*, giving rise to an obligation to pay damages.[3] According to this, if a breach of trust is a breach of a right *in rem*, i.e. a right availing against persons generally, it is, to that extent, also a tort. It will be seen later that it is not a tort for other reasons, but that does not release us from considering the validity of this reason in particular, and it has been much debated whether a breach of trust is an infringement of a right *in rem*, or of a right *in personam*, i.e. a right availing against a determinate person or determinate persons.[4]

At the outset, it is as well to say that discussion is here limited to the rights of the cestui que trust. But it

[1] E.g. Lewin, *Law of Trusts* (13th ed. 1928); Godefroi *Trusts* (5th ed. 1927), 59–62.
[2] *Ante*, p. 32.
[3] 30 *Harvard Law Review* (1917), 251.
[4] Most of the chief controversialists are referred to in W. N. Hohfeld, *Fundamental legal conceptions* (1923), 26.

TORT AND BREACH OF TRUST 109

is also necessary to add that it is not limited merely to his rights against persons other than the trustees. This has been rather overlooked by some writers who have selected for analysis the beneficiary's right of following the trust property or its proceeds, without considering other numerous rights which he has against the trustee himself. There is no need to say much of the details of these, but they must not be entirely forgotten. The beneficiary can sue the trustee for any of the many breaches of trust which he may possibly commit—wrongful investment, purchase of the trust property himself, keeping no accounts, mixing the trust property with his own, and so forth. And he can sue *only* the trustee for breach of these duties. Third parties cannot be made liable for them for the simple reason that they are not trustees. These rights of the beneficiary are therefore *in personam* against the trustee, and we need consider them no further.

Suppose, however, that the trustee alienates the trust property to a third person, what is the nature of the beneficiary's right against that third person? Is it *in rem* or *in personam*? Maitland has constantly been cited as holding that it is *in personam*. No doubt this was his ultimate opinion, but he did not reach it without hesitation. At first he thought the right did not easily fall under either heading, that it partook a little of both, and that while in history, and probably in ultimate analysis it is a right *in personam*, yet it is treated for many important purposes very like a right *in rem*.[1] But later he speaks of equitable estates and interests as rights *in personam* with a misleading resemblance to rights *in rem*, and the basis of his conclusion is that the cestui que trust has rights enforceable against the trustee, against all who claim through or under him as volunteers, against his creditors, and against those who acquire the

[1] *Equity* (1909), 23.

TORT AND BREACH OF TRUST

trust property with notice, actual or constructive, of the trust.[1] But at least one class of persons he cannot sue— *bona fide* transferees for value without notice of the trust. The argument is that the right does not avail against persons generally, because at least this class of persons (and Maitland contemplated the possibility of others)[2] is not liable to the cestui que trust. Therefore his right is *in personam*, not *in rem*.

Now Maitland was not alone in holding this view. It goes back to Coke, and it is supported by Langdell, Ames, Sanders, Gilbert and Lewin—a formidable battery of experts, ancient and modern. But it has not passed unchallenged. Several learned writers have maintained the exact reverse of it. Professor Austin W. Scott, of Harvard, may be taken as the champion of the view that the cestui que trust's right to claim the trust property from third persons is a right *in rem*, and he ranges on his side Austin, Salmond, Pomeroy and Huston. Very briefly his argument is this.[3] Starting with the conception of a right *in rem* as one which avails against persons generally, he contends that this exactly describes the right of the cestui que trust. He does not dispute for a moment that the cestui que trust cannot recover the trust property from a *bona fide* purchaser for value, but he urges that his right nevertheless avails against persons *generally*. What ground is there for saying that he has not got a right *in rem* simply because he cannot sue a *bona fide* purchaser for value? He has still got a right against persons generally. It might just as well be said that the holder of a cheque is not the owner of it—has not a right *in rem* to it—because a *bona fide* transferee for value of it may get a better title than the original holder.

[1] Equity (1909), 120, 122.   [2] *Ibid.* 120.
[3] 17 *Columbia Law Review* (1917), 269–290. A reply by Professor Harlan Stone (now a judge of the Supreme Court) appears at pp. 467–501.

TORT AND BREACH OF TRUST 111

The difficulty in deciding whether Maitland's view or that of Professor Scott is the more accurate lies in the uncertainty of what "generally" means. When it is said that a right *in rem* avails against persons "generally", how many, and what kinds, of exceptions are permissible before one can say that the generality has ceased and that the right, whatever be its nature, cannot be *in rem*? It is not easy to see how Professor Scott's argument can be answered if we must accept the dichotomy "*in rem—in personam*" as comprehensive; for it had already been shewn by Huston that the mere possibility of losing one's interest in property does not reduce ownership to mere obligation.

Another learned exponent of Equity has put forward a third view which postulates a trichotomy, instead of a dichotomy, of rights. Mr H. G. Hanbury thinks that Maitland's two propositions (*a*) that equitable rights are only rights *in personam*, and (*b*) that a *bona fide* purchaser for value is immune against equities, are capable of separation. For the doctrine of the following of trust funds by the beneficiary and of recovering the property *in specie* shews that his rights are a good deal higher than mere *jura in personam*. "Equitable rights and interests must, then, be regarded as hybrids, standing midway between *jura in personam* and *jura in rem*."[1] But it may be questioned whether this emphasis on the possibility of recovery *in specie* has much bearing on the problem whether a right is *in rem* or *in personam*. That distinction refers to the persons against whom the right avails, not to the possibility of recovering a specific thing from them. If I contract to buy the Pusey horn or an old silver altar-piece, I can be pretty sure of recovering such articles of rarity from the vendor, and not mere damages;

---

[1] 45 *Law Quarterly Review* (1929), 199. Developed at greater length in *La position actuelle de l'Équité*, etc. an offprint from *Bulletin de la Société de Législation comparée* (1929), 48–63.

112 TORT AND BREACH OF TRUST

but my right is nevertheless one *in personam*, not *in rem*. Possibly, however, the learned author attaches to the phrase right *in rem* a meaning different from that used in this chapter. Indeed the antinomy "right *in rem*— right *in personam*" has not been uniformly understood by various writers.[1] Incidentally, it is in commoner use in American courts than in English, where, indeed the phrases very rarely occur.[2]

The result seems to be that if we are forced to elect between right *in rem* and right *in personam*, we ought to regard the beneficiary's right against third persons as a right *in rem*. The right avails against persons generally and, if that were the only test of liability in tort, a breach of trust of this kind would be a tort, or, as Professor Scott has styled it, an "equitable tort". But this appears to be going too far. It does seem to be generally agreed that a tort gives rise to an action for unliquidated damages. Whatever differences of opinion there may be on other points in proposed definitions, there is no serious dispute as to this. And an action for breach of trust is not an action for unliquidated damages. The claim of the cestui que trust is in general a simple contract debt.[3] It is for compensation.[4] The measure of the trustee's liability personally is the loss caused to the trust estate, and where the remedy is against one who has the trust property, it is limited to that, or to the property into which it has been converted.[5]

Though a breach of trust can thus be marked off from liability in tort, it does not follow that breach of trust can never give rise to an alternative action in tort. A

---

[1] Hohfeld, *Fundamental Legal Conceptions* (1923), 68.

[2] See exceptionally Viscount Haldane L.C. in *Attenborough* v. *Solomon* [1913] A.C. 76, 85, and in *Sinclair* v. *Brougham* [1914] A.C. 398, 418.

[3] Lewin, *Law of Trusts* (13th ed. 1928), 952.

[4] *Ibid.* 940.

[5] Snell, *Equity* (20th ed. 1929), 176, 178.

TORT AND BREACH OF TRUST 113

trustee may have been guilty of negligence or of deceit, and negligence and deceit do not cease to be torts merely because it is a trustee who commits them. In just the same way, the same facts may give rise to alternative liability in tort or on contract. This is a matter to which we must revert when we come to deal with the effect of the Statutes of Limitations on alternative causes of action (*post*, Chap. XI).

Reverting to our own definition, it will be recollected that one essential of it is that tortious liability arises from the breach of a duty "primarily fixed by the law".[1] Is it possible to take this as yet another reason for differentiating a breach of trust from a tort? Can it be said that in a trust the duty is fixed primarily by the parties themselves, and not by the law? Does it not originate in agreement between the parties? The answer is "Not invariably". No doubt most trusts do spring from an agreement between the creator of the trust and the trustee, or at least from the assent of the trustee to undertake the trust after it has been created, e.g. where he has been appointed under a will without consulting him in the first instance. But this will not hold where the beneficiary is seeking to make some person other than the trustee liable, for assent is out of the question here. Nor will it hold in some forms of constructive trust. A total stranger to the trust may become a constructive trustee, not only without his assent, but against his vigorous protest. Any third person who receives the trust property with actual or constructive notice that it is such, or who gets it as a gift from the trustee without notice at all, becomes a constructive trustee of it.[2]

As, however, breach of trust is not redressible by an action for *unliquidated* damages, it is distinguishable from liability in tort, even if we confine ourselves to the

[1] *Ante*, p. 32.
[2] Snell, *Equity* (20th ed. 1929), 127.

W P

114 TORT AND BREACH OF TRUST

particular definition of tort which we have constructed. But it is better not to leave the matter there, but to take the much broader view with which this chapter began, and to regard trusts as a division of the law of property which is detachable with fair accuracy from the rest of the Anglo-American system. Trusts are so peculiarly within the province of Equity (in our technical sense of that word) and are so destitute of any true counterpart in continental law, that no injustice is done to jurisprudence of the most "general" type, if they are isolated in this way. There was a time when the Common Law Courts might have devised some form of action, such as case upon the action of account, which would have enabled them to compete with Chancery in the enforcement of trusts.[1] There was even a time when they actually made a defaulting trustee liable for damages as for a breach of implied contract.[2] But then they were trying to recall an opportunity that they had missed fatally at an earlier period. Trusts had fallen within the Chancellor's jurisdiction and there they remain to this day.

The separation of trusts from other parts of the law is not so clean cut as a pure theorist might wish. It has been pointed out in this chapter that trusts seem to be entangled with other legal conceptions, and in particular with contract. Logically, this is unfortunate, but it is inevitable that a completely logical scheme of the law is impossible. What jurists have to construct is the physiology of a living body, not the anatomy of a skeleton. Moreover the overlap of trusts with contract is comparatively inconsiderable. It is not serious enough to affect the main proposition that trusts should have a compartment to themselves. This conclusion is reinforced not only by the attitude of English and American

[1] Pollock, *Torts* (13th ed. 1929), 551–552. See also Holdsworth, *History of English Law*, iv, 418–419.
[2] Lewin, *Law of Trusts* (12th ed.), 15.

TORT AND BREACH OF TRUST 115

practitioners, but by the plan which has commended itself to the framers of the American Restatement of Case Law; they have made Trusts a separate topic. This is a wiser course than that taken by some writers on jurisprudence who have marshalled trusts under obligations *quasi ex contractu*.[1] The root of the matter lies in a remark of Sir Frederick Pollock's. It is embodied in a single line of editorial comment on an article discussing the place of trust in jurisprudence. "Why", he asks, "is Trust not entitled to rank as a head *sui generis?*"[2] We have not yet discovered any satisfactory reason why it should not be thus treated.

[1] E.g. Holland, *Jurisprudence* (13th ed. 1924), 250.
[2] 28 *Law Quarterly Review* (1912), 297.

8-2

Chapter VII

TORT AND QUASI-CONTRACT

IT has been pointed out in an earlier chapter that one of the difficulties in distinguishing tort from other forms of legal liability is not merely that the law of tort itself is a somewhat unsettled domain, but also that the confines of these other regions of the law are not clearly ascertained. Thus some of the borderland between tort on the one side and trusts and bailments on the other is disputable either because it is claimed by both parties or because it is not completely certain what is claimed. In differentiating tort from quasi-contract this difficulty is intensely aggravated, for the limits of quasi-contract are not so much untraced as untraceable. Here we have to deal with ill-explored country quite as much as with debatable boundaries. Consequently the bulk of this chapter must be occupied with an attempt to determine the province of quasi-contract, and, as opinions with respect to its scope differ considerably, any such effort must be rather hazardous. Not much further apology is needed for writing what may well appear to be primarily an essay on quasi-contract rather than an exposition on tort, for there is little enough on the subject by English writers.

We are unlucky in starting with an unpopular term. "Quasi-contract" is as irritating as any other unfamiliar phrase to practitioners. They may be excused for any feeling of annoyance on that score, for it is the fault of English law schools that they know so little of it. They may retain faint recollections of what the Roman lawyers had to say about the liability of Balbus to recoup Titius who had incurred expense in acting on behalf of Balbus

TORT AND QUASI-CONTRACT 117

in some emergency during his absence elsewhere; and they may have seen some hurried references in books on the law of contract to the *"indebitatus* counts" and in books on jurisprudence to "quasi-contract". But for the rest it is significant that, only some three years ago, a judge, who for almost the whole of his working life had been distinguished not only as a practitioner, but also as a teacher of the law, should have referred almost apologetically to "so-called quasi-contract".[1] Yet, paradoxically enough, nearly every Common Law practitioner with any extended experience has become well acquainted with the same thing under other names. He knows well enough what an "action for money had and received" is, and that a *quantum meruit* can be sued on a contract which has been broken in its essentials by the other party to it. Quite probably, too, he has advised a client to waive a tort and to sue instead on an implied contract, and has pioneered through the courts claims for contribution by one co-surety against another. Here we have the substance of the thing, though not its name of quasi-contract. What the practitioner cannot do, however, is to lay his hand on any book by an English lawyer which has adequately collected and treated under one title all these, and other cognate, topics. In the United States they have managed things better. Teaching of quasi-contract as a separate subject has long been common in the law schools there, with the inevitable result that books have been written by men who taught it. Two such monographs may be mentioned, for they will be often cited in this chapter. The first is Professor A. W. Keener's *Treatise on the Law of Quasi-Contracts*, published in 1893; it is reckoned as highly authoritative by American lawyers. A new edition of it is needed, as many decisions in the last forty years

[1] Fraser J. in *Hardie and Lane Ld.* v. *Chiltern* [1928] 1 K.B. at p. 681.

118 TORT AND QUASI-CONTRACT

require noting. The second is Professor F. C. Woodward's *Law of Quasi-Contracts* which appeared in 1913. For the purposes of an English lawyer there are two qualifications on the usefulness of these books. In the first place, both of them are, as a matter of course, primarily concerned with American law, though there is a good deal of reference to English law in them. Secondly, the American treatment of decided cases is, for a variety of reasons which cannot be detailed here, bolder than it is on our side of the Atlantic; and some of the criticisms of these learned authors are not likely to carry as much weight here as they might in other jurisdictions. In England, the literature on quasi-contract is of the scantiest. The wilderness and the solitary place possess it. It is no man's land, not in the sense that there are constant battles for it, but that nobody wants it. A certain amount of discussion about it is to be found in books on jurisprudence, but a good deal of it is of an abstract nature which might very well suit an ideal, or a comparatively new, system of law, but which has not much living application to English law, hampered as it is by a thousand years of history and almost strangled as it was at one time by procedural technicalities. On the more practical side, there are a few useful sections on quasi-contract in Dr Edward Jenks' *Digest of English Civil Law*,[1] and a very brief article on it in the *Encyclopædia of the Laws of England*.[2] The *Laws of England*, under the title "Constructive Contracts", is here, as elsewhere, a convenient starting-point for research into the cases.[3] In the Indian Contract Act[4] there is a chapter headed "Of certain relations resembling those created by contract",[5] and the comments of the learned

[1] 2nd ed. (1921), §§ 707–721.   [2] 2nd ed. xii, 165–167.
[3] Ed. Halsbury, vol. vii, §§ 945 *seq.*
[4] Ed. Pollock and Mulla (5th ed. 1924).
[5] *Ibid.* §§ 68–72.

TORT AND QUASI-CONTRACT 119

editor, Sir Frederick Pollock, upon it are very valuable. And that is all. No other efforts have been made to treat the topic in a connected fashion.[1]

It is a pity that the term quasi-contract cannot be eliminated in favour of some other more exact name, for some of the obligations comprised in it have nothing whatever to do with contract. It is not merely that in them the analogy to contract is faint; there is no analogy at all. "Contracts implied by law", and "constructive contracts" are historically more accurate expressions, but scientifically rather worse, than "quasi-contract". The temptation to select the first of these is strong, not only for historical reasons, but also because it is well-known to practitioners. But a "contract implied by law" is frequently not a contract at all, and occasionally has not the remotest resemblance to one. We cannot bow down in the house of Rimmon when the god has deserted his temple. "Innominate obligation" might do, but is much too strange to be acceptable to English lawyers. We are thus driven to adopt "quasi-contract", not because it is an accurate phrase, but because no better one is discoverable.

Some definition of quasi-contract had better be attempted even at this early stage. So far as current English law is concerned, genuine quasi-contract signifies *liability, not exclusively referable to any other head of the law, imposed upon a particular person to pay money to another particular person on the ground of unjust benefit.* The negative character of this definition at once invites criticism, but some justification of it will appear in the course of this chapter. In any event, "benefit" appears to be preferable to "enrichment", which would imply

[1] There is a fair amount of articles in the American law journals. See the titles "Assumpsit", "Money had and received", and "Quasi-contracts" in *Index to Legal Periodicals* (begun under the editorship of L. A. Jones in 1888; now edited by Eldon R. James).

120   TORT AND QUASI-CONTRACT

an actual increase of the defendant's estate. This in fact must sometimes be proved, but there are cases in which it is enough to shew that the defendant has got what he desired, and the question whether his estate has been thereby enriched is beside the mark.[1]

Another definition which has been offered is:

> When the law imposes upon one person, on grounds of natural justice, an obligation towards another similar to that which arises from a true contract, although no contract, express or implied, has in fact been entered into by them to that effect, such obligation is said to arise from quasi-contract.[2]

Historically, there is much to be said for this definition, but there are two drawbacks to it. First, it persists on the analogy to contract, which, as has been said above, is not always present. Secondly, the phrase "natural justice", though it is correct both historically and (if properly understood) even at the present day, sets up the risk of some confusion with equitable obligations, i.e. obligations which were formerly enforceable only in the Court of Chancery.

Yet another definition is:

> A quasi-contract right, or right of restoration, [is] a right to obtain the restoration of a benefit, or the equivalent thereof, conferred by the claimant, but unjustly retained by the defendant.[3]

But this does not separate quasi-contract from tort, for it would just as well describe detinue or trover; and it might well cover some breaches of trust. Moreover, the conferring of a "benefit" might include the transfer

[1] Woodward, *op. cit.* § 8. Keener, *op. cit.* 164–165.

[2] Jenks, *Digest of English Civil Law* (2nd ed. 1921), § 707.

[3] *Encyclopædia of the Laws of England* (2nd ed.), xii, 166. The writer of the article and the late Professor Sir T. E. Holland, *Jurisprudence* (13th ed. 1924), 247 note 2, attribute this definition to Keener, *Cases on the Law of Quasi-Contracts* (1888); but neither of them gives any further reference and the passage cited has not been traced.

TORT AND QUASI-CONTRACT   121

of land or of a chattel, and it is doubtful, to say the least of it, whether in the English law of quasi-contract anything except pecuniary compensation is recoverable. Finally, there are some instances of waiver of a tort in order to sue a quasi-contractual action in which the situation is more accurately described by saying that the defendant has reaped a benefit by inflicting an injury on the plaintiff, not that the plaintiff has "conferred" a benefit on the defendant.[1]

However, these suggestions may be but motes in other definitions as against a beam in the one which we have framed. In any event, the reader must be warned that it is no more than a description of what *true* quasi-contract appears to be in English law, for it will soon be perceived that quasi-contractual remedies have been applied to relations which by no amount of ingenuity can be scientifically reckoned as quasi-contractual.

The present law of quasi-contract cannot be understood without some historical sketch of its beginnings and development, and here the way has been paved by such experts as Ames[2] and Sir William Holdsworth.[3] The term appears in our law as early as Bracton, who imported it from Roman Law with the barest mention of its sub-headings as given in the *Institutes* of Justinian.[4] But there was so little in the English law of Bracton's time which corresponded with this foreign borrowing that he would have been merely unpractical if he had tried to make further use of it.[5] But though he was premature in pitchforking this classification into our law, the idea of it was bound to come sooner or later.

---

[1] E.g. *Lightly* v. *Clouston* (1808) 1 Taunt. 212. *Foster* v. *Stewart* (1814) 3 M. & S. 191.

[2] *Lectures on Legal History* (1913), Lect. xiv.

[3] *History of English Law* (3rd ed. 1923), iii, 416, 424–428, 450–451; vi, 521, 637–640; viii, 88–98.

[4] Fol. 100*b*.

[5] Maitland, *Bracton and Azo*, 158.

122 TORT AND QUASI-CONTRACT

There must always be circumstances which make one man civilly liable to another on grounds reducible neither to contract nor to tort. The principle that "one person shall not unjustly enrich [preferably 'benefit'] himself at the expense of another"[1] must penetrate any system of law. That principle is at the root of all genuinely quasi-contractual relations. We shall shew later that it will not account for all relations that have been called quasi-contractual.[2] The entry of the idea of quasi-contract into our law, is, as in all other parts of the system, implicated with procedure and much confused by it. The action of account was an early example of the mode in which a particular kind of quasi-contractual obligation was enforced, though the action was by no means limited to that type of claim. One who received money on behalf of another and who failed to account for it was amenable to this action, and, of course, the basis of his liability might quite well be a contract with the person to whom the money was owed.[3] But it was a common enough occurrence for A to hand money to B with a direction to pay it over to C, and here there was no contract between B and C. Yet it was recognized in 1367 that C could recover the money from B in an action of account.[4] Then another step was to apply the action of debt for this purpose. Nowadays one associates debt with a fixed sum of money due on a loan, but from very early times it went far beyond that. It could be used for the recovery of statutory penalties, forfeitures under by-laws, amercements inflicted by inferior courts, and judgment debts.[5] Such obligations are far removed from contract. Debt came to be employed in the assertion of a quasi-contractual claim similar to that in the case of 1367.

[1] Ames, *op. cit.* 162.
[2] Cf. Keener, *Quasi-Contracts*, 19.
[3] Ames, *op. cit.* 163.
[4] Y.B. Pasch. 41 Ed. III, f. 10, pl. 5 (*per* Cavendish).
[5] Pollock and Maitland, *History of English Law*, ii, 210.

TORT AND QUASI-CONTRACT 123

There is fair reason for supposing that this was recognized in Brooke's time and that *C* could sue *B* either in debt or in account.[1] Here then are some of the germs of quasi-contract. No one in that early period realized how the plant which sprang from this seed was to be labelled by later generations, but then there was little understanding of contract itself, much less of the subtler conception of quasi-contract. Again, it may be objected that some of the older *dicta* which have been used to shew debt and account as the sources of quasi-contract are taken from cases on bailment and that bailment is a division of the law distinct from quasi-contract.[2] So it may be to us in the twentieth century, but not to our ancestors who had to build the law without much leisure for considering its architecture. Moreover, "bail" was quite commonly used by them to express the fact that a man had done nothing more than deliver his chattel to another, and the word was just as untechnical as "deliver".[3] It is significant that "Bailment" has no place as a separate branch of the law in the Abridgments of either Statham[4] or Fitzherbert,[5] and that there are only ten cases under that caption in Brooke.[6]

We pass next to the influence of *indebitatus assumpsit* on the development of quasi-contract. This remedy has had more to do with its growth than anything else. It is

[1] Br. *Abr.* Debt, 129, citing an argument in Y.B. 36 Hen. VI, f. 9, pl. 5. Repeated in Br. *Abr.* Accompt, 61, but with a query as to whether debt will lie. Holdsworth, *op. cit.* iii, 425–426, cites Y.B. 33–35 Ed. I (R.S.) 238, as an example of debt on quasi-contract; but it appears to be rather an example of contract. It was not Alice (the beneficiary) who was suing, but the executor of the bailor.

[2] E.g. Laicon, and Prisot C.J., C.P. in Y.B. Hil. 39 Hen. VI, f. 44, pl. 7.

[3] Pollock and Maitland, ii, 169.

[4] *Circa* A.D. 1495.

[5] 1st ed. (1516). Winfield, *Chief Sources of English Legal History*, 225.

[6] 1st ed. (1568).

124   TORT AND QUASI-CONTRACT

true that it does not cover all the ground of quasi-contract left uninfluenced by debt or by account. Thus it did not take in the so-called quasi-contractual obligation arising upon record (e.g. judgments and recognizances); but its importance is such that the history of it is, in effect, the later history of quasi-contract.

It will be recollected that the action of *assumpsit* was delictal in origin because it was a special kind of trespass on the case, or deceit on the case; that it was extended to redress claims on pure contract; and that by the end of the seventeenth century there were three varieties of it: (i) special (or express) *assumpsit*, here it was simply the remedy on an executory contract; (ii) *indebitatus assumpsit*, where the claim was not on an express contract but on an implied one; (iii) the old action of *assumpsit*, from which (i) and (ii) sprang, and which was a remedy against anyone who had caused damage to another by misperforming a duty which he had undertaken.[1]

Now it was not certain until 1601 that *indebitatus assumpsit* applied to contract unless there had been an express promise by the defendant to pay money to the plaintiff. But in that year it was settled that "every contract executory imports in itself an *assumpsit*".[2] Hence *indebitatus assumpsit* came to be used as a remedy on a contract genuinely implied, i.e. a contract founded, not upon any fiction of law, but upon an interpretation of facts by the court which led it to the genuine conclusion that the parties had actually agreed to enter into the transaction which the law inferred from their conduct to be a contract. But a more violent extension of *indebitatus assumpsit* occurred when it was allowed by the courts to include a "contract implied by the law". Here, no attempt was made to ascertain whether the parties had created a genuine contract between themselves, but the law by a fiction imputed one to them. The sub-

[1] *Ante*, p. 45.   [2] *Slade's Case* 4 Rep. at 94*a*.

TORT AND QUASI-CONTRACT 125

stantial results gained by this fiction were in the main excellent, for it made enforceable many claims which were really quasi-contractual, which any good system of law must enforce, and for which there was no other remedy. But the fiction itself was often nowhere near the facts upon which it was supposed to be founded, and distorted·them out of all recognition into an "implied contract". The doctrine appears in its most unblushing form when the facts shewed not only no shadow of agreement between the parties, but merely a tort committed by one of them against which the other would presumably have vigorously protested from beginning to end. It is important that this distinction between a contract genuinely implied and a contract implied by a fiction of the law should be grasped, for some of the law reports will not be intelligible unless it is. Judges and counsel occasionally spoke of an "implied contract" by way of ellipsis for "contract implied by the law". A great master of the Common Law pointed out this ambiguity at a much later date, when the mischief had been in existence too long for anyone to hope that it could be extirpated. He criticized

the unfortunate terminology of our law, owing to which the expression "implied contract" has been used to denote not only a genuine contract established by inference, but also an obligation which does not arise from any real contract, but which can be enforced as if it had a contractual origin.[1]

Indebitatus assumpsit was not stretched to include "contracts implied by the law" without a struggle. It was not suggested for this purpose until the end of the seventeenth century, nor was it finally sanctioned until the beginning of the eighteenth century.[2] This is the

[1] Lindley L.J. *In re Rhodes* (1890) 44 Ch.D. at p. 107; so too Cotton L.J. at p. 105.
[2] Holdsworth, *op. cit.* iii, 450.

126 TORT AND QUASI-CONTRACT

point of contact between it and quasi-contract, and its history in the eighteenth century is a tale of progress from grudging admissions of this application of *indebitatus assumpsit* by Holt C.J. (who, indeed, flatly refused to allow it on some occasions) to its complete establishment as a popular remedy by Lord Mansfield, who was enthusiastically in its favour. Holt had much more ground than is generally admitted for his resistance to extending the scope of the action in this way. The importation of a starkly fictitious contract into transactions where there was no contract at all was distasteful to him. In the *City of York* v. *Toun*,[1] the City imposed a fine on the defendant because he declined to hold the office of sheriff of York, and it was sought to recover this fine by *indebitatus assumpsit*. Shower arguing for the defendant asked, "How can there be any privity or assent implied, when a fine is imposed on a man against his will?" And Holt C.J. said "We will consider very well of this matter; it is time to have these actions redressed".[2] He was scientifically correct when he said in a case before him in the next year that "the notion of promises in law was a metaphysical notion, for the law makes no promise where there is a promise of the party".[3] In some cases also he was theoretically accurate in preferring to assign the obligation alleged by the plaintiff to another compartment of the law to which it belonged more properly than to quasi-contract. Thus, in *Shuttleworth* v. *Garnet*,[4] the executor of a lord of a manor sued *indebitatus assumpsit* against a copyhold tenant for the customary fine payable on admission. The majority of the court allowed the action against the dis-

[1] (1698) 5 Mod. 444.
[2] Rokeby J. was against him. From the report in 1 Ld Raym. 502, Treby L.C.J. seems to have agreed extrajudicially with Holt.
[3] *Starke* v. *Cheeseman* (1699) 1 Ld Raym. 538.
[4] (1689) 3 Lev. 261.

TORT AND QUASI-CONTRACT 127

sent of Holt C.J. who said quite rightly that the claim was on "a duty arising out of an inheritance, a custom, and a tenure".[1] In other words, it was an incident of tenure in land law, and even at the present day it would be better to treat it in this fashion until copyhold tenure becomes extinct and the question falls to the ground.[2] Then again, quite apart from objections on jurisprudential grounds, Holt foresaw procedural difficulties. He thought that *indebitatus assumpsit* prejudiced the defendant, as compared with the action of debt,[3] and that it turned into matters of fact for the jury what were really matters of law for the judge. It will be seen shortly that Holt's fears on this score were unfounded and that Lord Mansfield regarded *indebitatus assumpsit* as a mode of procedure beneficial to both plaintiff and defendant. In fairness to Holt it must be said that he seems to have had no objection to the enforcement of claims which were truly quasi-contractual. What he did dislike was the glaring pretence that they were contractual.

In 1760, Lord Mansfield rescued the law of quasi-contract from the marsh of technicality into which it was sinking. It is usually said that he placed it on its modern basis. In one sense this is true. He certainly gave it a new centre of gravity, and one that was more natural to it. But in shifting the centre of gravity he set up an instability of quasi-contract in relation to our formal system of Equity which encountered a good deal of hostile criticism. Moreover the test which he adopted was sufficiently nebulous to make its application difficult in particular cases. On the whole, however, it was a great improvement on the theory of fictitious contract which had preceded it. As Sir William Holdsworth has

---

[1] To the like effect is his final remark in *Smith* v. *Aiery* (1703) 6 Mod. 128.

[2] Cf. Ames, *op. cit.* 162.

[3] Holdsworth, *op. cit.* viii, 91.

128   TORT AND QUASI-CONTRACT

pointed out, the very incoherency of the law made his statement of principle here far more acceptable and successful than his attempts to alter principles that had already been settled in the doctrine of consideration, and in the rule in *Shelley's Case*.[1] That statement of principle is embodied in the following extracts from his judgment in *Moses* v. *Macferlan*:[2]

If the defendant be under an obligation, from the ties of natural justice to refund, the law implies a debt, and gives this action [*indebitatus assumpsit*], founded in the equity of the plaintiff's case, as it were upon a contract ("*quasi ex contractu*", as the Roman Law expresses it).[3]

It lies only for money which, *ex aequo et bono*, the defendant ought to refund. It does not lie for money paid by the plaintiff, which is claimed of him as payable in point of honour and honesty, although it could not have been recovered from him by any course of law; as in payment of a debt barred by the Statute of Limitations, or contracted during his infancy, or to the extent of principal and legal interest upon an usurious contract, or for money fairly lost at play; because in all these cases, the defendant may retain it with a safe conscience, though by positive law he was barred from recovering. But it lies for money paid by mistake; or upon a consideration which happens to fail; or for money got through imposition (express or implied); or extortion; or oppression; or an undue advantage taken of the plaintiff's situation, contrary to laws made for the protection of persons under those circumstances.[4]

Now Mansfield certainly deserves much praise for giving some better reason for the enforcement of quasi-contractual obligation than the awkward pretence of a "contract implied by the law". But in the theory which he put forward the phrases "natural justice" and "*ex aequo et bono*" were a source of confusion in one direction and were difficult for judges to apply in another. The

---

[1] Holdsworth, *op. cit.* viii, 97.   [2] (1760) 2 Burr. 1005.
[3] *Ibid.* at p. 1008.   [4] *Ibid.* at p. 1012.

TORT AND QUASI-CONTRACT   129

confusion of *aequum et bonum* was likely to arise in connection with our technical system of Equity as administered by the Court of Chancery; and even in cases where there was no risk of collision with this technical equity, a practical judge might feel puzzled to know how he was to ascertain what "natural justice" might mean. We may examine the subsequent history of *Moses* v. *Macferlan* in the light of each of these defects:

(1) *The collision with Equity as administered in the Court of Chancery.*

It must be confessed that Lord Mansfield and some of his colleagues and successors used language, which, whether it was loose or deliberately provocative, was certain to upset any orthodox Chancellor. Thus a few years after *Moses* v. *Macferlan*, he described the action for money had and received (the typical claim in *indebitatus assumpsit*) as "a liberal action in the nature of a bill in equity".[1] And still later in the eighteenth century, Buller J. carried the equation of this action to Chancery "equity" very far when he said that the extension of the action had been on the principle of its being considered like a bill in equity, and that, in order to be successful in it, the plaintiff "must shew that he has equity and conscience on his side, and that *he could recover it in a court of equity*".[2] Nor did the mischief end here, for it spread from the legal forum to the lecture room. Sir William Holdsworth has pointed out that Blackstone's *Commentaries* were infected by this tendency to fuse or confuse technical "equity" with law.[3] In the early nineteenth century this led to adverse criticism by the Chancellor, Lord Eldon. He said that the law had suffered more by Courts of Common Law acting upon what they considered to be rules of equity than by any other

[1] *Clarke* v. *Shee* (1774) Cowp. 197, 199.
[2] *Straton* v. *Rastall* (1788) 2 T.R. 366, 370.
[3] 43 *Harvard Law Review* (1929), 8–13, 21–24.

W P

130   TORT AND QUASI-CONTRACT

circumstance; and that, as it was impossible for them to execute it, it was impossible for them to exercise equitable jurisdiction, e.g. on points of evidence.[1] And even some of the Common Law judges thought that Lord Mansfield had expressed himself too widely about the principle as to the action for money had and received. Such was the opinion of Lord Alvanley C.J. who, in approving what Lord Eldon had said, professed himself as disposed to be very cautious in admitting equitable matters to be agitated in a court of Common Law.[2] By the middle of the century, Pollock C.B. referred to the idea that the action for money had and received was an "equitable action" as exploded. "It is a perfectly legal action, and no good can result from calling it an equitable one."[3] Within the last generation, the doctrine of *Moses* v. *Macferlan* has been applied,[4] but with explanations that sharply distinguish it from Chancery equity. *Aequum et bonum* has been described as meaning no more than what is "fair and reasonable",[5] and "equity" as signifying not what is administered in the Court of Chancery, but the *jus naturale* of Roman Law.[6] The House of Lords in 1914 scouted the idea that there was any practical connection between Mansfield's "equity" and Chancery "equity".[7] So disappears the "Mansfield fallacy", as Mr H. G. Hanbury has styled it in a

[1] *Cooth* v. *Jackson* (1801) 6 Ves. Jr. at p. 39.
[2] *Johnson* v. *Johnson* (1802) 3 B. & P. 162, 169.
[3] *Miller* v. *Atlee* (1849) 13 Jur. 431.
[4] *Phillips* v. *London School Board* [1898] 2 Q.B. 447, 453. *Jacobs* v. *Morris* [1901] 1 Ch. 261, 268–269. In *re Bodega Co. Ld.* [1904] 1 Ch. 276, 286. *Lodge* v. *National Union Investment Co. Ld.* (1906) 76 L.J. Ch. 187, 193.
[5] Farwell J. in *Bradford Corporation* v. *Ferrand* [1902] 2 Ch. 655, 622–663.
[6] Farwell L.J. in *Baylis* v. *Bishop of London* [1913] 1 Ch. 127, 133, 136–137.
[7] *Sinclair* v. *Brougham* [1914] A.C. 398; Viscount Haldane L.C. at p. 417; Lord Sumner at pp. 454–456.

TORT AND QUASI-CONTRACT 131

recent trenchant article,[1] which leaves no room for any further misapprehension on the point. Perhaps his strictures are too severe in some respects. It seems harsh to reproach Mansfield for leaving "the sound soil of implied contract" for "the shifting sands of natural equity". Whatever faults the *aequum et bonum* theory may have had, it was not nearly so artificial as the doctrine of "implied contract", and it was probably not a whit more unstable. One has only to look at some of the decisions prior to *Moses* v. *Macferlan* to see how bewildered the courts were in applying the idea of implied contract and how embarrassed they were by its fictitious nature.[2] And there have been some curious decisions rendered since Mansfield's time owing to a throw-back to the theory of implied contract. But these will be discussed later.

(2) *The vagueness of "natural justice" and "aequum et bonum".*

Both in *Moses* v. *Macferlan* and in later decisions, Lord Mansfield put the theory of quasi-contractual obligation on a highly abstract level. In *Towers* v. *Barrett*,[3] he described the action for money had and received as "founded on principles of eternal justice". Whether it is consistent with the principles of eternal justice that a man should be able to retain a bet which he has won at horse-racing, or that a moneylender should be entitled to keep 300 per cent. on a loan, are questions that we need not stop to consider; for Mansfield was less likely than any other judge to administer justice in the

---

[1] 40 *Law Quarterly Review* (1924), 34–36.
[2] The learned author regards *Marriot* v. *Hampton* (1797) 7 T.R. 269, as giving "a truer understanding of the action [for money had and received]". It is somewhat difficult to see how it did so. Again Parke B. in *Kelly* v. *Solari* (1841) 9 M. & W. 54, seems rather to have expanded what Lord Mansfield had said than (as Mr Hanbury claims) to have restated the true principle on which the action is founded.
[3] (1786) 1 T.R. 133, 134.

9-2

132   TORT AND QUASI-CONTRACT

clouds, and both he and his successors on the bench, when it came to trying actual cases, toned down the vivid hues in which he had painted the action for money had and received. Practical limits were put upon "natural justice" in its application, and indeed it was held in at least one case where the defendant had actually been guilty of something very like sharp practice, that nevertheless he was not liable in an action for money had and received.[1] It is curious to mark the criticisms made upon the *aequum et bonum* principle by two judges of our own time, whose reputation as commercial lawyers suffers nothing by comparison with that of Mansfield himself. Lord Sumner, when he was in the Court of Appeal said:

> To ask what course would be *ex aequo et bono* to both sides never was a very precise guide, and as a working rule it has long since been buried....Whatever may have been the case 146 years ago, we are not now free in the twentieth century to administer that vague jurisprudence which is sometimes attractively styled "justice as between man and man".[2]

With this opinion of Lord Sumner, Scrutton L.J. expressed himself in entire agreement in the later case of *Holt* v. *Markham*[3] in which he deprecated the "well-meaning sloppiness of thought" which surrounded *aequum et bonum*.

In spite of the strength of these expressions, it is probable that they ought not to be, and were not intended to be, accepted without qualification. Otherwise some odd results would follow. What would have happened to much of our Common Law if "justice as between man and man" had been totally eliminated from it during the past one hundred and forty-six years,

[1] *Marriot* v. *Hampton* (1797) 7 T.R. 269.
[2] As Hamilton L.J. in *Baylis* v. *Bishop of London* [1913] 1 Ch. at p. 140.
[3] *Holt* v. *Markham* [1923] 1 K.B. at p. 513.

TORT AND QUASI-CONTRACT 133

it is hard to say in detail. But one thing is certain as a generalization. It would have lost much of the flexibility which is its chief justification and one of its great merits. Nor has this ceased to be true at the present day. *Aequum et bonum* is traceable as an ingredient in other standards employed in the judicial process. A judge must often either decide for himself what "reasonable" means, or, when sitting with a jury, direct them as to its signification. What does "reasonable" mean if it does not connote *aequum et bonum*, or "justice as between man and man"? The last phrase is often a mere piece of claptrap and the man on the Clapham omnibus is often a "sloppy thinker", but he understands how to put the phrase to practical use even if he cannot explain it. Sir Frederick Pollock has pointed out that the "reasonable man" and a "reasonable price" are only later instances of the "law of nature" under another name.[1]

Again, "public policy" is often the basis of a judicial decision, and it has been defined as "the opinions of men of the world, as distinguished from opinions based on legal learning";[2] or, as we have ventured to suggest elsewhere, "it is the judges themselves, assisted by the bar, who here represent the highest common factor of public sentiment and intelligence".[3] No one would have the face to say that men of the world, or the Bench, or the Bar, do not take account of *aequum et bonum* here.

Then, again, modern judges have not ceased to use the phrase "natural justice", or to base decisions on the doctrine which it represents and on nothing else.[4]

It is submitted that what Lord Sumner and Scrutton L.J. meant was that, whereas in Lord Mansfield's

---

[1] *Essays in the Law*, 68–74.
[2] Lord Haldane in *Rodriguez* v. *Speyer Bros.* [1919] A.C. at p. 79.
[3] 42 *Harvard Law Review* (1928), 97.
[4] *Valentini* v. *Canali* (1889) 24 Q.B.D. 166. A strong decision for it modified considerably the plain words of the Infants Relief Act, 1874.

134   TORT AND QUASI-CONTRACT

time quasi-contract was in its infancy and *aequum et bonum* was perhaps the best way of describing a judicial discretion for which there must have been great scope in developing this branch of the law, at the present day the main heads of quasi-contract have become so well settled that there is much less room for exercising in it the purely creative side of judicial discretion as compared with the merely interpretative side of it in applying technical rules embodied in scores of decisions during the last century and a half.

But it does not follow that no instances can occur nowadays in the law of quasi-contract in which the judges must fall back upon "natural justice", "*aequum et bonum*", or "justice as between man and man", loose and ambiguous as these phrases may be.

The criticisms of Lord Mansfield which have just been considered may be regarded rather as pruning some of the exuberance of his doctrine of quasi-contract, than as axes laid at the root of it. A much more serious question is whether the whole doctrine has not been uprooted and replaced by the older theory of a contract implied by the law, though Mansfield's colleagues seem to have been of opinion that the notion of "privity" was too cramped to support the action for money had and received, in general.[1]

Thus it has been said:

Without privity of contract the fact that the defendant is wrongfully in possession of money held for the benefit of the plaintiff, or even in possession of the plaintiff's own money, does not enable this form of action [for money had and received] to be maintained.[2]

If this be true, what becomes of the doctrine of

---

[1] *Per* Court of Common Pleas in *Hitchin* v. *Campbell* (1771) 2 W.Bl. at p. 830.

[2] 7 *Laws of England* (Halsbury), § 967.

TORT AND QUASI-CONTRACT 135

aequum et bonum even in the modified form to which the criticisms just mentioned have reduced it? However, investigation of the authorities cited in support of the quotation leads to a less sweeping conclusion than that which it puts forward.

In the first place, we can ignore some cases which are irrelevant to the proposition.[1] Secondly, a large proportion of the remainder turn upon agency. They appear to lay down the very sensible rule that if John is principal, and Peter is John's agent to whom John entrusts money for Andrew, then Andrew cannot recover the money from Peter unless Peter becomes Andrew's agent. Some of these decisions shew merely that Peter was purely the agent of John and not of Andrew. Thus in *Stephens* v. *Badcock*,[2] *J*, an attorney, who was accustomed to receive dues for the plaintiff, his client, went from home, leaving *B*, his clerk, at his office. *B*, in *J*'s absence, received money on account of the above dues for the client. He was authorized to do this, and he gave the payer a receipt signed, "*B* for Mr *J*". *J* was in bad circumstances when he left home and he never returned. The plaintiff sued *B* for money had and received. Held: *B* was not liable, for he had received the money as agent of *J* and was accountable to him for it, *J*, on the other hand being answerable to the client for the sum. There was no "privity of contract" between *B* and the plaintiff. The privity was between *J* and the plaintiff. Other decisions merely illustrate the principle; they do not carry it further and brief reference to them is sufficient.[3]

---

[1] *Oughton* v. *Seppings* (1830) 1 B. & Ad. 241; *Young* v. *Marshall* (1831) 8 Bing. 43; *Neate* v. *Harding* (1851) 6 Ex. 349; all these were cases of pure tort masquerading as contract, or turned into quasi-contract.

[2] (1832) 3 B. & Ad. 354.

[3] *Baron* v. *Husband* (1833) 4 B. & Ad. 611. *Howell* v. *Batt* (1833) 2 Nev. & M. (K.B. 381). *Cobb* v. *Beake* (1845) 6 Q.B. 930 (*A* sent cheque for agreed debt and costs to *B*, his solicitor, for transmission to *C* to whom the debt was due, but *A* gave no direction that this specific

136 TORT AND QUASI-CONTRACT

Though in all of them there is talk about no "privity of contract" between the plaintiff and the defendant, the decision might have been reached without dragging this in, and on the simple ground that the agent was the agent of the defendant, not of the plaintiff. But other decisions tackle more directly the problem, "What must the plaintiff prove in order to shew that the intermediary *is* his agent?" There must be "privity" between them, but it is difficult to say what this means. In quite a number of cases no explanation of the word is vouchsafed, nor is the phrase "privity *of contract*" used. In a decision of Lord Ellenborough's it was laid down that there must be some appropriation of the money by the defendant to the use of the plaintiff, and it was held that mere information given by the defendant's principal to the plaintiff that he (the principal) had directed the defendant to pay the plaintiff was not sufficient.[1] Yet it might be inferred from later decisions that if the defendant (i.e. the agent) tells the plaintiff that he is holding the money of *A*, the defendant's principal, on behalf of the plaintiff, then, there is privity between them and the defendant is liable.[2] But the inference would be inconsistent with yet another line of decisions which indicate that "privity" signifies either actual contract between *B*, the agent, and *C* the person whom *A*, the principal of *B*, intends to benefit, or else something closely resembling contract. As to actual contract, in *Malcolm* v. *Scott*,[3] *A* requested the firm, *B*, to hold a sum of money at the disposal of *C*, and *A* in-

cheque was to be passed to *C*). *Barlow* v. *Browne* (1846) 16 M. & W. 126 (defendant held to be agent of executor, not of plaintiff). *Black* v. *Siddaway* (1846) 15 L.J.Q.B. 359 (treasurer of money club not an agent for a non-member of the club). *Watson* v. *Russell* (1864) 5 B. & S. 968.

[1] *Williams* v. *Everett* (1811) 14 East, 582 (a much-cited case).

[2] *Moore* v. *Bushell* (1857) 27 L.J. Ex. 3. See too 7 *Laws of England* § 968, and other authorities cited there.

[3] *Malcolm* v. *Scott* (1850) 5 Ex. 601.

TORT AND QUASI-CONTRACT 137

formed *C* of this direction to *B*. *B* advised *C* of the request. It was held that the *B* firm was not liable to *C* for money had and received, because "they were under no obligation to pay over the money until they bound themselves by a contract with the plaintiff to do so".[1] "The law is clear. The defendants are under no obligation to pay over the money to the plaintiff, unless they have made a binding agreement with him to do so."[2] But this seems not only to put an end to any distinction between contract and quasi-contract, but also (as will be shewn later) to be inconsistent with the law of agency abstractedly from any notion of quasi-contract. It goes beyond other cases which require no more than some sort of analogy with contract in order to constitute privity, though it is a moot point how much analogy is needed. Thus it has been held in one decision that consideration is necessary in all cases, "though in an action for money had and received, a direct consideration moving from the plaintiff is seldom shewn";[3] in another, that there must be an express promise to pay;[4] in yet another, that there can be no recovery unless the law will imply a contract to pay on request from the relation which the parties bear towards each other.[5] All this makes it puzzling to say what the law is. The notion that some sort of contract, or some ingredient of contract, must be implied led to some queer results. Occasionally what is astonishing is not so much the artificiality of imputing a contract where none existed, but the waste of energy in imputing it where it already existed. It might well have been argued that there was liability on a plain contract, and yet recourse was had to the

---

[1] *Malcolm* v. *Scott* (1850) 611.   [2] *Ibid.* 610.

[3] *Lilly* v. *Hays* (1836) 5 Ad. & El. 548, 550. So too *Walker* v. *Rostron* (1842) 9 M. & W. 411; good consideration had to be found.

[4] *Barlow* v. *Browne* (1846) 16 M. & W. 126.

[5] *Robbins* v. *Fennell* (1847) 11 Q.B. 248.

138 TORT AND QUASI-CONTRACT

action for money had and received.[1] Again, some decisions are inexplicable, because there was held to be no privity even when the defendant ought to have been liable on quasi-contract as a stakeholder.[2]

The result seems to be this. In the triangular relation, John—Peter—Andrew, to which we have referred, the action for money had and received is maintainable by Andrew only where Peter is the agent of Andrew and not merely the agent of John. If this be so, all that "privity" means is the creation of agency between Peter and Andrew. And, as agency can arise in many ways otherwise than by contract (e.g. by implication of law from the conduct of the parties or from the necessity of the case),[3] no contract need be proved. Short of this, what must be proved, is a question to which no certain answer can be returned. One can do no more than refer to the authorities which have been already quoted. They are limited to a particular form of agency, and if they impugn the *aequum et bonum* doctrine, they do so only in this special instance.

A much more powerful and general reversion to the implied contract theory appears in the recent decision of the House of Lords in *Sinclair* v. *Brougham*.[4] A building society, acting *ultra vires*, engaged in banking. In the winding-up of the society, it was held that depositors in this bank were not entitled to recover moneys paid by them on an *ultra vires* contract of loan, on the footing of money had and received by the society to their use. Such action applied only "where the law could consistently impute to the defendant at least the fiction of a promise".[5] Here, it could not be imputed

[1] *Hooper* v. *Treffry* (1847) 1 Ex. 17.
[2] *Jones* v. *Carter* (1845) 8 Q.B. 134. The decision was prior to the relevant Gaming Acts.
[3] Bowstead, *Agency* (7th ed. 1924), 16.
[4] [1914] A.C. 398.
[5] At p. 417.

TORT AND QUASI-CONTRACT 139

where money had been paid under a contract which was
ultra vires.

The fiction...becomes inapplicable where substantive law, as
distinguished from that of procedure, makes the defendant incapable of undertaking contractual liability. For to impute a
fictitious promise is simply to presume the existence of a state of
facts, and the presumption can give rise to no higher right than
would result if the facts were actual.[1]

So Viscount Haldane L.C., and so too Lord Sumner:

All these causes of action are common species of the genus *assumpsit*. All now rest, and long have rested, upon a notional or
imputed promise to repay. The law cannot *de jure* impute
promises to repay, whether for money had and received or otherwise, which, if made *de facto*, it would inexorably avoid.[2]

It might be thought that *Sinclair* v. *Brougham* finally
disposes of the *aequum et bonum* theory, but this is not
so. First, there are other varieties of quasi-contract
besides those redressed by the action for money had and
received. Such are claims arising out of salvage and
general average.[3] The fiction of an implied contract has
no room there. Secondly, even in those cases in which
the House of Lords insists that we must now accept the
implied promise theory, the influence of *aequum et bonum*
does not necessarily disappear. It has been the ground-
work of a number of decisions which the House of Lords
had no idea of upsetting. And it must still be used as
an aid to the courts in determining whether they will,
in any particular circumstances imply a contract or not,
assuming that there is no previous authority which
covers the point. Indeed there is nothing in the speeches

[1] At p. 417.
[2] At p. 452. See too Lord Dunedin at pp. 432–433, and Lord Parker
at p. 440.
[3] *Post*, pp. 155, 182. But it is doubtful whether general average falls
under quasi-contract.

140   TORT AND QUASI-CONTRACT

of the noble and learned lords which is inconsistent with this.[1] It matters very little in substance whether we describe this guide as "*aequum et bonum*", or "natural justice", or "what is reasonable", except that the courts do not much relish the first two of these terms, while they would see nothing objectionable in the third. But all three mean much the same thing in the English Common Law. It may be doubted whether, except in some special cases, there is much to be gained by veiling the question, "What is reasonable?" behind the question, "Can we imply a promise?" We have already mentioned some examples of the awkward consequences to which the fiction of implied contract, or "privity", has led. Others are not far to seek. An action for money had and received lies for the recovery of money paid over on an illegal transaction before the transaction is carried out. Here there is no contract, for the agreement was illegal from the beginning. As there is none, is one to be implied? If so, it is curious that no trouble has been taken in several decisions to discover it.[2] Again, in some instances of waiving a tort, and suing in quasi-contract, the fiction is transparent to the point of absurdity. In *Lightly* v. *Clouston*,[3] the defendant was held liable in an action for money had and received for decoying away the plaintiff's apprentice. This was pure tort, and Le Blanc J. admitted the hollowness of the pretence about "privity", but, after stating the true principle that the money claimed by the plaintiff belonged to him "in justice and equity", he went out of his way to find the following extraordinary implied contract: "I should also be inclined to consider that, as there was a contract [*sc.* between the apprentice and the defendant], the

[1] See [1914] A.C. at pp. 432–433, 453–454.
[2] *Hastelow* v. *Jackson* (1828) 8 B. & C. 221. *Taylor* v. *Bowers* (1876) 1 Q.B.D. 291, 295–296. *Barclay* v. *Pearson* [1893] 2 Ch. 154.
[3] (1808) 1 Taunt. 212. See too *Foster* v. *Stewart* (1814) 3 M. & S. 191.

TORT AND QUASI-CONTRACT 141

master [the plaintiff] might avail himself of it, as the apprentice was under an incapacity of making any contract, except for the benefit of his master".[1] In other cases of waiver of a tort not the faintest attempt has been made to discover any "privity". Thus, in *Oughton* v. *Seppings*,[2] the defendant, a sheriff, wrongfully seized under a writ of *fi. fa.* the plaintiff's pony. It was held that the plaintiff could waive the trespass to her possession of the pony, and sue an action for money had and received (the proceeds of sale of the pony by the defendant). Not a word was said about "privity" in the judgments.[3]

On the whole, then, we have preferred to omit any reference to implied contract in the definition which we have framed, and to adopt rather the idea of unjust benefit.

This general historical sketch may be concluded with a statement of the reasons why *indebitatus assumpsit* was so popular as a remedy. The obvious cause might seem to be that it redressed many forms of grievance which could not be met by other actions. But that is not altogether satisfactory. It does not tell us why it was preferred to debt or to some sort of action on the case. It was often said to be "a liberal action", but this merely

---

[1] 1 Taunt. at p. 200. See too *Neate* v. *Harding* (1851) 6 Ex. 349, 352. Keener, 180–181, says of Martin B's judgment there: "It is certainly a novelty in the law, to establish a contract between a plaintiff and a defendant by proving that the defendant tortiously took the plaintiff's money and deposited it with a third party, the deposit with a third party creating a contract between the plaintiff and the defendant, where but for the deposit there would have been no such relation".

[2] (1830) 1 B. & Ad. 240.

[3] Cf. *Young* v. *Marshall* (1831) 8 Bing. 43. It is worth while noting that judicial opinion is divided as to whether "contract" when used in a statute includes implied contracts based on fictions. In *Brocklebank* v. *R.* [1925] 1 K.B. 52 Bankes and Sargant L.JJ. held that it did, while Scrutton L.J. held that it did not. It is scarcely necessary to add that, in any event, each statute must be construed on its own merits.

142 TORT AND QUASI-CONTRACT

puts the question one step further back. Why was it a liberal action? Holt C.J., as has been noticed, thought that it prejudiced the defendant as compared with debt,[1] and expressed apprehensions as to other possible procedural defects in it.[2] Lord Mansfield, on the other hand, regarded it as beneficial to both parties, and there is no doubt that it proved to be so.[3]

First, as to the plaintiff. The declaration in the action for money had and received was very simple. It occupied no more than a dozen lines. All that the plaintiff need allege was that the defendant was indebted to him in so much money had and received by the defendant to the use of the plaintiff, and that he thereupon promised the plaintiff to repay it, "and with this slender machinery", said Samuel Warren, writing in 1845, "may be recovered any sum of money, however large, which *ex aequo et bono*, the defendant ought to refund".[4] These "*indebitatus* counts", or "common counts", compared most favourably with a declaration in special form (e.g. on an executory contract) where there must be set out all the facts necessary to explain the intention of the parties and the nature of the transaction; the precise consideration and promise; the plaintiff's performance of all that he was bound to do; the defendant's non-performance or breach of contract; and the plaintiff's damages.[5]

Next, as to the defendant. To the plaintiff's declaration he need put in no more than a mere denial, and that put in issue not only the defendant's receipt of the money, but also the existence of all those facts which made his receipt of it a receipt to the use of the plaintiff.[6]

[1] Holdsworth, *op. cit.* viii, 91.
[2] *Ante*, p. 127.
[3] *Moses* v. *Macferlan* (1760) 2 Burr. 1005, 1010.
[4] *Introduction to Law Studies* (2nd ed.), 230–321.
[5] *Ibid.* 486–487. So too 2 Williams' Saund. (ed. 1871), 742 note (7).
[6] Warren, *op. cit.* 320–321.

TORT AND QUASI-CONTRACT 143

The defence was any "equity" that would rebut the action.[1] But it must be added that there might be circumstances in which permission to sue this action instead of another, which was applicable, would have greatly prejudiced the defendant, and in such cases Lord Mansfield was as emphatic as any judge in refusing to allow the·plaintiff to sue it.[2]

The procedural advantages of *indebitatus assumpsit* were almost entirely swept away by nineteenth century statutory reforms; but the action for money had and received and the actions akin to it are still used, partly because there are many claims to which they alone are appropriate, partly because the tincture of *aequum et bonum* which still flavours them makes it sometimes worth while to use them in preference to some other remedy.

The advantages of one application of *indebitatus assumpsit* call for special notice, for they are by no means obvious in modern textbooks. This application is known as waiver of a tort in favour of the action for money had and received. More must be said of it later, but here it is enough to explain that it occurs where *A* has committed a tort against *B*, and *B* is permitted by the law to waive his right of action in tort and to sue, on the same facts, the action for money had and received. But why should he ever do this? It is generally admitted that he must, in the first instance, establish the commission of a tort. If he is forced to take all the trouble of doing this, what sense is there in his saying in effect, "I have made out my case in tort, but I wish to make no claim upon it. I prefer to claim as for money had and received"? The selection of this course seems the more remarkable, because some passages in the reports might

[1] *Sadler* v. *Evans* (1776) 4 Burr. 1984, 1986.
[2] *Lindon* v. *Hooper* (1776) 1 Cowp. 414. Cf. Patteson J. in *Ashmole* v. *Wainwright* (1842) 2 Q.B. at p. 845.

144 TORT AND QUASI-CONTRACT

raise the inference that the only person who gained by the plaintiff's choice was the defendant.[1] Again, in other cases, while it is expressly stated, or clearly implied, that the action for money had and received was more beneficial to the plaintiff than an action in tort, there is no hint of why it was so.[2]

In fact it benefited both parties. All the procedural advantages attended it which have been noticed as characteristics of *indebitatus assumpsit* in general. The plaintiff and the defendant both relieved themselves of the difficulty and precision of special pleading. Both, on the other hand, took risks which, however, were worth taking. The plaintiff might be surprised by the defendant putting up any *bona fide* defence on pleading the general issue,[3] and the defendant could not know so exactly as in other actions what the framework of the plaintiff's claim was.[4]

Then, in particular, the plaintiff reaped several other benefits. If he waived trover in favour of money had and received, he need not set out to prove the exact value of the thing converted (as he must in trover). That might be a difficult task, for a jury might well have a lower opinion of its value than the plaintiff, quite apart from the evidential difficulties of assessment. By condescending on a definite amount, as he would do in an action for money had and received, the plaintiff simplified the machinery of proof of his loss, because he could fix that at the sum for which the defendant had sold the article (where he had done so); and he could be pretty certain of getting that particular sum. Again, the action for

[1] "We are clear that the party may waive the tort; which, if he does, it is to his own prejudice, and in favour of the defendant." Lord Mansfield in *Feltham* v. *Terry* (1772) Lofft, at p. 208.
[2] *Lamine* v. *Dorrell* (1705) 2 Ld Raym 1216. Pollock C.B. in *Rodgers* v. *Maw* (1846) 15 M. & W. at p. 448.
[3] *Lindon* v. *Hooper* (1776) Cowper, at pp. 417, 419.
[4] Cf. Littledale J. in *Burnett* v. *Lynch* (1826) 5 B. & C. at p. 609.

TORT AND QUASI-CONTRACT 145

money had and received was not extinguished by death as were most actions in tort, and the plaintiff could thus have a remedy where he would otherwise have had none.[1] Yet again, he might be released from giving a statutory notice which might be requisite if he sued in tort.[2] Even with the simplification of procedure in the nineteenth century, there may still be reasons for waiving a tort. One of them relates to the survival of actions. The Administration of Estates Act, 1925[3] (re-enacting the Civil Procedure Act, 1833, s. 2), puts very short periods of limitation on suing in tort where the remedy in tort survives. But these do not apply to the action for money had and received.[4] At the present day, also, it is possible for the plaintiff, by waiving a tort, to procure as compensation an amount which it is doubtful whether he could get if he relied on the tort of conversion.[5]

The special benefits which accrued to the defendant where the plaintiff waived a tort were that he could plead such matters as set-off or payment into court.[6] In particular, if it were trover that the plaintiff waived, the defendant was liable, not for the full value of the goods, but only for the sum for which they had actually been sold; for, in selling, he was regarded as the agent of the plaintiff.[7] In the action for money had and received, the plaintiff "cannot then come for damages; he cannot say, if the goods are sold, that they were double the value the defendant sold them for. Here nothing can be recovered

[1] Bayley J. in *Foster* v. *Stewart* (1814) 3 M. & S. at p. 202.
[2] *Irving* v. *Wilson* (1791) 4 T.R. 485.
[3] Sect. 26.
[4] Thus in *Phillips* v. *Homfray* (1883) 24 Ch.D. 439, an action in tort was not maintainable, for the injuries to the land had been committed much more than six months preceding the trespasser's death.
[5] *Bavins* v. *L. & S.W. Bank* [1900] 1 Q.B. 270.
[6] *Smith* v. *Hodson* (1791) 4 T.R. 211. *Lightly* v. *Clouston* (1808) 1 Taunt at p. 115. *Orton* v. *Butler* (1822) 5 B. & Ald. 652. *Young* v. *Marshall* (1831) 8 Bing. at p. 44.
[7] *King* v. *Leith* (1787) 2 T.R. at p. 145.

W P

146   TORT AND QUASI-CONTRACT

but what is conscientiously due; nothing but the real value".[1] Further, a plea in abatement was applicable in this action, but not in trover.[2] As with the plaintiff, so with the defendant, procedural reforms have reduced considerably the advantages of the action. The Common Law Procedure Act, 1852, actually improved the position of the defendant in actions on the border-line of contract and tort, by providing that any plea which should be good in substance should not be objectionable on the ground of its treating the declaration either as framed for a breach of contract, or for a wrong.[3]

Before we pass to examine in detail quasi-contractual obligation, it will be as well to consider what has been called by a very learned American writer *quasi-assumptual obligation*. Mr Street[4] distinguishes quasi-contract from quasi-assumpsit as follows:

> In the ordinary quasi-contract we have to deal with a positive legal duty to pay or surrender a specific sum of money either definable in fact or reducible to certainty, or to turn over a measurable or ponderable quantity of chattels or their proceeds. In the quasi-assumptual obligation, on the other hand, we have to deal with positive obligations whereby a man is bound to do particular acts other than to pay money or chattels, or is bound to do his acts in a particular way, or is bound to warrant particular states of fact, or is bound to refrain from acting altogether.[5]

The examples which he gives are

(i) Statutory obligations like those in *Couch* v. *Steel*[6] (duty on shipowners to keep on board a supply of medicines).

(ii) Statutes which require carriers to observe certain precautions in running trains or managing ships.

---

[1] Lord Mansfield in *Feltham* v. *Terry* (1772) Lofft, at p. 208.
[2] *Orton* v. *Butler* (1822) 5 B. & Ald. 652.
[3] Sect. 74. Repealed S.L.R. Act, 1883, s. 3 (subject to s. 7).
[4] *Foundations of Legal Liability* (1906), ii, chap. xxv.
[5] *Ibid.* p. 236.   [6] (1854) 3 E. & B. 402.

TORT AND QUASI-CONTRACT 147

(iii) Statutory obligation on public officers to perform the functions of their office. These first three, Mr Street says, are usually dealt with under the head of negligence.

(iv) Those who ply a common calling; e.g. the innkeeper's duty to entertain, the common carrier's duty to convey for all the public alike.

(v) The whole law of negligence is, in one aspect, quasi-assumptual.

(vi) Implied warranties in sale.

(vii) Contracts for the benefit of third persons.

(viii) An agent's implied warranty of authority.

(ix) Implied promise not to prevent the other party to a contract from performing his part of the agreement.

(x) Exoneration of, and contribution among, persons acting jointly, as in suretyship.

(xi) Equitable estoppel.

The objections to quasi-assumpsit as a separate head of the law are twofold. First, Street does not apply his own definition consistently. Thus the duty of a co-surety to contribute his share of a debt which another co-surety has already paid is "a positive legal duty to pay...a specific sum of money". In other words it falls within Street's definition of quasi-contract, not of quasi-assumpsit. Secondly, all the obligations which he mentions are just as adequately distributed under quasi-contract or some other division of the law. Most of them are treated fully later, and it need only be said here that the first five fall under ordinary liability in tort, (vi) is genuine implied contract, and so are (ix) and (x). (vii) is quasi-contract *qua* its enforceability by the third person. (viii) is doubtful and its correct place must be postponed for further discussion, but there is no necessity to invent quasi-assumpsit for it. (xi) from the English point of view is merely a rule of evidence.

148   TORT AND QUASI-CONTRACT

It would therefore seem that quasi-assumpsit is superfluous. Historically there is much to be said for it, for *assumpsit* in origin squares with no one department of the law in the current books of jurisprudence. But we are sufficiently emancipated from its history nowadays to avoid making it a separate heading, especially as the term quasi-assumpsit is almost totally unknown to English practitioners.

We now proceed to investigate the most conspicuous quasi-contracts in English law. They may be grouped as follows:

(A) *Pseudo-quasi-contracts*.[1] These are cases in which the idea of quasi-contract is now entirely inapplicable.

(B) *Pure quasi-contracts*, i.e. where the obligation is quasi-contractual, and the facts do not give rise to any alternative liability, whether in tort, contract, or on any other ground. Here, if the plaintiff had no remedy in quasi-contract, he would have none at all.

(C) *Quasi-contract which is alternative to some other form of liability.* Here the facts equally well would support an action in tort, or on contract, or otherwise.

(D) *Doubtful quasi-contracts*, where it is not certain whether the obligation should be regarded as quasi-contractual or should be placed under some other species of obligation.

It may be urged that (C) is really quite as much pseudo-quasi-contract as is (A), that at the present day if the plaintiff can get what he wants in an action in tort or under some other head of liability there is no point in giving him on precisely the same facts an alternative remedy, and that to do so is inconsistent with the idea of *aequum et bonum*, or "natural justice", or "reasonableness", which (either in a neat form or disguised by "implied contract") lies at the root of quasi-contract. The answer to this is that if an analysis of quasi-con-

[1] The phrase is barbarous, but we can think of no other.

TORT AND QUASI-CONTRACT 149

tract is to be of any practical value in English law it must take account of facts; that if the courts have decided in a large number of instances that the obligation is quasi-contractual (whatever else it may also be), then it is idle to say that they were wrong in doing so; and that to adopt any such course is really to substitute the personal judgment of a theorist as to whether a benefit accruing to the defendant is "unjust",[1] for that of the courts themselves. It is true that some of these instances under (C) are mere survivals of procedural distinctions which are now largely extinct and that they would not figure as quasi-contract in an ideal system of law; but it is equally true that even at the present day the action for money had and received is governed by considerations, substantial and procedural, which do not apply to actions in tort or on contract, and that its abolition in cases where, on the same facts, there is an alternative remedy might lead to serious injustice. To put the matter in a nutshell, if the English law of quasi-contract were "restated" today *more Americano*, it would be extremely unwise to eliminate from it the varieties falling under (C).

The different headings can now be taken in detail:

(A) *Pseudo-quasi-contracts.*

Under whatever form of obligation these fall, it ought not to be quasi-contract.

(1) *Contracts of record.* Examples are judgments and recognizances. Judgment debts have not a shadow of likeness to contract. Recognizances are faintly analogous to it in that there is an assent which is compelled. But neither of them correspond to any sound definition of quasi-contract in modern law,[2] and they had better be

---

[1] See definition of quasi-contract, *ante* p. 119.

[2] Keener, *op. cit.* 16, and Woodward, *op. cit.* § 1, accept them as such; so does Jenks, *Digest of English Civil Law*, § 716. But this does not square with the tests of quasi-contract given in these works.

150   TORT AND QUASI-CONTRACT

dismissed as "procedural obligations". Foreign judgments have also been described as creating quasi-contractual obligation.[1] Historically, it is true that the remedy on a judgment debt was debt (in the technical sense of the old action for debt) or *indebitatus assumpsit*[2] which here, as in other instances supplanted debt; but later judicial pronouncements adopt the broad principle that the judgment of a British or foreign court of competent jurisdiction imposes an obligation on the defendant to fulfil it, and the courts of this country are bound to enforce it where it originates in a court outside English jurisdiction just as much as they will enforce an English judgment.[3] This leaves us free to say that the obligation to fulfil an English judgment is one created judicially by the state, while the obligation created by a foreign judgment is part of a substantive branch of the law (Conflict of Laws) which has its own principles and which had better be respected as such. At any rate, a foreign judgment is unhampered by the awkward fiction attaching to English judgments—that they are "contracts" of record.[4] It is probably better to refer other obligations arising in foreign law which might be treated as quasi-contractual to the same general head of Conflict of Laws.[5]

(2) *The duty of a finder of goods.* According to Coke C.J. in *Isaack* v. *Clark*,[6] "If a man findes goods,

---

[1] 7 *Laws of England* (Halsbury), § 1000. Jenks, *op. cit.* § 716.

[2] *Dupleix* v. *De Roven* (1705) 2 Vern. 540 (foreign judgment).

[3] *Per curiam* in *Schibsby* v. *Westenholz* (1870) L.R. 6 Q.B. 155, 159. Parke B. in *Williams* v. *Jones* (1845) 13 M. & W. at p. 265.

[4] *Walker* v. *Witter* (1778) 1 Dougl. 1.

[5] In *Batthyany* v. *Walford* (1887) 36 Ch.D. 269, the duty of a *fidei commisse* under Austrian law to hand property to his successor in as good condition as when he received it was held by the C.A. to be in the nature of an implied contract, and to be unaffected by the rule *actio personalis moritur cum persona*, which would have destroyed the claim if it had been one in tort.

[6] (1614) 2 Bulst. 306, 312.

TORT AND QUASI-CONTRACT 151

an action upon the case lieth for his ill and negligent keeping of them, but no trover and conversion, because this but a *non fesans*." This action upon the case would presumably be for negligence, and as that is now an independent tort, the finder's liability is tortious, not quasi-contractual. Nor is there anything in the authorities which negatives this view.[1] The right of the finder to be paid reasonable compensation for salving lost property is, of course, another matter; where it exists, it is quasi-contractual.[2]

(3) *Duties arising from a public calling or profession.* It was pointed out in an earlier chapter that Blackstone included under "implied contracts" the "class of contracts implied by reason and construction of law" which "arises upon this supposition, that every one who undertakes any office, employment, trust, or duty, contracts with those who employ or entrust him, to perform it with integrity, diligence, and skill".[3] Among the examples which he gives are the liability of the innkeeper to secure his guest's goods; of the common carrier for the goods carried; of the innkeeper to entertain all persons (and, *semble*, of the common carrier to accept goods proffered to him for carriage); of the sheriff who does not execute a writ sent to him, or who wilfully makes a false return to it; of the sheriff or gaoler who allows a prisoner on mesne process to escape; of an attorney who betrays the cause of his client; of a common

[1] Story, *Bailments*, §§ 85–87. Addison, Torts (8th ed. 1906), 580. 1 *Laws of England*, Halsbury, § 1079. The Indian Contract Act, § 71, makes a finder who takes goods into his custody subject to the same responsibility as a bailee. The placing of this section under what is in effect quasi-contract is infelicitous.

[2] "No similar doctrine [compensation for salvage] applies to things lost upon land, nor to anything except ships or goods in peril at sea." Bowen L.J. in *Falcke* v. *Scottish Imperial, etc. Co.* (1886) 34 Ch.D. 234, 248. Cf. Woodward, *op. cit.* § 207, for American decisions. For Salvage see *post*, p. 155.

[3] *Ante*, p. 28. Blackst. *Comm.* iii, 165.

152 TORT AND QUASI-CONTRACT

farrier who lames a horse; of a common tailor or other workman who does not perform his business in a workmanlike manner.[1]

Now there has been much debate as to how the duties of these people who exercise "public callings" of this sort should be classified in modern law. And an important distinction ought to be taken in the first instance between (*a*) refusal to exercise the calling at all, and (*b*) incompetence in the exercise of it when once it has been undertaken. This distinction has not always been observed, and both types of obligation have been referred to quasi-contract.[2] It is submitted, however, that tort or contract will nowadays adequately account for one or the other without the necessity of having recourse to quasi-contract.

(*a*) To begin with, there has probably been a considerable reduction since Blackstone's time in the number of callings which can be regarded as public in the sense that those who profess them commit a legal wrong if they refuse to exercise them when called upon to do so. No one now would seriously contend that an attorney, a farrier,[3] or a tailor is compelled to accept any one who offers himself as a client or customer. Indeed, the list seems to have shrunk to the innkeeper, the common carrier, and the sheriff. The shift of economic conditions perhaps accounts for the change. As to the innkeeper and common carrier, from early times an action upon the case lay against them if they refused to exercise their callings. In 1502, this was looked upon as settled law in the case of an innkeeper who denies me lodging in his inn,[4] and in 1683 a common carrier who

[1] *Comm.* iii, 165–166.   [2] E.g. Keener, *op. cit.* 18.

[3] Street, *op. cit.* ii, 237, says the duty is now extinct. In 1502 the whole court agreed that case lay against a smith who refused to shoe a horse; *Anon.* Keil. 50, pl. 4; and the duty was recognized as existing in 1683; *Jackson* v. *Rogers*, 2 Show. 327.

[4] *Anon.* Keil. 50, pl. 4.

TORT AND QUASI-CONTRACT 153

refused the plaintiff's pack, though he had accommodation for it, was held liable.[1] The action was based on the "custom of the realm". This we can now identify with the Common Law, and we can regard the innkeeper and common carrier as now liable in tort, for in these circumstances they are under a duty "towards persons generally", and that duty is "primarily fixed by the law".[2] It is impossible to make it square with liability in quasi-contract. How can an innkeeper or common carrier who refuses to exercise his trade be said to have received an "unjust benefit"? And there is no analogy to contract except the professed willingness on their part to contract with any one who offers; but that is characteristic of every tradesman in England. So, too, an action against the sheriff who will not execute a writ is now better classified as one in tort.

(*b*) Suppose, however, that a person who professes a "public calling" actually exercises it in any given case and misperforms it. Here, in current law, his liability may be reduced to either contract or tort, and often to alternative liability in either. As to contract, when once I have entered into an agreement with an innkeeper, a common carrier, or the like, it is an implied[3] term of the contract that he shall conduct his work with reasonable skill.[4] It is nothing to the purpose that he denies that he ever expressly agreed to shew more skill than he actually possesses. He might just as well allege that he was unaware of the warranties implied by statute on a

---

[1] *Jackson* v. *Rogers*, 2 Show. 327. Does the duty apply to passengers as well as to goods? Crompton J. in *Denton* v. *G.N.R. Co.* (1856) 5 E. & B. 860, inclined to think that it does. Story, *Bailments*, § 591, regarded the duty as the same in both cases. No reference later than *Denton's Case* has been traced.

[2] *Ante*, p. 32.

[3] "Tacit" is really more exact, but not so familiar; Salmond and Winfield, *Contracts*, p. 47.

[4] See *Warbrook* v. *Griffin* (1609) 2 Brownlow, 254.

154   TORT AND QUASI-CONTRACT

sale of goods, or that he did not know that frustration of the enterprise would defeat a contract. All these are terms in contracts, and they are terms which are implied by the law, not in the fictitious sense of quasi-contract, but as genuinely depending on the agreement of the parties who are always taken to be aware of the law of the land when they enter into a contract. These terms may be more stringent with respect to persons like the innkeeper, the common carrier, or the attorney; but that is a difference in degree, not in kind.

Next as to tort. Quite independently of any contract between the parties, there is liability for the tort of negligence in the case of any one who professes skill in any matter and who does not shew a reasonable amount of it, provided the law has imputed to him a duty to take care in the first instance. *Imperitia culpae adnumeratur* is as sound a rule in English law as in Roman law. We have noticed how the law veered about with respect to the common carrier on this point, and how it was ultimately settled with respect to these "competence" cases in general.[1] It is submitted that even the liability of the sheriff who does not pay a judgment debt which he has levied is now more aptly regarded as tortious than quasi-contractual, though the earlier authority is certainly the other way.[2]

Two other suggestions for classifying liability of the "public calling" sort have been made.

According to one, it should be relegated to the law of status. It has been thought that this would be its position in early law.[3] For present purposes, however, this is an undue straining of the meaning of status. Where is one to stop on this hypothesis? Has a barber or a

---

[1] *Ante*, pp. 60–62.

[2] *Speake* v. *Richards* (1617) Hob. 206. Cf. Keener, 19.

[3] Holdsworth, *op. cit.* ii, 464–465; iii, 385–386. Phillimore L.J. in *Steljes* v. *Ingram* (1903) 19 T.L.R. 534.

TORT AND QUASI-CONTRACT 155

cobbler a status at the present day? If not, what is the line separating him from a solicitor or a surgeon? Even if status be limited to those who are legally bound to enter into a contract with any one who demands that relation of them (e.g. the innkeeper and common carrier), it seems unnecessary when the law of tort will cover that obligation; and it is also awkward to contend that they have a status for that purpose but not for misperforming the contract when they have once entered into it.

Another suggestion is that the obligation should be placed under quasi-tort.[1] It is not clear whether this is confined to refusal to act at all or whether it extends to acting incompetently as well. But tort sufficiently accounts for the one and tort and contract for the other. There is probably room in a scientific arrangement of our law for quasi-tort, but it would appear more appropriate to vicarious responsibility in tort than to refusal to exercise a public calling.

(B) *Pure quasi-contracts.*

In many quasi-contracts under this class and the next one (C), the remedy is the action for money had and received. Further sub-classification is too difficult to attempt even if it were possible, for no one formula will cover all the cases to which this action is applicable;[2] and, moreover it is not the only quasi-contractual remedy. *Quantum meruit* and the action for money paid are others, and these do not exhaust the list. In fact, the classification which we have adopted is a cross-section through the remedies, but no further grouping has been made and there is nothing significant in the order in which we propose to discuss the otherwise heterogeneous topics falling under each main head.

(1) *Salvage.* The obligation of the owner of a ship or cargo to compensate one who rescues his property

[1] Holdsworth, *op. cit.* viii, 89.
[2] Scrutton L.J. in *Holt* v. *Markham* [1923] 1 K.B. at p. 514.

156 TORT AND QUASI-CONTRACT

from peril is quasi-contractual.[1] It is independent of contract. The fact that the property has been saved imposes on the owner legal liability to remunerate the salvor who has conferred a benefit on him, though he has made no contract on the subject.[2] Indeed in Admiralty jurisdiction the broad view is taken that salvage is a matter of public policy as well as of private right, for in claims for saving life the shipowner often pays for something from which he has derived no benefit at all, but he is made to do so in the interests of humanity and commerce.[3]

(2) *Total failure of consideration.* This might have been regarded merely as grounding liability for breach of contract. If consideration fails totally, it is scientifically just as much a breach of contract as if it fails partially. This was clearly perceived by Holt C.J. in his opposition to the extension of *indebitatus assumpsit* to this kind of claim.[4] But within a few years he reluctantly yielded to the prevailing current of decisions that the action would lie for the recovery of money paid under bargains which had collapsed.[5] The modern theory, now long settled, is that the contract is totally rescinded in such cases.[6] In fact, unless that has happened, the action will not lie.

[1] Cf. Keener, *op. cit.* 356. Woodward, *op. cit.* §§ 206–207.

[2] *Five Steel Barges* (1890) 15 P.D. at p. 146. Kennedy, *Law of Civil Salvage* (2nd ed. 1907), 4–6.

[3] Kennedy, *op. cit.* 7–8.

[4] "Where there is a bargain, tho' a corrupt one, or where one sells goods that were not his own, I will never allow an *indebitatus.*" *Anon* (1697) Comb. 446–447. *Dewbery* v. *Chapman* (1694) Holt, 35.

[5] *Holmes* v. *Hall* (1704) 6 Mod. 161.

[6] Keener, *op. cit.* 303. Examples, old and new, are *Giles* v. *Edwards* (1797) 7 T.R. 181; *Stone* v. *Rogers* (1837) 2 M. & W. at p. 448; *Rowland* v. *Divall* [1923] 2 K.B. 500. Other authorities are cited in Addison, *Contracts* (11th ed. 1911), 136; Chitty, *Contracts* (17th ed. 1921), 56, 64–66; Leake, *Contracts* (7th ed. 1921), 69; 7 *Laws of England* (Halsbury), § 798; 2 Smith L.C. (13th ed. 1929), 1, 22–23; Woodward, *op. cit.* Index, "Consideration"; Jenks, *op. cit.* § 713 (v).

TORT AND QUASI-CONTRACT 157

There must have been something equivalent to saying, "I rescind this contract"—a total refusal to perform it, or something equivalent to that which would enable the plaintiff on his side to say, "If you rescind the contract on your part, I will rescind it on mine."[1]

(3) *Money paid under mistake.* This is a genuine example of quasi-contract.[2] The payee is under an obligation to refund the money. Both parties may have acted in apparent agreement, but such agreement is vitiated by the mistake. At one time the money was recoverable by an action upon the case for money had and received, and this was allowed as an alternative to the action of account.[3] Later, ordinary *indebitatus assumpsit* was held to be applicable.[4] The payment, though usually made under a supposed contract, may equally well take place under some other imagined obligation, e.g. the duty to pay tithe rent-charge.[5]

(4) *Quantum meruit.* This has been described as a source of quasi-contract, but unfortunately it is also a source of considerable misapprehension on this point. The difficulty arises from several causes. One is that *quantum meruit* has several applications, some of which have nothing to do with true quasi-contract. Another is that the information procurable on the topic is extraordinarily scattered and is all the harder to ascertain, either because it is ancillary to the discussion of other matter, or because obsolete statements about it are reproduced in books on the current law.

Quantum meruit is used in three distinct senses:

---

[1] Parke B. in *Ehrensperger* v. *Anderson* (1848) 3·Ex. 148, 158.

[2] Keener, *op. cit.* chap. ii. Woodward, *op. cit.* §§ 10–19. Jenks, *op. cit.* § 711. *Barber* v. *Brown* (1856) 1 C.B.N.S. 121. The Indian Contract Act, § 72, includes it under a head corresponding to quasi-contract.

[3] *Cavendish* v. *Middleton* (1628) Cro. Car. 141. Holdsworth, *op. cit.* viii, 94.

[4] *Bonnel* v. *Foulke* (1657) 2 Sid. 4.

[5] *Baylis* v. *Bishop of London* [1913] 1 Ch. 127.

158 TORT AND QUASI-CONTRACT

(i) A claim by one party to a contract, on breach of it by the other party, for reasonable remuneration for what he has done. More exactly, the rule may be thus stated. Where one party has disabled himself from performing the contract, the other party is entitled to treat the contract as at an end. In that event, he is not only entitled to damages for breach of the contract, but if he has performed what is due from him, wholly or in part, he also has a right to sue on a *quantum meruit* for what he has done. "This right does not arise out of the original contract, but is based on an implied promise by the other party arising from the acceptance of an executed consideration."[1] Thus the aggrieved party has two quite distinct remedies: (a) he can sue for breach of contract; (b) he can treat the contract as at an end, and sue *quantum meruit*. In (a) the liability is contractual, in (b) it is quasi-contractual. It has no relation to the original contract, for that is gone.[2] In fact (b) is excluded if the contract is still open.[3] Nor has it any relation to a new or substituted contract, for none has been made. In *Prickett* v. *Badger*,[4] a strong court of Common Bench emphatically placed the liability of the defendant in such an action on a contract implied by law (i.e. on quasi-contract) and not on one to be inferred by a jury from the conduct of the parties.[5] The action

[1] *Planché* v. *Colburn* (1831) 8 Bing. 14. Salmond and Winfield, *Contracts*, pp. 286–289. Jenks, *op. cit.* § 714. 7 *Laws of England* (Halsbury), § 901. *Cutter* v. *Powell* and notes thereon in 2 Smith L.C. (13th ed. 1929), 1, 20–26, 40.

[2] *Indebitatus assumpsit* was at one time used for the same purpose as *quantum meruit*. *Dutch* v. *Warren* (1726) 1 Stra. 406.

[3] *Weston* v. *Downes* (1778) 1 Doug. 23. It was precisely because Lord Mansfield was "a great friend to the action" that he refused to endanger it by making such an extension of it. Cf. *Longchamp* v. *Kenny* (1779) 1 Doug. 132. *Towers* v. *Barrett* (1786) 1 T.R. 133.

[4] (1856) 1 C.B.N.S. 296.

[5] See, too, *Mavor* v. *Pyne* (1825) 3 Bing. 285. *Inchbald* v. *Western and Co.* (1864) 17 C.B.N.S. 733.

TORT AND QUASI-CONTRACT 159

in (*b*) was preferred to that in (*a*) on purely procedural grounds. In substance, the liability might well be urged to begin and end on grounds of a breach of contract, and therefore to be contractual. But, just as in waiver of a tort in favour of suing *indebitatus assumpsit*, the procedural advantages of the "common counts" were too alluring to be resisted,[1] so too the law allowed a *quantum meruit* as a remedy alternative to an action for breach of contract, and that has persisted to the present day.

(ii) Another application of *quantum meruit* is as a mode of redress on a new contract which has replaced an earlier one. The position is that the parties (or one of them), have not observed the terms of the earlier contract, but it can be implied from their conduct that they have substituted another contract for the first. If they do so, and one party does not fulfil his side of the second contract, the other can sue *quantum meruit* upon it for what he has done.[2] The obligation sued upon is genuinely contractual and is not quasi-contractual. "If I order from a wine merchant twelve bottles of whiskey at so much a bottle and he sends me ten bottles of whiskey and two of brandy and I accept them, I must pay a reasonable price for the brandy."[3]

(iii) In a third signification, *quantum meruit*, or *quantum valebat*, is merely a rule of law that if, in a contract, no price or remuneration has been fixed for goods sold or work done, a reasonable price or remuneration will be implied. Usually it will be a jury that assesses the amount of this. The only difference between *quantum meruit* and *quantum valebat* was that the former applied to labour, the latter to goods.[4] These counts fell into

---

[1] *Ante*, p. 143.
[2] *Munro* v. *Butt* (1858) 8 E. & B. 738. *Sumpter* v. *Hedges* [1898] 1 Q.B. 673. *Steven* v. *Bromley and Son* [1919] 2 K.B. 722.
[3] Atkin L.J. in *Steven* v. *Bromley and Son* [1919] 2 K.B. at p. 728.
[4] Blackst. *Comm.* iii, 162–163.

160   TORT AND QUASI-CONTRACT

disuse and were superseded by the general application of the *indebitatus* counts. A claim for a *quantum meruit* of this kind is, of course, substantially possible at the present day, though it does not usually go by that name. It is an incident in assessing the amount due under an ordinary contract where the amount is blank. It has no connection with quasi-contract.[1]

(5) *Stakeholder.* A stakeholder is liable to an action for money had and received at the suit of the party in whose favour is determined the event on the ascertainment of which the deposit was made.[2] It might be thought that the basis of this liability is contractual rather than quasi-contractual; and where the deposit is by both parties it would appear to be the former; so also where it is by one party only, *qua* that party; and expressions have been used which support this view. A consideration might well be found in the fact that the stakeholder, if he makes a profit on the money while it is entrusted to him, is entitled to keep it.[3] On the other hand, it is possible for the deposit to have been made by one party only, or even by a third party for the benefit of one or other of two other persons (e.g. a prize in a boat race), and there the obligation is on genuine quasi-contract.[4]

(6) *Money paid over on an illegal purpose.* This is recoverable before the purpose is carried out. The obligation is quasi-contractual, for the success of the action depends on the abandonment of the illegal contract (if any) that led to the payment of the money.[5]

---

[1] *Lagos* v. *Grunwaldt* [1910] 1 K.B. 41, 47–48.

[2] *Cowling* v. *Beachum* (1823) 7 Moore (C.P.) 465. Jenks, *op. cit.* § 713 (vi). 7 *Laws of England* (Halsbury), § 976.

[3] Parke J. in *Harington* v. *Hoggart* (1830) 1 B. & Ad. 577, 589–590.

[4] *Sadler* v. *Smith* (1869) L.R. 5 Q.B. 40.

[5] *Hastelow* v. *Jackson* (1828) 8 B. & C. 221. *Barclay* v. *Pearson* [1893] 2 Ch. 154. Jenks, *op. cit.* § 713 (vii). Keener, *op. cit.* 267 *seq.* Woodward, *op. cit.* § 152.

TORT AND QUASI-CONTRACT 161

(7) *Money paid at the request of another*. Where *A*, at the request of *B*, pays money to *C*, a promise by *B* to repay the amount will be implied, even though *B* has not thereby been relieved from any legal claim.[1] The request may be direct or indirect, e.g. where *B* has placed *A* under a liability to pay *C*. Thus, an auctioneer who has been forced to pay dues to the Excise authorities in respect of a sale of *B*'s property can recover the amount from *B*.[2]

(8) *Compulsory payment of another's debt or discharge of another's liability*. Where *A* is under a legal liability to do something, and *B*, under threat or reasonable apprehension of legal proceedings against *B*, or legal restraint of *B*'s goods, does what *A* is bound to do, the law will generally imply a contract on *A*'s part to indemnify *B*.[3]

The action by which this quasi-contractual obligation is enforced is usually the action for money paid.[4] The obligation itself is important for it has several well-known sources. It frequently originates in genuine contract, and, where that is the fact, it must be treated as such. But there are many instances in which it is purely quasi-contractual. In the earlier decisions, more emphasis is laid on the existence of "privity" between the plaintiff and the defendant than in the later.[5] We

---

[1] 7 *Laws of England* (Halsbury), § 946.

[2] *Brittain* v. *Lloyd* (1845) 14 M. & W. 762.

[3] Jenks, *op. cit.* § 709. 7 *Laws of England* (Halsbury), § 947. With the English law the Indian Contract Act, § 69, may usefully be compared. "A person who is *interested in the payment of money which another is bound by law to pay*, and who therefore pays it, is entitled to be reimbursed by the other." Sir Frederick Pollock notes that the words italicized go farther than any English authority, for they might include the apprehension of any kind of loss or inconvenience, or at any rate of any detriment capable of being assessed in money. Pollock and Mulla, *Indian Contract, etc. Acts* (5th ed. 1924), p. 369.

[4] 7 *Laws of England*, §§ 946–957.

[5] E.g. *Griffinhoofe* v. *Daubuz* (1855) 5 E. & B. 746.

W P

162 TORT AND QUASI-CONTRACT

have already had occasion to discuss this vague phrase.[1] That some sort of relationship between plaintiff and defendant is usual, which distinguishes them from being utter strangers to one another, is clear; but what exactly the relationship is, has never been defined, and some of the decisions as to its closeness are hard to reconcile. At any rate it falls far short of contract, or even of agreement. What possible agreement is there between B who pays money to abate a nuisance, and A who has caused the nuisance on B's land? Or put it that B lends a horse to A; that A takes the horse to an inn, and has it detained there against a bill which he runs up; and that meanwhile B has sold the horse to C, who discovers later that he must pay A's bill in order to get the horse. Here C can recoup himself against A in an action for money paid. But the liability of A is certainly not contractual.[2] And this is the view which is now adopted. "The right to indemnity or contribution in these cases exists, although there may be no agreement to indemnify or contribute, and although there may be, in that sense, no privity between the plaintiff and the defendant."[3]

Some examples of this variety of quasi-contract, which have acquired specific names, may be mentioned:

(i) *The surety's right of indemnity* against the principal debtor, where the right is not based on a contract between them, is quasi-contractual.[4] It is quite likely that A may have become surety for a loan by B to C without any knowledge, much less any consent, on C's part.

---

[1] *Ante*, p. 134.

[2] Willes J. in *Johnson* v. *R.M.S.P. Co.* (1867) L.R. 3 C.P. 38, 45. Another example of the same sort is where the plaintiff is a tenant of the defendant and has paid under compulsion taxes which are primarily payable by the defendant as landlord. *Earle* v. *Maugham* (1863) 14 C.B.N.S. 626.

[3] *Lindley* L.J. in *Edmunds* v. *Wallingford* (1885) 14 Q.B.D. 811, 815.

[4] Keener, *op. cit.* 400. Woodward, *op. cit.* § 253.

TORT AND QUASI-CONTRACT 163

(ii) *Contribution.* Where one of several persons jointly, or jointly and severally, liable under a contract is called upon to perform the contract in full, or to discharge more than his own proper share, he has, as a general rule, a right to call upon the persons jointly, or jointly and severally, liable with himself to contribute to the liability which he has incurred and the payment of which will be treated as a payment to the use of all the co-debtors.[1] This principle is commonly associated with the right of one co-surety who has paid more than his share to claim recoupment from the other co-sureties, but contribution is a wider term than that and includes cases that are not matters of suretyship at all.[2] Just like the right of a surety to indemnity, the right to contribution may be the result of an express contract; but it may also be independent of it, and is then quasi-contractual. In Equity, the doctrine was definitely detached from liability on contract even where that might have existed. "Questions of contribution often depend not upon contract, but upon the general principles of equity....In *aequali jure,* the law requires equality."[3] On the Common Law side, Lord Mansfield together with most of the other judges were, in 1757, of the like opinion, and indeed the Chief Justice went out of his way to import liability on an implied contract into a transaction which might well have been regarded as an ordinary contract between debtor and surety, for the surety had become such at the defendant's request.[4] A generation

[1] 7 *Laws of England* (Halsbury), § 958, and authorities there cited. Several of these are wide of the mark, but there are enough left to establish the proposition in the text.

[2] *Holmes* v. *Williamson* (1817) 6 M. & S. 158. *Burnell* v. *Minot* (1820) 4 Moore (C.P.) 340. *Edgar* v. *Knapp* (1843) 6 Scott (N.R.) 707. Neither Keener nor Woodward considers contribution apart from co-sureties and joint tortfeasors.

[3] Turner L.J. in *Spottiswoode's Case* (1855) 6 De G.M. & G. 345, 371–372.

[4] *Decker* v. *Pope* cited in 1 Selw. N.P. (13th ed. 1869), 91.

11-2

164 TORT AND QUASI-CONTRACT

later, the Court of Exchequer put the principle of contribution in terms broad enough to have been uttered by Mansfield himself. "The bottom of contribution is a fixed principle of justice, and is not founded on contract. Contract indeed may qualify it." "Contribution is founded on equality and established by the law of all nations."[1] It is true that Lord Campbell C.J. at a later date said of the right of contribution that "we must look to the implied engagement of each, to pay his share, arising out of the joint contract when entered into",[2] and it has been thought that this expressed his view that the basis of contribution is contract, and not quasi-contract.[3] If he meant to state it as a general proposition, it cannot stand against the sounder theory; and indeed the Court of Exchequer not long afterwards held that when two parties employ an arbitrator without any provision as to the payment of his costs, and one of them pays a sum to take up the award, "in reason, justice and law he is entitled to recover from the other a moiety of the sum so paid".[4] But as the case before Lord Campbell was one in which there was an express prior contract between co-sureties, it may be that he did not intend his opinion to go beyond the facts. It has also been thought that the quasi-contractual theory runs directly counter to the rule in Equity that, as soon as the creditor's claim against the surety is established, he can, without first paying the debt, compel his co-surety to contribute with him.[5] Some of the *dicta*, if not the actual decisions, in certain American jurisdictions have gone far in support of adopting genuine implied contract as the foundation of contribution; but both here

[1] *Deering* v. *Winchelsea* (1787) 2 B. & P. 270, 272, 274.
[2] *Batard* v. *Hawes* (1853) 2 E. & B. 287, 296.
[3] Keener, *op. cit.* 405. Woodward, *op. cit.* p. 400.
[4] *Marsack* v. *Webber* (1860) 6 H. & N. 1, 6.
[5] Woodward, *op. cit.* p. 398, citing *Wolmershausen* v. *Gullick* [1893] 2 Ch. 514.

TORT AND QUASI-CONTRACT 165

and there the better view is that it is not necessarily implicated with contract at all. There may be instances of co-suretyship where there is no vestige of agreement between the co-sureties; e.g. where *A* has become surety for *B*'s debt, and at a later date *C* also becomes surety for the same debt.[1]

So with contribution among joint tortfeasors. Where the right exists, it may spring from contract; but if there be no such contract, the claim to contribution is essentially quasi-contractual. Thus, one who is cast in damages on the score of vicarious responsibility in tort may be able to reimburse himself against his agent, who has acted in the course of his employment, but possibly in direct contravention of the employer's orders.[2] American law is rich in illustration of successful claims for such indemnity in cases which are quite unconnected with vicarious responsibility.[3]

(9) *Liability of husband for wife's necessaries.* This is usually treated in books on contract, but in *Manby* v. *Scott*,[4] it was stated that the husband was liable on "an *assumpsit* in law for necessaries", and at that date (1663) a wife could not contract at all on her own account. Nowadays, there are still circumstances in which her husband is held liable for her necessaries without any consent on his part to the ordering and supply of them,[5] and this makes quasi-contract a more rational ground for his liability than contract.[6]

---

[1] See generally Rowlatt, *Principal and Surety* (2nd ed. 1926), 3–6, 179, 222, 228. Keener, *op. cit.* 400–408. Woodward, *op. cit.* §§ 253–254. Hewitson, *Suretyship* (1927) 133, 155–158 (the citation of *England* v. *Marsden* on p. 158 is irrelevant to suretyship, and must, in any event, be qualified by *Edmunds* v. *Wallingford* (1885) 14 Q.B.D. 811).

[2] *Wooley* v. *Batte* (1826) 2 C. & P. 417.

[3] Woodward, *op. cit.* §§ 255–259. Keener, *op. cit.* 408–410.

[4] (1663) 1 Siderf. 109. 2 Smith L.C. (13th ed. 1929), 421. So too *Seaton* v. *Benedict* (1828) 5 Bing. 28.

[5] Salmond and Winfield, *Contracts*, pp. 481–482.

[6] So too Keener, *op. cit.* 22–23, and Street, *op. cit.* ii, 204–205.

166   TORT AND QUASI-CONTRACT

(10) *Liability of lunatics and drunkards for necessaries.*
Under the Sale of Goods Act, 1893, s. 2, their liability
for necessaries is placed on a statutory basis. They must
pay a reasonable price for them. Before the Act, the
liability of the lunatic was held to be quasi-contractual
In re Rhodes,[1] where Cotton L.J. said: "What the law
implies on the part of such a person is an obligation,
which has been improperly termed a contract....I think
that the expression 'implied contract' is erroneous and
very unfortunate".[2] An opinion of Pollock C.B. in
Gore v. *Gibson*[3] puts the liability of the drunkard on the
ground of a contract implied by law from the circumstances.[4]

Cotton L.J. laid down a more sweeping, but quite
reasonable, rule in the case above cited: "Whenever
necessaries are supplied to a person who by reason of
disability cannot himself contract, the law implies an
obligation on the part of such person to pay for such
necessaries out of his own property".[5]

(11) *Unauthorized gains of agent.* An action for money
had and received can be sued by a principal against his
agent for any money of the principal in the agent's hands
or, for any unauthorized profit made by the agent.[6] It
will also lie against any person who has agreed to bribe
the agent. The liability of the agent here is genuinely
quasi-contractual, for though agency is often based on
an express contract between principal and agent, yet
this is not always so. Of course, the contract induced by
the bribe may often constitute the tort of deceit, and the

---

[1] (1890) 44 Ch. D. 94, 105.
[2] So too Keener, *op. cit.* 9, 20; Street, *op. cit.* ii, 204; Indian Contract
Act, § 68.
[3] (1845) 13 M. & W. 623, 626. *Molton* v. *Camroux* (1848) 2 Ex.
487, cited in *Benjamin on Sale*, 70, note (*t*) was not on necessaries.
[4] So too Street, *op. cit.* ii, 204.
[5] *In re Rhodes* (1890) 44 Ch. D. at p. 105.
[6] *Hovenden* v. *Millhoff* (1900) 83 L.T. 41.

TORT AND QUASI-CONTRACT 167

liability in quasi-contract must then be regarded as alternative to liability in tort,[1] and would more correctly be discussed under the next main division (C). The allowance of such alternative remedies might be justified, if for no other reason, *propter odium furum*. Other ways in which quasi-contract arises in connection with agency need not be detailed here.[2]

(C) *Quasi-contract which is alternative to some other form of liability.*

(1) *Account stated.*[3] This phrase has three different meanings.[4]

(i) A claim to payment by one party, which is admitted by the other to be correct. This is no more than an admission of debt out of court, and, while it is no doubt cogent evidence that the debt is due, yet it may, like any other admission, be shewn to have been made in error.[5] It does not seem necessary to erect this subsidiary rule of evidence into a quasi-contractual obligation. It is presumptive proof of an obligation, but not an obligation in itself.

(ii) When, after mutual dealings between *A* and *B*, several items of claim are brought into account on either side, and being set against one another a balance is struck, the consideration for the payment of the balance is the discharge of the items on each side. "It is then the same as if each item was paid and a discharge given for each, and in consideration of that discharge the balance was agreed to be due."[6] This is a genuine

---

[1] *Grant* v. *Gold Exploration Syndicate* [1900] 1 Q.B. at pp. 244–245.

[2] Keener, *op. cit.* Index, "Agency". Woodward, *op. cit.* Index, "Principal and Agent". 7 *Laws of England* (Halsbury), § 975. Jenks, *op. cit.* § 710.

[3] Jenks, *op. cit.* § 715. 7 *Laws of England* (Halsbury), § 715.

[4] Lord Cave in *Camillo Tank S.S. Co. Ld.* v. *Alexandria Engineering Works* (1921) 38 T.L.R. 134, 143.

[5] Cf. Lord Abinger C.B. in *Lubbock* v. *Tribe* (1838) 3 M. & W. at pp. 612–613.

[6] Blackburn J. in *Laycock* v. *Pickles* (1863) 4 B. & S. at p. 506.

168   TORT AND QUASI-CONTRACT

account stated (the older name for it was *insimul computassent*). It must be reckoned as quasi-contract, but scientifically contract would satisfactorily cover it, for all the points requisite to a valid contract seem to be met. Presumably it might alternatively be treated as such.

(iii) Cases where *A* has made a claim against *B*, and *B* has, for valuable consideration, agreed to accept it as correct. The consideration may be a reduction of the claim, a consent to wait for payment, or any other species of consideration. Here, again, there seems to be no need to resort to quasi-contract in order to explain what is, on the face of it, an ordinary contract.

(2) *Money paid to recover goods wrongfully detained.*[1] As a general rule payments made to recover goods wrongfully detained (other than goods distrained for rent) are not deemed to be voluntary, and may be recovered. Thus in *Astley* v. *Reynolds,*[2] the plaintiff had pawned goods with the defendant, and, in order to get the goods, paid what he knew to be an excess of interest. He was held to be entitled to recover this excess in an action for money had and received. This might be regarded as a case of pure tort redressible by detinue or trover, but the court thought that the plaintiff might have such an immediate want for his goods that an action of trover would not meet his needs. Indeed, even at the present day the action for money had and received may be preferable to one in tort, for it has distinct advantages over replevin.[3]

(3) *Waiver of a tort.* Doubts have been expressed as to whether this heading of quasi-contract is not more

---

[1] Keener, *op. cit.* 426–430. Woodward, *op. cit.* § 216. 7 *Laws of England* (Halsbury), § 974. Jenks, *op. cit.* § 713, makes the rule apply to detainer of the person of the plaintiff, his wife, child, or servant; but no authority is cited for this extension.

[2] (1731) 2 Stra. 915. See to *Ashmole* v. *Wainwright* (1842) 2 Q.B. 837.

[3] *Green* v. *Duckett* (1883) 11 Q.B.D. 275.

TORT AND QUASI-CONTRACT 169

correctly merged in the law of tort or in the law of damages; but in fact it has been generally regarded as independent of tort.[1] It is a historical survival, and an example of purely tortious liability which has agglutinated to itself an alternative quasi-contractual remedy. The reasons for preferring the latter have already been stated.[2]

What happens, then, is that the plaintiff has, on the same facts, a claim either in tort or on quasi-contract, and elects to sue in quasi-contract, thus waiving the tort. But how far is it possible to do this? Can any tort be waived in favour of quasi-contract? According to Tindal C.J. "No party is bound to sue in tort, where by converting the action into an action of contract [i.e. quasi-contract], he does not prejudice the defendant".[3] But this does not help us much nowadays, and it is inconceivable how waiver can apply to some torts. If the tort committed were assault and battery, how can the action for it be waived and an action for money had and received be sued instead? What money has been "had and received" by the defendant? Some sort of limit there must be, but what it is cannot be inferred from the authorities as they now stand.[4] We can do no more than mention torts which, it has been held, can be waived. They are usually conversion, trespass to land or goods, deceit, and occasionally action upon the case, and the action for extorting money by threats.

An early example of waiver of trover occurred in 1678,[5] but the decision generally quoted in connection

---

[1] Woodward, chap. xx and § 270. Keener, 24 and chap. iii. Most of the authorities cited by the learned authors are American. The chief English authorities are referred to in 7 *Laws of England* (Halsbury), § 982.

[2] *Ante*, p. 143.

[3] *Young* v. *Marshall* (1831) 8 Bing. at p. 44.

[4] Salmond, *Torts*, § 43 (2).

[5] *Howard* v. *Wood* 2 Lev. 245.

170 TORT AND QUASI-CONTRACT

with this is *Lamine* v. *Dorrell* (1705).[1] Holt C.J., who was not remarkable for his attachment to *indebitatus assumpsit*, admitted that the right to sue it here had crept in by degrees. It was propped up by the veriest fiction, for Powell J. said,

> It is clear the plaintiff might have maintained detinue or trover for the debentures; but when the act that is done is in its nature tortious, it is hard to turn that into a contract, and against the reason of *assumpsit*. But the plaintiff may dispense with the wrong, and suppose the sale [of the debentures by the defendant] made by his consent, and bring an action for the money they were sold for, as money received to his use. It has been carried thus far already.

The rule was recognized in 1834 as a well-established one.[2]

There are several cases recognizing waiver of trespass to goods (which the trespasser has subsequently turned into money)[3] or to land.[4] But there may be circumstances in which it will not be allowed. In *Lindon* v. *Hooper*,[5] it was held that waiver of trespass and replevin for wrongful distress damage feasant was not permissible, because the defendant would be so much embarrassed in pleading by not knowing what sort of right the plaintiff might set up. Yet it was admitted that there had been many cases of such waiver where there was no likelihood of the defendant being taken by surprise.

There is also a weight of authority for waiver of deceit.[6] But here again there may be exceptions. Deceit

---

[1] 2 Ld Raym. 1216.

[2] *Marsh* v. *Keating*, 1 Bing. N.C. 198, 215–216.

[3] *Oughton* v. *Seppings* (1830) 1 B. & Ad. 241. *Rodgers* v. *Maw* (1846) 15 M. & W. at p. 448. *Neate* v. *Harding* (1851) 6 Ex. at p. 351.

[4] *Powell* v. *Rees* (1837) 7 A. & E. 426.   [5] (1776) Cowp. 414.

[6] *Hill* v. *Perrott* (1810) 3 Taunt. 274 (the reasoning in the decision is criticized by Keener, *op. cit.* 197). *Abbotts* v. *Barry* (1820) 2 B. & B. 369. *Holt* v. *Ely* (1853) 1 E. & B. 795. *Kettlewell* v. *Refuge Assurance Co.* [1908] 1 K.B. 545; affirmed [1909] A.C. 243.

TORT AND QUASI-CONTRACT 171

is the appropriate action, and waiver is not possible, if the right to rescind a contract induced by fraud no longer exists because restoration of the property is not feasible.[1]

It is better to refer to this head of waiver of deceit or fraud the obligation to compensate a person for having obtained his services by fraud. There is no need to make it, as do some of the books, a separate division of quasi-contract.[2] If the defendant by fraud has induced the plaintiff to perform a service for him, without intending to pay for it, this is a plain instance of deceit. The plaintiff can sue upon it as such, or he can waive the tort and sue in quasi-contract. Whether the theory of this quasi-contractual obligation is that no man must take advantage of his own fraud,[3] or that a contract is implied to pay for the services, the same result is reached. In *Rumsey* v. *N.E.R. Co.*,[4] a railway passenger by a train on which he was allowed to carry only a certain weight of luggage because he had a cheap excursion ticket, concealed the fact that he had not an ordinary ticket and thereby procured a porter to put luggage in excess of that weight on the train. Held, that the circumstances raised an implied contract for the carriage of the luggage for hire, and that therefore the Company were justified in detaining the luggage until the hire was paid. Erle C.J. seemed to be bent on finding a genuine contract between the parties, for he dragged in the doctrine of consideration, though he admitted that there was no obligation on the part of the Company to carry the goods safely. Williams J. regarded the case as like waiver of a tort and suing on an

---

[1] *Clarke* v. *Dickson* (1858) E.B. & E. 148.

[2] 7 *Laws of England* (Halsbury), § 945.

[3] *Hill* v. *Perrott* (1810) 3 Taunt. 274. See, too, *Abbotts* v. *Barry* (1820) 2 B. & B. 369.

[4] (1863) 14 C.B.N.S. 641. Keener, *op. cit.* 165, treats this under waiver of a tort.

172 TORT AND QUASI-CONTRACT

implied contract. Willes J. took the ground that no man is allowed to take advantage of his own fraud, and that the passenger could not be heard to say that, though the luggage was carried with his consent, he did not contract to pay for the carriage. The peculiarity of the case lies in the use of quasi-contractual obligation as a defence alternative to the defence of fraud. It was, in fact, not a waiver of one action for another but of one defence for another; but the principle is much the same in either event.

In *Howard* v. *Wood*[1] we have an example of waiver of action upon the case for disturbance in an office. The defendant had wrongfully taken the fees of a stewardship which properly belonged to the plaintiff. He was allowed to recover these by *indebitatus assumpsit*. Either conversion,[2] or case for disturbance, would have been equally, if not more, appropriate. It was argued that the defendant had received the fees to his own use, not to the use of the plaintiff, and Scroggs C.J. said during the hearing that a man might as well sue *indebitatus assumpsit* for money taken by force from his person.[3] However, in a considered judgment on behalf of himself and his brethren he allowed the action, but only because that course had been taken in previous cases. "If this were now an original case, we are agreed it would by no means lie." There is reason to think that waiver in such a case is still permissible.[4]

It is generally agreed that the obligation to restore money extorted by threats is quasi-contractual, but some of the English and American writers treat it as an independent division of quasi-contract instead of as a particular instance of waiver of a tort.[5] Yet the latter

---

[1] (1678) 2 Lev. 245. 2 Show. 21. Freeman K.B. 478. T. Jones, 126.

[2] 2 Lev. at p. 22.   [3] Freeman, at p. 479.

[4] Keener, *op. cit.* 188. 7 *Laws of England* (Halsbury), § 983.

[5] Jenks, *op. cit.* § 713 (ix). 7 *Laws of England* (Halsbury), § 973. Keener, *op. cit.* chap. xi. Woodward, *op. cit.* §§ 211–227.

TORT AND QUASI-CONTRACT 173

appears to be the more appropriate way of handling it, at any rate in English law. There is no real doubt that if I obtain your money by unlawful intimidation, I have committed a tort.[1] If you wish to recover your money by the action for money had and received, you are entitled to do so, but by so doing you are waiving a tort. There is nothing in the authorities which negatives this view. Even if you part with your money in consequence, not of a threat, but of a fraudulent misrepresentation, you are merely waiving another tort (deceit) if you sue the action for money had and received.[2] Of course, it is often a difficult problem to say whether there is present what the law would call "intimidation" or a "threat". At any rate, it is probable that getting another person to do something against his will by stating that otherwise you will do to him something which you have a legal right to do is not, in a civil court, an unlawful threat.[3] That is the rule whether the action be in tort or for money had and received.[4]

It may be as well to add that an action for money paid will not lie for the recovery of a voluntary payment made

---

[1] Salmond, *Torts*, § 152 (2).

[2] See *Steele* v. *Williams* (1853) 8 Ex. 625 (fee wrongfully extorted (whether knowing it to be wrongful or not does not appear) by parish clerk for search in register).

[3] *Hardie and Lane, Ld.* v. *Chilton* [1928] 2 K.B. 306. Cf. *R.* v. *Denyer* [1926] 2 K.B. 258.

[4] *Brocklebank, Ld.* v. *R.* [1925] 1 K.B. 52. Jenks, *op. cit.* § 713 (*x*) gives the extortion of money *colore officii* as a separate example of facts which raise quasi-contractual obligation; but this seems to be only a particular instance of a wider rule: it is immaterial whether the person who makes the extortion is an official or any one else. This is so even if such extortion be referred to a heading of "money paid under compulsion", rather than to "money extorted by threats".

The Indian Contract Act, § 72, requires a person to whom money has been paid, or anything delivered, under coercion, to repay or return it, and this is placed under what is, in effect, quasi-contractual obligation. See Sir Frederick Pollock's note as to the meaning of coercion, Pollock and Mulla, *Indian Contract, etc. Acts* (5th ed. 1924), 387.

174 TORT AND QUASI-CONTRACT

by one person on behalf of another, without his request. A curious exception occurs in the recovery of reasonable burial expenses from the executors of a deceased person by one who has buried the deceased without being requested to do so. The common principles of decency and humanity and the convenience of the public are the best reasons for such liability.[1]

So much for torts which certainly can be waived. After this, we are on uncertain ground. The doctrine of waiver was pushed to extreme lengths in *Lightly* v. *Clouston*.[2] The defendant had induced the plaintiff's apprentice, in breach of his apprenticeship, to work for the defendant. The plaintiff was allowed to waive the tort and sue *indebitatus assumpsit* for work and labour done for the defendant by the apprentice. Mansfield C.J. said that it was long settled in cases of sale that, if the plaintiff chose to sue for the produce of the sale, he might do so, and that the like principle applied here. It was not competent to the defendant to argue that he got the labour, not by contract, but by wrong. A few years later this decision was followed with some hesitation in *Foster* v. *Stewart*[3] by Lord Ellenborough C.J., though he thought that, for the better preservation of the simplicity of actions, he would have been more inclined to hold that where seduction is the cause of action, the

---

[1] *Rogers* v. *Price* (1829) 3 Y. & J. 31. One who buries a wife living apart from her husband is similarly entitled to recover suitable expenses from the husband. The principle is perhaps the same in both cases. *Ambrose* v. *Kerrison* (1851) 10 C.B. 776. Willes J., *contra* in *Bradshaw* v. *Beard* (1862) 12 C.B.N.S. 344, 348–349.

The Indian Contract Act, § 70, dealing with the obligation of a person enjoying a non-gratuitous benefit goes far beyond English law. Sir Frederick Pollock points out that it would entitle one who finds and restores lost property, apart from any question of reward having been offered, to be compensated for his trouble if he did not intend to act gratuitously. Pollock and Mulla, *Indian Contract, etc. Acts* (5th ed. 1924), 378–379.

[2] (1808) 1 Taunt. 112.   [3] (1814) 3 M. & S. 191.

TORT AND QUASI-CONTRACT 175

action ought to be in tort for that. It is uncertain whether these decisions would be followed at the present day. Their dates are material in the sense that many of the procedural advantages given by the action of *indebitatus assumpsit* have been wiped out by later legislation, so that there is not so much reason for giving a wide scope to waiver now. Again, it is difficult to find a complete answer to counsel's argument in *Foster* v. *Stewart*,[1] that, if waiver were allowed there, "as well might it be said, that if a man take the goods of another, the owner of the goods may have *assumpsit* against him for goods sold". On the other hand, we have just seen that waiver is possible where the tort is extortion by threats and there is not much difference between that and waiving the conversion which is constituted by taking a man's goods without any threat. Moreover, we have noticed earlier that even nowadays the action for money had and received may be very useful to a plaintiff when an action in tort will not help him; for the former action may survive the death of the parties while the latter may not. Upon the whole, it may be conjectured that, even if *Lightly* v. *Clouston* and *Foster* v. *Stewart* are still law, the courts would not now be disposed to add to the list of torts which, it has been decided, can be waived.

Assuming that the case is one of a tort in which waiver is possible, is it necessary that the tort must be established in evidence before it can be waived? From a review of the authorities, the answer seems to be, "Yes".[2] But this is subject to two qualifications. First, proof of what is mainly a technical ingredient in the tort will not be insisted on; e.g. where the tort alleged is conversion, and the trustee in bankruptcy wishes to

[1] (1814) 3 M. & S. at p. 196.
[2] E.g. in *Oughton* v. *Seppings* (1830) 1 B. & Ad. 241, evidence of trespass to possession, even though slight, had to be given.

176 TORT AND QUASI-CONTRACT

waive it, he is not bound to shew any disaffirmance of a fraudulent preference of the bankrupt which constituted the conversion.[1] Secondly, waiver is not prevented merely because an action in tort is impossible owing to the death of the defendant.[2] After all, the tort is there, but it cannot be sued on owing to what is quite as much a rule of procedure as of substantive law. A distorted converse of the proposition that the tort must be established is that no waiver will be allowed if there is no contract upon which the plaintiff could sue if he had been permitted to waive the tort.[3] If "contract" here means a genuine contract and not merely a contract implied by the law (i.e. quasi-contract), this seems to be a confusion of the doctrine of waiver of tort for the purpose of suing in quasi-contract with the doctrine of alternative actions in tort or contract on the same facts.[4]

Finally, if the plaintiff has once elected to sue in tort, he cannot then waive the tort and sue in quasi-contract. He cannot have it both ways, or, as has been repeatedly said in cases of this type, he cannot blow both hot and cold at the same time.[5] Conversely, if he chooses to sue in quasi-contract, he cannot afterwards sue in tort. What constitutes election seems to be quite as much a matter of fact as of law.[6]

[1] *Heilbut* v. *Nevill* (1870) L.R. 5 C.P. 478.

[2] *Powell* v. *Rees* (1837) 7 A. & E. 426. *Phillips* v. *Homfray* (1883) 24 Ch. D. 439.

[3] *Read* v. *Hutchinson* (1813) 3 Camp. 352. *Meyer* v. *Everth* (1814) 4 Camp. 22.

[4] *Ante,* p. 65.

[5] *Birch* v. *Wright* (1786) 1 T.R. 378, 387. *Hardie* and *Lane, Ld.* v. *Chiltern* [1928] 1 K.B. 663. In *Andrews* v. *Hawley* (1857) 26 L.J. Ex. 323, the Court of Exchequer apparently allowed the plaintiff to recover, on the same facts, either on a count for tort or on a count for money had and received, but they declined to commit themselves definitely to one ground of action or the other, and it is impossible to say whether they regarded the plaintiff as waiving a tort, or indeed whether they held that any tort at all had been committed.

[6] *Rice* v. *Reed* [1900] 1 Q.B. 54, 66.

TORT AND QUASI-CONTRACT 177

(D) *Doubtful quasi-contracts.*

In the class of cases now under discussion, there is no doubt that the defendant is liable to the plaintiff, but it is debatable whether his liability is quasi-contractual or has some other source.

(1) *Implied warranty of authority.* This arises where one contracts as agent on behalf of another who has given him no authority to do so, but the supposed agent honestly believes that he has such authority. Of course, he cannot make his supposed principal liable, nor is he himself liable for deceit; but the third party with whom he professed to make the contract can sue him on what is known as "implied warranty of authority".

Discordant views have been expressed as to the correct basis of this action. *Collen* v. *Wright*,[1] the highly authoritative decision in which the doctrine appears, unquestionably bases it upon contract.

The obligation arising in such a case is well expressed by saying that a person, professing to contract as agent for another, impliedly, if not expressly, undertakes to or promises the person who enters into such contract, upon the faith of the professed agent being duly authorized, that the authority which he professes to have does in point of fact exist. The fact of entering into the transaction with the professed agent, as such, is good consideration for the promise.[2]

Some half century later, the House of Lords affirmed the rule in *Collen* v. *Wright*, without examining further its scientific foundation; and they declined to limit it to circumstances in which the transaction with the supposed agent results in a contract.[3] No reasonable objection can be taken to the rule itself, which may well have existed before *Collen* v. *Wright*,[4] but it has been

[1] (1857) 8 E. & B. 647.
[2] *Ibid.* at pp. 657–658.
[3] *Starkey* v. *Bank of England* [1903] A.C. 114.
[4] Lord Lindley in [1903] A.C. at pp. 119–120.

178 TORT AND QUASI-CONTRACT

urged that the principle at the back of it is not contract but either quasi-contract,[1] quasi-tort,[2] or quasi-assumpsit.[3] It does not clearly appear in any of these views why the obligation cannot be a contractual one. Presumably the argument is that, as both parties purported to contract on the assumption that one of them was the agent of *X*, the falsity of this assumption negatives any *consensus ad idem* and, consequently, the creation of any contract. It may be replied to this that the law undoubtedly is that a man who unreasonably misleads another party by mistakenly saying what is not the fact, is nevertheless bound by his words;[4] and that one who holds himself out as contracting in this manner does genuinely contract, or, rather, the law says that he does. Perhaps it is a fair rejoinder to this that the principle on which he is liable is estoppel, and not contract at all; and that the most which can be conceded to a rule of evidence which peremptorily excludes any denial of the assent requisite to a contract is that it may leave the transaction like a contract, but that it is certainly not a contract itself. If that be so, the liability on implied warranty of authority is perhaps a true instance of quasi-contract, though it may not be easy to see that the defendant has got an unjust *"benefit"*.

(2) *Customary duty*. We have relegated this subheading to "Doubtful quasi-contract", in order to dispose of the sweeping implication that all such duties must be regarded as quasi-contractual. As a matter of fact, some of them are correctly described as such, of others it is difficult to say whether they are so or not, and others again belong to some other variety of obligation.

---

[1] Woodward, *op. cit.* p. 124.
[2] Holdsworth, *op. cit.* viii, 89.
[3] Street, *op. cit.* ii, 237–238.
[4] Salmond and Winfield, *Contracts*, § 63.

TORT AND QUASI-CONTRACT 179

Of the first class, the following are examples. A custom, which is very exceptional, permits an action by an incumbent against the executor of his predecessor in the living for lack of repair of the ecclesiastical buildings. In *Sollers* v. *Lawrence*,[1] Willes L.C.J. said of this action:

> It is not considered as a tort in the testator, but as a duty which he ought to have performed....And for this reason, it is not contrary to the rule that *actio personalis* (which is always understood of a tort) *moritur cum persona*; as actions on the case for all sorts of debts and duties are now daily brought against executors.[2]

Opinions have differed as to whether the custom is a custom and nothing else, or whether it has become part of the Common Law.[3]

The obligation to pay the customary fees for knighthood is also quasi-contractual, and a claim in *indebitatus assumpsit* has been held maintainable for them.[4] So too the obligation to pay a fine for not undertaking the office of sheriff in a city when called upon by the authorities to do so.[5]

Next comes the class of cases in which it is doubtful whether the obligation is to be regarded as merely a genuinely implied term in a contract, or as quasi-contractual. An early instance of this sort was *City of London* v. *Goree*.[6] Money was claimed from the defendant upon a custom to pay scavage (a toll exacted for exposing for sale foreign wares which had been entered in the custom-house). *Indebitatus assumpsit* was held to lie. "This is a duty that ariseth *ex quasi contractu*,

---

[1] (1743) Willes, 413.
[2] Cited with approval by Cotton L.J. *obiter* in *Batthyany* v. *Walford* (1887) 36 Ch. D. 269, 280. See also Keener, *op. cit.* 18–19.
[3] *Bryan* v. *Clay* (1852) 1 E. & B. 38.
[4] *Duppa* v. *Gerard* (1689) 1 Show. 78.
[5] *City of York* v. *Toun* (1698) 5 Mod. 444.
[6] (1676) 3 Keb. 677. 2 Lev. 174. 1 Vent. 298.

180   TORT AND QUASI-CONTRACT

and not *ex delicto*." No express promise to pay the toll was made. If none can be implied except the fictitious one "implied by law", the duty must be reckoned as quasi-contractual.[1] On the other hand, in a case very little later in date, where the defendant was held liable for customary weighage on goods brought into the Port of London, the action that was sued was ordinary *assumpsit*, not *indebitatus assumpsit*, and the facts were treated as if they raised an ordinary contract, for one of the arguments against the plaintiffs was the lack of consideration; consideration was found, however, in the master's liberty to bring the goods into the port.[2] About the same time, *indebitatus assumpsit* was held to lie for £20 forfeited by the defendant under the constitutions and ordinances of the Barber Surgeons of London because he would not serve the office of steward in their company.[3] It has been said of this case that the obligation to pay a penalty for breach of a by-law is obviously simply imposed by law and is not contractual.[4] But this depends on the by-law. Some by-laws are certainly unconnected with contract, e.g. those of railway companies which make trespass punishable. Others, however, may well be reckoned as implied or express terms in a contract. A club by-law may forbid members to entertain guests in the club dining-room. That is one of the terms of the contract of membership of the club. And the same applies to a by-law imposing a fine on a member of a society (whose membership is not gratuitous) be-

[1] Holdsworth, *op. cit.* viii, 96, is decidedly of opinion that it has nothing contractual about it, but is simply imposed by law. Ames, *op. cit.* 161, takes it to be quasi-contractual.

[2] *Mayor of London* v. *Hunt* (1681) 3 Lev. 37. As to consideration, it must be noted, however, that there were sporadic efforts on the part of some judges to discover it as a prop for quasi-contractual obligation. This sprang from a desire to get the parallel between contract and quasi-contract as close as possible.

[3] *Barber Surgeons of London* v. *Pelson* (1679) 2 Lev. 252.

[4] Holdsworth, *op. cit.* vii, 96.

TORT AND QUASI-CONTRACT 181

cause he declines to hold office in it. And this in effect is the view adopted in a later decision.[1]

Finally, some customary obligations are not quasi-contractual at all, though they have been regarded as such. The duty of the common carrier to receive goods and to carry them safely, and the duty of the innkeeper to receive guests and to keep their goods secure, have already been considered.[2] The liability of a copyhold tenant to pay a customary fine on admission is really an incident of tenure, though *indebitatus assumpsit* has been allowed for its redress.[3]

(3) *Statutory duty.* Very much the same as with customary duties, it has been broadly stated that quasi-contracts, or "constructive contracts", include duties created by statute to pay a sum of money to, or for the benefit of, another person.[4] No doubt the amount can be recovered as a debt, but there is no need or justification to argue from that to the existence of quasi-contractual liability in all circumstances. Each statute must be taken on its merits, and it may be that the obligation which it sets up is rightly to be deemed as a compulsory incident in a contract which is otherwise freely entered into, or where there is no such contract, as a statutory duty towards a particular person. The authorities are consistent with this view. Usually the action sued was that of debt which was colourless as to the jurisprudential nature of the liability behind it. Where the action was for money had and received, it was generally alternative to an "action at law on the statute", which was given no further detailed description.[5]

---

[1] *Tobacco Pipe Makers' Co.* v. *Loder* (1851) 16 Q.B. 765, 780. Cf. Keener, *op. cit.* 16.
[2] *Ante*, p. 151.
[3] *Shuttleworth* v. *Garnet* (1689) 3 Lev. 261. *Ante*, p. 126.
[4] Jenks, *op. cit.* § 718. 7 *Laws of England* (Halsbury), § 1001.
[5] E.g. *Lloyd* v. *Burrup* (1868) L.R. 4 Ex. 63.

182   TORT AND QUASI-CONTRACT

(4) *Liability of minor for necessaries.* A minor is, of course, liable for necessaries supplied to him, but upon what principle? The law, here, has passed through stages of variation from one doctrine to another. At first, the minor's liability may have been contractual.[1] But then another mode of making him pay, otherwise than by action for debt, was *assumpsit* on a *quantum meruit,* and in this the plaintiff could recover, not necessarily the price which had been fixed for the goods, but only a reasonable price.[2] This, it has been argued, is such an alteration of the obligation into which the minor entered by the contract that there is a new obligation which is quasi-contractual.[3] In England, at least one judge has gone further than this, and has denied that a minor can make a contract of purchase at all in the strict sense of the word.[4] Whether either of these views is correct is somewhat doubtful. It is possible to urge against them that, at any rate at the present day, the rule as to only a reasonable price being recoverable is no more than a statutory[5] term implied in a contract which a minor is perfectly competent to make; that it is similar to many other statutory terms in a contract, e.g. implied warranties as to title and quality in sales of goods; and that these do not affect the existence of the contract or the possibility of making it.[6] However, be the theory what it may in England, there is respectable authority abroad for regarding the obligation as quasi-contractual.[7]

(5) *General average.* This is the apportionment of loss among all the parties interested in ship or cargo, in proportion to their interest, where the loss is caused

[1] Holdsworth, *op. cit.* viii, 52.
[2] *Ibid.*   [3] Keener, *op. cit.* 21.
[4] Fletcher Moulton L.J. in *Nash* v. *Inman* [1908] 2 K.B. 1, 8–9.
[5] Sale of Goods Act, 1893, s. 2.
[6] See a further criticism in Keener, *op. cit.* 21.
[7] Keener, *op. cit.* 21. Street, *op. cit.* ii, 204. Indian Contract Act, § 68.

TORT AND QUASI-CONTRACT 183

intentionally and for the common safety, as by cutting away masts or throwing cargo overboard. There is no agreement among English judges as to whether liability, arising from general average is quasi-contractual or contractual.[1] One view would make it a term implied in the contract of affreightment, just as those who contract with reference to a custom impliedly make it part of the contract. Another view is that the liability is wholly independent of contract and arises "by virtue of the equitable doctrine of the Rhodian law, which as part of the law maritime has been incorporated in the municipal law of England".[2] This opinion is perhaps concerned rather with historical origin than with scientific classification, but it need not be pushed much further in the latter direction to make quasi-contract the basis of general average, for it would neatly illustrate "natural justice". In any event, the controversy is not so unpractical as might be thought.[3]

This concludes the examination of the contents of quasi-contract. Before we attempt to distinguish it from liability in tort, one other question has to be settled which leads up to the final problem. Is it a characteristic of a claim on quasi-contract that it must always be for a liquidated sum of money? It may be stated at the outset that, whatever be the answer to this, the claim must be for money and not for specific goods.[4] On the other hand, the courts do not insist on proof by the plaintiff that the money claimed did actually come into the hands of the defendant. Consequently, they have

[1] Lowndes, *General Average* (6th ed. 1922), § 3.
[2] Vaughan Williams L.J. in *Milburn* v. *Jamaica Fruit Importing Co.* [1900] 2 Q.B. 540, 550.
[3] Lowndes, *op. cit.* p. 31, note *g*.
[4] In at least two instances of quasi-contract under the Indian Contract Act, the possibility of recovering goods *in specie* is contemplated. Sect. 72 provides that "a person to whom money has been paid, or anything delivered, by mistake or under coercion, must repay or return it".

184   TORT AND QUASI-CONTRACT

allowed the plaintiff to sue for money had and received where a presumption can be raised that goods received by the defendant have been converted into money, and thus things which can easily be turned into money have been treated as equivalent to money for this purpose.[1] But it is that money which will be recovered and not the things themselves. Thus in *Longchamp* v. *Kenny*[2] the plaintiff and the defendant had each received some masquerade tickets from *C* to dispose of, for which they were to account after the masquerade, by paying their value or returning the tickets. The defendant got possession of one of the tickets which had been delivered to the plaintiff. The plaintiff paid five guineas (the value of the ticket) to *C*, in order to prevent *C* from arresting him for not returning the ticket. It was held that the plaintiff could recover from the defendant in an action for money had and received. Lord Mansfield said: "It is certain that where the demand is for a specific thing, an action cannot be maintained in this form". But he held that, as the defendant came prepared as to the nature of the claim and was not taken by surprise, he was liable. If he had sold the ticket and received value for it, he held the price to the plaintiff's use, and, as the defendant had not produced the ticket, it was a fair presumption that he had sold it.[3]

Another preliminary is to settle the meaning of "liquidated" and "unliquidated" damages.

The term "liquidated damages" is applied to such damages as constitute a liquidated demand payable in money. It therefore includes liquidated sums payable as damages under a statute, or by reason of a breach of contract, such payment having been previously agreed upon by the parties thereto.

[1] 7 *Laws of England* (Halsbury), § 970.
[2] (1779) 1 Doug. 132.
[3] *Hunter* v. *Walsh* (1816) 1 Stark 224, is a *nisi prius* ruling of Lord Ellenborough to the like effect.

TORT AND QUASI-CONTRACT 185

This would be clearer if the very word defined were not twice used in the definition. But there is more light thrown on it by the same author's explanation of the converse phrase.

The term "unliquidated damages" is employed in cases where a plaintiff does not claim a predetermined and inelastic sum, but seeks to recover such an amount as the court, in its discretion, is at liberty to award, though the pleadings may specify a particular amount.[1]

Now it has been asserted that in an action for money had and received, the claim must always be for a defined and ascertained sum.[2] This had better be investigated before cases of quasi-contract, other than money had and received, are considered at large, and it is somewhat doubtful whether the proposition with regard to money had and received represents the law. In favour of it is an inference from *Harvey* v. *Archbold*[3] that the plaintiff must give evidence of the particular sum to which he is entitled; and in *Garbett* v. *Veale*[4] it was held that the action was inapplicable where the sum could have been ascertained only upon a settlement of partnership accounts which the court could not take without the consent of the parties interested. *Edwards* v. *Bates*[5] was a direct decision against bringing the action before ascertainment that anything was due to the plaintiff. And in the much more modern case of *Grant* v. *Gold Exploration Syndicate*,[6] some judicial *dicta* indicate that the sum claimed must be "quantified" which, judging by the context in which the word is used, seems to mean "ascertained at the time of bringing the action". On

---

[1] Arnold, *Damages and Compensation* (2nd ed. 1919), 5–6.
[2] 7 *Laws of England* (Halsbury), § 970.   [3] (1825) 3 B. & C. 626.
[4] (1843) 5 Q.B. 408. So too *Bovill* v. *Hammond* (1827) 6 B. & C. 149.
[5] (1844) 8 Scott N.R. 406.
[6] [1900] 1 Q.B. 233. Collins L.J. at p. 248. A. L. Smith L.J. at pp. 244–245. Vaughan Williams L.J. at p. 256.

186 TORT AND QUASI-CONTRACT

the other hand, *Parker* v. *Bristol etc. R. Co.*[1] is the other way. Pollock C.B.,[2] regretted that *Ashmole* v. *Wainwright*[3] had broken in upon a broad and general principle of the action for money had and received that it must be brought "for a definite, clear, and certain sum, and not for some unknown sum, which is to depend upon the verdict of the jury." But, as the rest of the Court of Exchequer were against him and were satisfied with that decision, he said that he felt bound by the case. "While I yield to that authority, I am not convinced by it." He added that the principle as to certainty of the sum had prevailed for many years in Westminster Hall and was worth preserving.

As to quasi-contract in general, it cannot be maintained that it extends only to liquidated claims. It is true that Bowen L.J. in *Phillips* v. *Homfray*[4] held that the action, which was certainly quasi-contractual in character, could not have been brought if the damages had been unliquidated and uncertain; but his remarks cannot well be regarded as of wider application than to the type of action before him, which was in effect waiver of a tort. Moreover, if *Lightly* v. *Clouston*[5] and *Foster* v. *Stewart*[6] are still good law,[7] there is at least one instance in which, where a tort is waived, the quasi-contractual claim may be for an unliquidated amount. In the former of these cases (the latter was precisely similar to it), the defendant induced the plaintiff's apprentice to break his apprenticeship and help to work the defendant's ship home. The plaintiff was held to be entitled to waive the tort and sue *indebitatus assumpsit*. The value of the services of the apprentice in navigating the defendant's

[1] (1851) 6 Ex. 702. [2] At p. 706.
[3] (1842) 2 Q.B. 837.
[4] (1883) 24 Ch. D. 439, 455, 466.
[5] (1808) 1 Taunt. 212.
[6] (1814) 3 M. & S. 191.
[7] *Ante*, p. 174.

TORT AND QUASI-CONTRACT 187

ship was an unliquidated amount.[1] But, quite apart from waiver of tort, much stronger examples of quasi-contract can be found in which there is no pretence of the claim being one for a liquidated amount. Such is a claim for salvage. There is no absolute rule or fixed scale of remuneration. Unless it has been ascertained by a valid agreement, it is dependent on the discretion of the court, and the factors for arriving at a decision include not only such variables as peril, weather, time spent, and value of the property salved, but also things that are completely incapable of exact calculation; e.g. the encouragement of enterprise and the discharge of what is due to the general interests of commerce.[2] Again, in *quantum meruit* of the genuine quasi-contractual type,[3] the effective claim may well be for an indefinite amount.

[1] As to the American authors, Woodward, *op. cit.* § 3, makes it an essential of quasi-contract that the obligee shall be compensated, not for any loss or damage suffered by him, but for the benefit which he has conferred on the obliger. He adds that the obligation is "to pay the equivalent or the *reasonable worth* of the benefit received". This justified the inference that, in his opinion, the claim may be for an unliquidated amount. It is not easy to say what view was held by Keener. At p. 166 he implies that where a tort is waived the quasi-contractual claim may be for an unliquidated sum, for he says that it does not follow that the measure of recovery is to bear any relation to the amount of profit made by the defendant, and that the plaintiff should recover such sum as a jury would have been authorized to give, had there been a contract between plaintiff and defendant that the latter should pay a reasonable value for user of plaintiff's property. No authority is cited. The same implication is raised as to waiver on p. 166, where the amount recoverable is stated to be the sum which it is against conscience that the defendant should keep. No English authority is cited. On the other hand, at p. 173, he cites a mere *dictum* of Lord Mansfield in *Lindon* v. *Hooper* (1776) Cowp. 414, 419, that in waiver of a tort it will be fatal to the plaintiff if the amount is not ascertainable. At pp. 298–300, in discussing quasi-contractual remedies used as alternative to contractual ones, he seems positive that the principle is restitution, not compensation; but *Dutch* v. *Warren* (1720) 1 Stra. 406, which he cites was clearly a case in which the "restitution" consisted of unliquidated damages.

[2] Kennedy, *Law of Civil Salvage* (2nd ed. 1907), chap. vi.
[3] *Ante*, pp. 158–159.

188 TORT AND QUASI-CONTRACT

In *Prickett* v. *Badger*,[1] the plaintiff actually claimed £143. 5s. but a jury, on the judge's direction that the plaintiff was entitled to recover a reasonable remuneration for his services, awarded him only £50. Yet again, the statutory liability of lunatics and drunkards to pay a reasonable price for necessaries can only be unliquidated in character.[2]

The conclusion is therefore irresistible that, though the amount claimable in many forms of quasi-contract is liquidated, in several others it is not; and that the certainty or uncertainty of what is due is irrelevant to the determination of whether liability is quasi-contractual or not.

We are now in a position to distinguish liability on quasi-contract from liability in tort. It will be recollected that the latter has been defined as arising "from the breach of a duty primarily fixed by the law: such duty is towards persons generally and its breach is redressible by an action for unliquidated damages".[3]

In view of what has just been said, we can at once rule out "unliquidated damages" as any test for such distinction. Nor can it be said that it lies in the fact that, while in tort the duty is primarily fixed by the law, in quasi-contract it is primarily fixed by the parties. This is true of many species of quasi-contract, but it is not true of all. Salvage, and quasi-contract arising from statute (to mention no other instances), cannot be distinguished from tort in this way. But a real difference is to be found in the scope of the duty. In tort it is towards persons generally, in quasi-contract it is towards a particular person.[4]

An additional test has been suggested but without much enthusiasm. "Quasi contracts are superficially

[1] (1856) 1 C.B.N.S. 296.
[2] *Ante*, p. 166.   [3] *Ante*, p. 32.
[4] This, in effect, is the view of Woodward, *op. cit.* § 5.

TORT AND QUASI-CONTRACT 189

unlike the duty not to commit a tort, but are like most contracts in that the obligation is positive rather than negative: the obligor is required to act rather than to forbear."[1] But this will not suffice, for the modern tort of negligence may consist in omission as well as in commission.[2] In other words tortious obligation may arise from breach of a positive duty as well as from breach of a negative duty. In mediaeval law, it would have been nearly (but not quite) accurate to say that omission grounded no civil liability,[3] but we are concerned with the law as it is here and now.

[1] This, in effect, is the view of Woodward, *op. cit.* § 5.
[2] 42 *Law Quarterly Review* (1926), 199–201.
[3] *Ibid.* 191–192.

Chapter VIII

TORT AND CRIME

OVER a hundred and fifty years ago, Lord Mansfield said, "there is no distinction better known, than the distinction between civil and criminal law; or between criminal prosecutions and civil actions".[1] The whole attitude of English lawyers towards these distinctions is epitomized in this quotation. They have repeatedly assumed that these distinctions are well known and that they are clear, but very few of them from Lord Mansfield downwards have tried to explain what they are, and, upon the whole, the result at the present day is that, while every lawyer feels that there are obvious differences, none can state in exact terms what they are.

At the outset of the Common Law, the position was much the same. Both in theory and in practice there was a perception of the distinction between civil and criminal proceedings, but there was no sharply cut division between them. The two were a viscous intermixture.[2] Every cause for a civil action was an offence, and every cause for a civil action in the King's court was an offence against the King punishable by amercement, if not by fine and imprisonment. Even the line between Pleas of the Crown—a phrase which until quite modern times was equivalent to criminal cases—and Common Pleas was a blurred one,[3] and appeals of felony might well defy any classification. Then came another element of confusion, and a strong one. That was the double aspect of trespass in its old wide sense. It could be dealt

[1] *Atcheson* v. *Everitt* (1775) 1 Cowp. at p. 391.
[2] Winfield, *History of Conspiracy* (1921), 92.
[3] Pollock and Maitland, ii, 572–573.

TORT AND CRIME

with criminally on presentation at the tourn or before the King's judges, and such trespasses became the misdemeanours of later law.[1] Yet a civil action was also available. In fact, it is extraordinary how these civil actions supplemented to some extent the meagre list of crimes in our early law.

"The man who has put a cat into his neighbour's dovecot", says Sir William Holdsworth, "or who has extracted wine from his neighbour's casks and filled them with sea-water; the man who has removed his neighbour's landmark, or destroyed his neighbour's sea wall; the man who has laid waste his neighbour's fields, or besieged his house—all are sued by an action of trespass."[2]

And yet nowadays there is not a single one of these acts that is not also a crime. It is worth repeating here that so late as 1694, the defendant to a writ of trespass was theoretically liable to fine and imprisonment.[3] The same learned author has pointed out that the Star Chamber, while it widened the horizon of our criminal law, also tended to obscure still more the indeterminate boundary between crime and tort; for, though it treated certain acts as criminal, the Common Law courts remedied the same or similar acts by civil actions on the case for damages.[4] Thus, historical antecedents leave us with nothing exact. Writers of the nineteenth and twentieth centuries have at least made efforts—some of them very strenuous ones—to remove the uncertainty. In the previous chapter on Tort and Quasi-contract, it was said that the chief difficulty of separating these topics was the perfunctory way in which the limits of quasi-contract had been treated by English authors. No such complaint can be made against those who have ex-

[1] Holdsworth, *History of English Law*, iii, 317–318.
[2] *Ibid.* iii, 370.
[3] Pollock, *Torts*, 590.
[4] Holdsworth, *op. cit.* viii, 306.

192 TORT AND CRIME

pounded criminal law. It is certainly not the lack of effort that is chargeable with the somewhat disappointing results which have been achieved. Such failure as there is must be attributed to the intractability of the subject-matter.

The following are some of the leading definitions of a crime:

(1) Sir James Stephen regarded it as

an act or omission in respect of which legal punishment may be inflicted on the person who is in default either by acting or omitting to act.

But he was not much satisfied with his own definition.[1]

(2) Crimes are wrongs whose sanction is punitive, and is in no way remissible by any private person, but is remissible by the Crown alone, if remissible at all.[2]

So the late lamented Professor Kenny in his brilliant *Outlines of Criminal Law*. He expended so much care on searching for the distinction between crime and tort that we shall have occasion to refer later to his analysis more often than to any other. It is safe to assume that every one is acquainted with the details of it and his reasons for rejecting wholly or in part other definitions.

(3) The term "crime" or "criminal offence" is applicable only to acts (and omissions) for which the law awards punishment.[3]

(4) A crime is an unlawful act or default which is an offence against the public, and renders the person guilty of the act or default liable to legal punishment...it is as an act or default contrary to the order, peace, and well-being of society that a crime is punishable by the state.[4]

(5) The only certain lines of distinction are to be found in the nature of the remedy given, and the nature of the procedure to

[1] *History of Criminal Law* (1883), i, 1, 2, 3.
[2] 13th ed. (1929), 15–16.
[3] Harris, *Criminal Law* (14th ed. 1926), 1.
[4] 9 *Laws of England* (Halsbury), § 499.

TORT AND CRIME 193

enforce the remedy. If the remedy given is compensation, damages, or a penalty enforced by a civil action, the wrong so redressed is a civil wrong. If the remedy given is the punishment of the accused, which is enforced by a prosecution at the suit of the crown, the wrong so redressed is a crime or criminal in its nature. Even this test sometimes fails to establish a clear line of difference.[1]

These are fair specimens and we need burden the text with only one more. In one shape or another, other modern books have embodied it.

(6) Blackstone's analysis is to be gleaned from these passages in his *Commentaries*.[2] He first says that a crime is "an act committed, or omitted, in violation of a public law". Then he goes on:

The distinction of public wrongs from private, of crimes and misdemeanours from civil injuries, seems principally to consist in this: that private wrongs, or civil injuries, are an infringement or privation of the civil rights which belong to individuals, considered merely as individuals: public wrongs, or crimes and misdemeanours, are a breach and violation of the public rights and duties, due to the whole community, considered as a community in its social aggregate capacity.

And it is clear from a later sentence that he regards punishment as an essential consequence of crime, and an additional distinction between crimes and civil injuries.

When we turn to the law reports, we find that judicial definitions of crime are extremely scanty and not very informative. Here are three samples extending over a century. "The proper definition of the word 'crime' is

---

[1] Holdsworth, *op. cit.* viii, 306. The last paragraph is supported by a citation of *A-G. v. Bradlaugh* (1885) 14 Q.B.D. 667, where the proceedings, though conducted at the suit of the Crown, were nevertheless held to be civil, not criminal.

[2] Vol. iv, 5–7.

WP

194 TORT AND CRIME

an offence for which the law awards punishment."[1] "An illegal act which is a wrong against the public welfare seems to have the necessary elements of a crime."[2] "An offence against the public law."[3]

Nor is any help to be derived from the legislature. When Parliament has had occasion to define a "crime", sometimes its interpretation of that word, though doubtless useful for the purposes of the particular statute in which it is contained, merely affords opportunities for parody from a scientific point of view.[4] Sometimes, however, the signification attached to the word has gone pretty near a good general working definition,[5] though not such as would be likely to be adopted if the law were "restated" or codified.

Another line of approaching the subject is to attempt a definition of "criminal proceedings" and to contrast them with "civil proceedings" rather than to define crime.[6] This is unquestionably a more practical adventure, for it is no exaggeration to say that in the law courts there has scarcely ever been any need to define crime, while there are scores of *dicta* or decisions on the distinction between criminal and civil "proceedings", or "causes" or "matters". Indeed, this accounts for the poverty of information about "crime" in the law reports. But the moment we pass from crime in the abstract to litigation in connection with it, consequences of importance at once emerge according to whether the proceedings are criminal or not. They differ from civil

[1] *Mann* v. *Owen* (1829) 9 B. & C. 595, 602.

[2] Lord Esher M.R. in *Mogul S.S. Co.* v. *McGregor, Gow and Co.* (1889) 23 Q.B.D. at p. 606.

[3] Viscount Cave in *Clifford* v. *O'Sullivan* [1921] 2 A.C. at p. 580; and the Judicial Committee of the P.C. in *Nadan* v. *R.* [1926] A.C. at p. 489, and in *Chung Chuck* v. *R.* [1930] A.C. at p. 250.

[4] E.g. Prevention of Crimes Act, 1871, s. 20. Prevention of Crime Act, 1908, Sched.

[5] Conspiracy and Protection of Property Act, 1875, s. 3.

[6] E.g. Russell, *Crimes* (8th ed. 1923) i, 1.

TORT AND CRIME 195

cases in the rules of evidence, in waiver of the rules of procedure, in the Crown's power of pardon, and in other ways.

It has been said that a civil proceeding has for its object the recovery of money or other property, or the enforcement of a right for the advantage of the persons suing, while a criminal proceeding has for its object the punishment of a public offence.[1] And it has also been indicated that the mildest grade of punishment—a fine —suffices to make the proceeding a criminal one.[2] But it is the phrase "criminal cause or matter" rather than "criminal proceeding" which has evoked most judicial interpretation. No appeal lies (except under the Criminal Appeal Act, 1907), from any judgment of the High Court in any criminal cause or matter.[3] It is well settled that this term must be taken in its widest sense. It applies to "a decision by way of judicial determination of any question raised in or with regard to proceedings, the subject-matter of which is criminal, at whatever stage of the proceedings the question arises".[4] Thus an application for a writ of habeas corpus on extradition proceedings,[5] and the taxation of costs on a judgment for the accused in a criminal information for libel are criminal causes or matters.[6] It is obvious that many decisions of this nature can be of no assistance in determining the difference between crimes and civil injuries. If crime is in the air, so to speak, the cause or matter is

[1] 9 *Laws of England* (Halsbury), § 499. Practically the same as Platt B. in *A-G.* v. *Radloff* (1854) 10 Ex. 84, 101–102.

[2] Pollock C.B. in same case, at p. 109.

[3] Supreme Court of Judicature (Consolidation) Act, 1925, s. 31, s-s. 1 (*a*), re-enacting in effect Judicature Act, 1873, s. 47.

[4] Lord Esher M.R. in *Ex parte Woodhall* (1888) 20 Q.B.D. at p. 836. This was approved in effect by the H.L. in *Provincial Cinematograph, etc. Ld.* v. *Newcastle-upon-Tyne, etc.* (1921) 125 L.T. 651. See too [1921] 2 A.C. at p. 580.

[5] *Ex parte Woodhall* (1888) 20 Q.B.D. 832.

[6] *R.* v. *Steel* (1876) 2 Q.B.D. 37.

13-2

196 TORT AND CRIME

a criminal one by a species of infection. But this much does seem to be clear. The cause or matter is criminal if the source of it is something which may result in imprisonment, or in a fine, with imprisonment as a possibility on non-payment of the fine.[1] But it would be wrong to deduce from this that such imprisonment or fine can be seized upon as the test of *crime*. Thus, in *Seaman* v. *Burley*[2] a judgment to enforce payment of a poor-rate by distress warrant was held by the Court of Appeal to be a judgment in a criminal cause or matter, because the proceedings *might*, though they *need not*, end in imprisonment. Yet two of the Lord Justices (Kay and A. L. Smith) seemed to regard the non-payment of the rate as not a crime; but the whole court attached no importance to the question whether it was or not, and concentrated attention on whether the proceeding was a criminal cause or matter.

Let us turn back to the various definitions of crime at the beginning of this chapter and see which, if any, of them can be adopted or adapted. It will be noticed that, however much they differ in other respects, there is one element common to them all. A crime always involves *punishment*. If an exact meaning can be attached to that term, then we can mark off crimes from civil injuries. But before we investigate this, we must dispose of an additional suggested test. Dr Kenny regarded the sanction of crime not only as punitive, but as "remissible by the Crown alone, if remissible at all". Now "sanction" in this context signifies punishment. It does not refer to any part of a criminal proceeding prior to punishment, e.g. a *nolle prosequi*; for Kenny himself rejected the supposed distinction between crimes and civil injuries that the redress of the former can be initiated

---

[1] Bramwell L.J. in *R.* v. *Whitchurch* (1881) 7 Q.B.D. 534. *Robson* v. *Biggar* [1908] 1 K.B. 672.
[2] [1896] 2 Q.B. 344.

TORT AND CRIME 197

by the Crown only, and he expressly uses "sanctions" as equivalent to "punishments".[1] "Remission" must therefore refer to pardon by the Crown, for the only way in which the Crown can remit a punishment is by pardon. If, then, it can be ascertained what the scope of pardon is, that ought to indicate also the scope of crime. This, unfortunately, is precisely where the definition breaks down. Coke tells us that a pardon cannot affect civil rights, but he does not explain what civil rights are.[2] And we learn from the law reports that crimes which are pardonable are only those which are against the public laws and statutes of the realm,[3] and that pardon extends to sentences of a punitive character.[4] But while the tendency of a wrong to injure the public is a factor by no means to be ignored in considering the criminality of such wrong it is too vague to rest the whole weight of a definition of crime upon it. And the description of pardon as applicable to sentences of a punitive character appears to put the question only one step further back—"What is punishment?" Other writers merely state that the prerogative of pardon applies to nothing but crime. This leads to a vicious circle. What is a crime? Something that the Crown alone can pardon. What is it that the Crown alone can pardon? A crime. Thus, it does not seem advisable to accept this part of Dr Kenny's definition.

What then is punishment? We should instantly

[1] *Criminal Law*, 14. He says just before this that interference by the Crown with *continuation* of proceedings is a mark of their being criminal, but it would appear that he is explaining Austin's analysis of criminal procedure.

[2] 3 Inst. 236.

[3] *Bentley* v. *Episc. Eliens.* (1731) 2 Stra. 912 (pardon does not extend to "crimes" constituted by breaches of the private statutes of a college. They are in the nature of domestic rules for the better ordering of a private family).

[4] *In the Matter of a Special Reference from the Bahama Islands* [1893] A.C. 138.

198 TORT AND CRIME

recognize a sentence of death, of penal servitude, of whipping, as such. A pecuniary fine, whether with or without imprisonment in default of payment is also in general a punishment,[1] but if a pecuniary payment is a civil debt, the order to pay it is not punitive. As to imprisonment, it cannot be said offhand whether it is a punishment or not. As a general rule if it is merely coercive, it is not.[2] If the delinquent is sent to prison simply to compel him to do something, and if he is to be released the moment he does it, then his incarceration is only coercive. Such is the case where a bailiff is sent to gaol because he will not make good his liability for excessive charges extorted by him in levying a distress.[3] Nothing but recourse to the statutes imposing imprisonment in any particular circumstances will help to decide whether it is coercive or punitive. The wrongful act itself gives no reliable assistance, and it is worth while repeating that decisions as to what is a criminal cause or matter within the Judicature Acts may quite conceivably throw no light whatever on whether a crime has been committed or not, and that they may well be a source of confusion as to the meaning of imprisonment. For instance, non-payment of a poor-rate is a criminal cause or matter, because it may result in imprisonment;[4] non-payment of a general district rate is not a criminal cause or matter, because such a rate is a mere civil debt.[5] Yet it may equally result in imprisonment. And in each case the imprisonment is only coercive and not punitive. Probably too, in neither case would the court have held the non-payment to be a crime, though in fact there was

[1] *Parker* v. *Green* (1862) 2 B. & S. 299, 309, 311.
[2] Kenny, *op. cit.* 14.
[3] *Robson* v. *Biggar* [1908] 1 K.B. 672. *R.* v. *Daly* (1911) 75 J.P. 333.
[4] *Seaman* v. *Burley* [1896] 2 Q.B. 344.
[5] *Southwark, etc. Water Co.* v. *Hampton U.D.C.* [1899] 1 Q.B. 273.

TORT AND CRIME 199

no necessity to pronounce whether it was such or not. It does not, however, seem to be an invariable rule that coercive imprisonment is never applicable to crime. A parent who does not send his child to school commits a criminal offence,[1] and he is liable to imprisonment if he will not pay the fine imposed on him for this.[2] Yet surely such imprisonment is coercive, not punitive. Still, in the vast majority of cases it is safe to say that coercive imprisonment is not a punishment.

Before summing up, one or two other points may be noted. Occasionally the idea of evil in punishment is stretched to breaking-point. One of the sanctions which can be imposed on a parent who does not send his child to school is not a fine, not imprisonment, but an order that the child shall go to a certified industrial school.[3] This is a proceeding which presumably benefits both child and parent; but perhaps it may be regarded as punitive in depriving the parent of the liberty of selecting the school to which the child is to be sent.

Again, two words used in connection with criminal law have a troublesome ambiguity. They are "penalty" and "offence". When they occur in statutes they generally connote a criminal act,[4] but judges have certainly not considered themselves bound always to interpret them in this way.[5] Non-payment of a cab fare is recoverable as a penalty before a justice of the peace; yet it is purely a civil debt.[6]

Finally, in determining whether disobedience to a statute is a misdemeanour (assuming that the statute itself is silent on the point except for the imposition of

---

[1] *Mellor* v. *Denham* (1880) 5 Q.B.D. 467.
[2] Education Act, 1921, s. 45.
[3] *Ibid.*
[4] *R.* v. *Paget* (1881) 8 Q.B.D. 151.
[5] Platt and Martin BB. in *A-G.* v. *Radloff* (1854) 11 Ex. 84. *Derbyshire C.C.* v. *Borough of Derby* [1896] 2 Q.B. 53.
[6] *R.* v. *Kerswill* [1895] 1 Q.B. 1.

TORT AND CRIME

a penalty), it is a question of construing the statute in each case; and the test has been stated as being whether the duty created is towards the public and whether the remedy is intended to be enforced in the interests of the public.[1]

The result, then, may be thus propounded. The essence of punishment is its inevitability. When once liability to it has been pronounced, no option is left to the offender as to whether he shall endure it or not. He can get rid of it, in general, only by suffering it. Contrast this with a civil case. There, if he is adjudged to pay a debt, or is cast in damages, or is put under an injunction, he can always compromise or get rid of his liability with the assent of the injured party.

Now the only tolerably certain test of crime is, "Does the conduct complained of render the offender liable to punishment?" Another consideration, which is a guide rather than a secondary test, is, "Does such conduct have an evil effect on the public?" But while it would be neither wise, nor indeed possible as matters now stand, to reject this as a guide, it is too nebulous to be incorporated in a definition. A crime may, therefore, be defined as *a wrong the sanction of which involves punishment*; and punishment signifies death, penal servitude, whipping, fine, imprisonment (but not, as a rule, non-coercive imprisonment), or some other evil which, when once liability to it has been decreed, is not avoidable by any act of the party offending.

We may be reproached with having expended a good deal of energy in getting no further than Blackstone and his successors have done. That may be so, but at least the line of investigation has been an independent one, and hitherto most writers, with the exception of Dr Kenny, have assumed that punishment needs no explanation. It may likewise be urged that the attempt

[1] Bowen L.J. in *R. v. Tyler*, etc. [1891] 2 Q.B. at p. 594.

TORT AND CRIME

to define crime is unpractical, and that it would have been better to centre attention on criminal proceedings. But it has been shewn that this would be a mere exchange of one obscure topic for another. Nor is it clear why, in the interests of scientific exposition, we should be driven to put what is really a piece of substantive law wholly under the law of procedure.

Tort can be distinguished from crime in that the sanction for crime is punishment, while the sanction for tort is an action for damages. These damages may be exemplary or punitive, but they are not within the definition of punishment which has just be developed.

But it must not be hastily inferred that damages can never be awarded in connection with a crime. We do not refer to the fact that the same circumstances may constitute both a crime and a tort, for that is hardly worth stating. What we are here considering is that it is possible in some criminal proceedings to claim unliquidated damages. This will appear when the various pecuniary payments procurable in such proceedings are examined.

A fine is often one of the punishments that can be inflicted for crime. It has usually an upward limit, but its amount within that limit is in the discretion of the court. It is therefore indefinite until the court has fixed it, and in that sense is quite as uncertain as the amount of damages claimable in an action in tort until these are assessed by the judge or jury. Till that moment the sum is as unliquidated in the one case as in the other. But the very notable difference is that whereas the damages in a civil action go to the injured party, the fine in a criminal proceeding does not (subject to exceptions shortly to be noticed) enure to the injured party, but to the Crown. In other words, a fine cannot be described as "damages" at all, for it benefits the injured party nothing. And so far we could rule out fines as having no bearing on the matter under discussion.

202 TORT AND CRIME

But there are circumstances in which pecuniary compensation is payable by a convicted criminal to the injured private party, who is therefore actually benefited. In the first place, "fine" includes (at any rate in a Court of Summary Jurisdiction) "any pecuniary penalty or pecuniary forfeiture or pecuniary compensation payable under a conviction".[1] Thus, on a summary conviction for wilful or malicious damage (not exceeding £20) to property, the court, in addition to inflicting fine or imprisonment, may award reasonable compensation to the party aggrieved.[2] Again, it is possible for criminal courts in general to award compensation in other circumstances. Under the Probation of Offenders Act, 1907, s. 1 (3), such damages for injury or compensation for loss as the court thinks reasonable may be ordered to be paid by the offender. This is in addition to any other order which the court may make. More generally still, where an accused person has been convicted of felony, the court may, on the application of any person aggrieved, immediately after conviction, award any sum not exceeding £100 by way of satisfaction or compensation for any loss of property suffered by means of the felony.[3] This compensation is in addition to, and not a substitute for, the punishment appropriate to the crime.[4]

Now these species of compensation[5] are undoubtedly just as much unliquidated as are damages for a tort; and they unquestionably benefit the injured private party and not the Crown. But there is one feature peculiar to

[1] Summary Jurisdiction Act, 1879, s. 49.
[2] Criminal Justice Administration Act, 1914, s. 14.
[3] Forfeiture Act, 1870, s. 4.
[4] *R.* v. *Lovett* (1870) 23 L.T. 95.
[5] Discretionary rewards payable in connection with the apprehension of persons charged with crime are irrelevant to the discussion. Their source is not any property of the accused, and the person whom they benefit is not necessarily the person injured by the crime. Information with respect to them will be found in Russell, *Crimes* (8th ed. 1923), 1888–1891.

TORT AND CRIME 203

them all which marks them off from damages in tort. In every case they are obtainable only *in addition to* some punishment, or order in the nature of punishment, inflicted or made by the court. They are not the primary remedy in the criminal proceeding; but only a secondary one. In a civil action, on the other hand, the claim for damages .can always be made in priority to any other claim. It is true that under the Probation of Offenders Act, 1907, it is possible for the court to award the compensation if, in the opinion of the court, "it is inexpedient to inflict any punishment". But even then the court must, before it can make the award, pronounce an order of some sort, whether it be a dismissal of the charge, a discharge on recognizances, or a release on probation; and none of these courses is permissible unless the court holds that the offence charged is proved.

Hence, in crime unliquidated damages benefiting the injured party are not claimable in the first instance; in tort they are.

Chapter IX

TORT AND THE LAW OF PROPERTY

IT may be a matter of speculation to students of English law why the Law of Tort and the Law of Property should overlap to some extent in point of literary treatment. Those who are familiar with Dr Cheshire's book on the *Modern Law of Real Property* may have been puzzled to find there topics which might just as well be placed under the law of tort, and indeed are often so placed. Such are limitations on rights with respect to water[1] which are also handled in Salmond's *Law of Torts*;[2] so too the rights of a tenant in fee simple in general. Is there any need to describe the same things under both heads of the law? The question is of some importance on both theoretical and practical grounds. On the theoretical side it is of interest from the point of view of jurisprudence; and it is certainly a practical consideration for those who propose to write books on either of these subjects and who wish to ascertain their correct boundaries. The object of this chapter is to probe the relations of the Law of Property to the Law of Tort, and it will be seen that the upshot of the investigation is that repetition of the sort which we have described is probably unnecessary either in theory or in a practical exposition of English law.

In theory, one might expound the law solely by reference to legal rights, leaving all legal duties to be inferred from the statement of rights. Thus, if it is stated that I may lawfully abstract water from a stream, as riparian owner, the inference is that all other people are under a duty not to prevent me from abstracting it. If it is

[1] 2nd ed. (1927), 119.
[2] 7th ed. (1928), §§ 74–80.

TORT AND THE LAW OF PROPERTY 205

stated that I am lawfully entitled to personal security, the inference is that all other people are under a duty not to meddle with my person. If it is stated that I am entitled to my good reputation, the inference is that all other people are under a duty not to cast aspersions on my character. On this hypothesis the law of tort could be eliminated as a separate division of the system. All the duties comprised in it could be deduced from statements of the various rights *in rem* comprised under the rights to property, to personal security and to reputation. But, for historical reasons, English law has never reached this abstraction. To begin with, like any other legal system, it has been compelled to plod along from the simple idea of a "wrong" to the complicated idea of a "right". A legal right is such a commonplace conception to a modern lawyer that he can scarcely imagine that it has ever been otherwise. Yet people in early times cannot grasp what is really a complicated matter, and it is a long journey that must be traversed before they can either acquire the capacity, or feel the need, for understanding it.[1] The Register of Writs, the importance of procedure until comparatively recent times, and the evolution of trespass and trespass upon the case, all testify to this. "Wrongs" and "remedies" are much more simple and intelligible things than are "rights".

But even when the idea of legal rights did become familiar, English law has wavered from beginning to end between adopting rights or wrongs as the *clou* of legal exposition. This is strikingly illustrated by the Law of Tort. Roughly speaking, it deals with injuries, (i) to property, (ii) to the person, (iii) to reputation. Now, with respect to (i), the books on real property law generally deal with the *rights* relating to such property and practically ignore the wrongs by which such rights

[1] Street, *Foundations of Legal Liability* (1906), iii, 6–7.

206 TORT AND THE LAW OF PROPERTY

may possibly be infringed. These are, and long have been, treated under the Law of Tort (e.g. trespass, nuisance, breaches of strict duties). At least this is so as regards breaches of rights *in rem*. Breaches of rights *in personam* (e.g. waste), are more within the province of a book on real property law than of one on tort. As to personal property, the hesitation of writers in deciding whether this shall be explained solely from the point of view of right, or whether it shall include also infractions of such rights, is still more noticeable. The leading textbooks, with more or less consistency or felicity, emphasize the "rights" side. Yet conversion of chattels and trespass to them are important chapters in the Law of Tort and, on the whole, had better be left to that subject.

Next, as to (ii) and (iii). Here there is practically no attempt to analyse these from the "rights" standpoint. In general, they are examined under the law of "breaches of duties" or "wrongs"; that is to say, so far as civil remedies are concerned, under the Law of Tort. Examples are assault, battery, false imprisonment, defamation.

Thus, there has been a curious divergence in the treatment of (i) as compared with that of (ii) and (iii). In (i) the oscillation in favour of "rights" has been marked, though it cannot be said that there has been a definite and exclusive selection of this mode of exposition. In (ii) and (iii), emphasis is definitely and almost exclusively laid on "wrongs" or "breaches of duties". Why, then, should "rights" have secured such a prominence in real property law? Perhaps because of the extreme importance of land in our early law and indeed at the present day. Personal security and reputation may seem equally important, but from the view-point of "right" there is not so much to say about them as there is about land. At any rate this was so in our

TORT AND THE LAW OF PROPERTY 207

earlier history. The answer to "what may I do?" is much longer in land law than in the law affecting personal security and reputation. Or, to put the converse, in the latter it is much easier to answer the question, "what am I forbidden to do to my neighbour?" than the question, "what may I do?" Again, Sir Frederick Pollock has clearly shewn us why much of "what really belonged to the law of property was transferred, in forensic usage and thence in the traditional habit of mind of English lawyers, to the law of torts".[1] He points out that the remedies for restitution of property (the writ of right, and the like, and the writ of debt), were so clumsy and perilous to the plaintiff that they were thrust into the background by the adaptation of writs of penal redress, i.e. the writ of trespass and the writs cognate to it. So too, detinue was superseded to a large extent by trover. "In this way the distinction between proceedings taken on a disputed claim of right, and those taken for the redress of injuries where the right was assumed not to be in dispute, became quite obliterated."[2]

The result then seems to be that breaches of rights *in rem* connected with property fall within the domain of tort rather than within that of the law of property. Historical antecedents and practical convenience are too strong to be ignored, even if logic might dictate otherwise. It would be tempting to set out a framework of the law based upon rights as an ideal for a code, but that would be more relevant in a book on jurisprudence and, in any event, it would take in many other topics which are beside the purpose of these lectures.

[1] *Law of Torts* (13th ed. 1929), 14.   [2] *Ibid.* 13.

Chapter X

TORT AND QUASI-DELICT

THIS chapter must begin with a doubt as to whether any such idea as quasi-delict or quasi-tort has been isolated in English law, and it must end with another doubt as to its practical value, even if we assume that it exists. Until quite recently it has lain in a dark and dusty corner of the Anglo-American system and a good deal of searching for it has resulted in little more than piecing together a "beggarly account of scraps and fragments".

Roman Law, to which the phrase quasi-delict owed its origin, unfortunately leaves us in some obscurity as to its exact basis. Four cases of it are mentioned in Justinian's *Institutes*, and Professor Buckland has pointed out that the common quality of these is uncertain, but that they were, at any rate, all instances of vicarious liability.[1]

Quasi-delict appears pretty early in our law in the *De legibus Angliae* of Bracton, but his treatment of it may be dismissed as the importation of an exotic which instantly withered on English soil. In classifying obligations, he includes those "quasi ex maleficio, ut si judex scienter male judicaverit", and he adds that the liability of the *judex* is reckoned as such because, though it does not arise from contract, yet he is deemed to have erred in some respect, even though by inadvertence.[2]

---

[1] *Text-Book of Roman Law* (1921) 594. In Roman-Dutch Law, Professor Lee regards their common link as "absolute liability", i.e. "cases in which the law draws an irrebuttable inference of culpa and of consequent liability". *Introduction to Roman-Dutch Law* (2nd ed. 1925), 307.

[2] Fol. 99.

TORT AND QUASI-DELICT 209

This is a direct borrowing from Justinian's *Institutes*.[1] Shortly afterwards, Bracton speaks of actions which spring "quasi ex maleficio" in that they do not relate to agreements, nor strictly to delicts, but resemble delicts more than contracts.[2] This is all that Bracton says of quasi-delict. It corresponded to nothing real in our law and it was dropped by those who compiled the epitomes of the *De legibus Angliae* known as Britton and Fleta. Succeeding centuries saw no trace of its influence, except perhaps in the liability of the master of a merchant ship to the merchant and passengers for the torts of the crew.[3] If we turn to the law reports, references to quasi-delict are very uncommon. Lindley L.J. in 1895 thought that quasi-torts existed in English law, but he did not specify what they are.[4] In 1916, Phillimore L.J. made the rather fantastic suggestion that, while liability for breach of promise of marriage should be regarded as contractual, the exemplary damages recoverable in the action for such breach should be considered as arising out of quasi-tort.[5] There are no doubt other *dicta* of judges on the topic, but we do not know any machinery for discovering them except casual reading or examination of all the reports, for "quasi-delict" and "quasi-tort" are non-existent in the indexes to the reports, or, for that matter, in law dictionaries. In any event, we can set aside House of Lords cases in which the term appears in appeals from the Scottish Courts. In Scots law, delict signifies an offence committed with an injurious, fraudulent or criminal purpose, while quasi-delict implies gross negligence or imprudence which is not fraudulent, malicious or criminal;[6] or, as

[1] *Inst.* 3.13.2; 4.5 pr.
[2] Fol. 103. Cf. Maitland, *Bracton and Azo* (1894), 141, 177.
[3] Holdsworth, *History of English Law*, viii, 250.
[4] *Taylor* v. *M.S. & L.R. Co.* [1895] 1 Q.B. 134, 138.
[5] *Quirk* v. *Thomas* [1916] 1 K.B. 516, 533.
[6] Bell, *Principles of the Law of Scotland* (10th ed. 1899) §§ 543, 553.

WP   14

210 TORT AND QUASI-DELICT

has been said by Lord Watson, delicts proper embrace all breaches of the law which expose their perpetrators to criminal punishment, while quasi-delict is generally applied to any violation of the common or statute law, which does not infer criminal consequences, and which does not consist in any breach of contract, express or implied.[1]

Nor do writers on jurisprudence take any appreciable account of quasi-delict in English law. Where they do not contemptuously reject the term (as John Austin did), they are content to reproduce the Roman Law relating to it. Exceptionally, Street makes the distinction between delict and quasi-delict correspond, for modern purposes, to that between act and omission. "In delict, or tort proper, we should say, liability is founded upon the doing of a positive injurious act. In quasi-delict liability results from omissive breach of duty." And he gives as examples the unjustified refusal of an innkeeper to entertain a wayfarer, or of a common carrier to convey a passenger or his goods; and "a considerable part of the law of negligence".[2] But Street made no further development of quasi-delict, and, indeed, his later treatment of the very examples which he gives is inconsistent, for it is so framed as to connect them with "quasi-assumptual obligation", the definition of which includes "positive obligations" as well as negative ones.[3]

Of periodical literature on the subject, we are also almost totally destitute. An important exception is an article by Professor Nathan Isaacs in the *Yale Law Journal* on *Quasi-delict in Anglo-American Law*[4] in which he has given much careful consideration to the topic.

[1] *Palmer* v. *Wick, etc. Shipping Co. Ld.* [1894] A.C. 318, 326.
[2] *Foundations of Legal Liability* (1906), vol. i, Introd. xxvi, note 2.
[3] *Op. cit.* vol. ii, 236.
[4] 31 *Yale Law Journal* (1922), 571–581.

TORT AND QUASI-DELICT

He points out that, if we follow the school of thought which seeks to find a foundation for the law of tort in the presence of some wrongful state of mind on the part of the defendant, we encounter the difficulty that the formula "no responsibility without fault" will not apply to many acts and omissions which are reckoned as torts and which it is neither customary nor even possible to separate entirely from that branch of the law. Moreover, this difficulty has been aggravated by the increase during the latter part of the nineteenth century of torts in which liability without fault is conspicuous.[1]

For these anomalous cases he regards quasi-delict as an appropriate term, and he reduces them to three varieties, with the necessary warning that such classification must depend on the particular definition of tort which happens to be adopted by the reader.[2]

(1) The main head is that of harms inflicted otherwise than through breach of contract or through tort, for which restitution is none the less required by law on equitable grounds. This would include all cases of strict liability[3] and of vicarious liability. Two other examples given are equitable waste and trespass *ab initio*. On the definition of tort which we have adopted[4] the duty not to commit waste is not towards persons generally, and the analogy borne by waste to a tort is thus fainter than that borne by strict liability and vicarious responsibility. Perhaps, then, it might be better classified not as a quasi-delict, but as liability arising from agreement between the parties (or their predecessors in title), with respect to the property wasted. And trespass *ab initio* is not so entirely free from fault on the part of the

---

[1] 31 *Yale Law Journal* (1922).   [2] *Ibid.* 576.

[3] Professor Isaacs styles it "absolute" liability. We have tried to shew elsewhere that this term is infelicitous, and that there is no such thing as "absolute" liability. Moreover, it is doubtful whether it ever has existed in English law. 42 *Law Quarterly Review* (1926), 37–51.

[4] *Ante*, p. 32.

212   TORT AND QUASI-DELICT

defendant as to make it detachable from the law of tort, even on the "no responsibility without fault" hypothesis. True, the doctrine of trespass *ab initio* makes a man retrospectively liable for a wrong to possession of land, though in fact he had committed no wrong whatever until he abused his right, but still that retrospective liability would never have come into existence if he had not abused his right, i.e. if he had not done some intentionally wrongful act which vitiated his right from the very beginning. Moreover, the doctrine is an archaic survival which we have grown so accustomed to regard as an incident in expounding trespass that, on the score of convenience, it had better be left there.

(2) Statutory liability sounding in tort. This, says Professor Isaacs, must be distinguished from liability arising from true statutory torts. His examples of quasi-delicts of this sort are:

(i) Liability for a dog not known to be vicious. For the purposes of English law, this presumably refers to the Dogs Act, 1906, sect. (1) of which makes the owner of a dog liable for injury done by his dog to cattle, irrespective of whether he knew of any previous mischievous propensity of the dog or whether he were negligent or not. This seems to be merely a species of the strict liability referred to in (1).

(ii) Sale of goods in bulk which the law adjudges to be in fraud of creditors, though no fraud is in fact perpetrated. Here, again, we must seek for our own illustration in English law, and it is to be found in the law of bankruptcy.[1] The avoidance of such transfers of property seems to be placed quite as well on quasi-contractual grounds as on quasi-delict.

(iii) Constructive notice may indirectly impose quasi-delictal liability on one who acted without actual notice of the situation, and thereby unintentionally caused an

[1] Williams, *Bankruptcy* (13th ed. 1925), 14–15.

TORT AND QUASI-DELICT 213

injury. The learned author gives no further details as to this, and, as the doctrine of constructive notice has nearly a dozen different applications in English law, some of which have no likeness to the law of tort, it is not possible to accept this example without more knowledge of what it implies.

(iv) Statutes creating penalties, in so far as liability flows to one who has suffered no harm, e.g. where an informer can sue for the penalty. But, with us, this kind of liability belongs rather to public law than to private law.

(3) Waiver of contract and suing in tort. This heading is not very acceptable to a modern English lawyer. Professor Isaacs refers to it "standardized contracts", such as those with a banker, a carrier, or a warehouseman, which constitute relationships independent of contract.

We therefore proceed as if such a relation as that of passenger and carrier, or of shipper and carrier, or of depositor and banker resulted from contract, but constituted a fact in itself independent of contract, much as marriage, whether resulting from a contract or not, constitutes a relationship free from the ordinary incidents of contract. Just as the husband owes certain duties to his wife which we hardly think of as contractual duties, so the banker, carrier, warehouseman, and a host of others owe duties to us by virtue of their relation to us. Hence we sue them in tort without reference to the contract for failure to perform these seemingly non-contractual duties.[1]

The following English authorities are cited. In *Marzetti* v. *Williams*,[2] a banker was held liable for dishonouring the cheque of a customer when he had sufficient money in the customer's account to meet the cheque. The court deemed it immaterial whether the plaintiff framed his declaration in contract or in tort.

---

[1] 31 *Yale Law Journal*, 578.   [2] (1830) 1 B. & Ad. 415.

214 TORT AND QUASI-DELICT

Weall v. *King*[1] and *Green* v. *Greenbank*[2] related to the liability of a warrantor on sale for deceit. All three cases have been treated earlier in these lectures[3] and further details of the decisions in them need not be repeated. It is submitted that the true explanation of them is given there. After stripping them of their procedural shell, it appears that the same set of facts might give rise to alternative remedies in contract and in tort. If this be so, it is unnecessary to borrow the head of quasi-delict in order to account for them, and it is difficult to accede to Professor Isaacs' statement that "in all these cases, we must bear in mind that although the action sounds in tort, we have no true tort". It does not follow that, because the ramifications of a standardized contract are extensive, they either cease to be terms in the contract, or that the breach of them cannot give rise to alternative liability in tort. If a railway company negligently injures my luggage, I can sue them either for breach of a term in their contract of carriage or for the tort of negligence, and it seems merely to complicate matters if we pray in aid such a disputable term as quasi-delict. Professor Isaacs rightly points to the historical confusion caused by the curious development of *assumpsit*. We have already examined this in some detail on our own account, but we do not gather from it that the English courts ever found refuge from the confusion in the blessed words "quasi-delict" or "quasi-tort". If these phrases helped no one in time past to explain standardized contracts, there is still less reason for using them at the present day as a compartment for such contracts.[4] Finally, this third head of quasi-delict has no link, except the mere name, with the first two heads, which are affiliated to the idea that there can be

---

[1] (1810) 12 East, 452.
[2] (1816) 2 Marshall, 485. [3] *Ante*, pp. 67–68, 79–80.
[4] Cf. Salmond, *Law of Torts* (7th ed. 1928), pp. 5–6.

TORT AND QUASI-DELICT 215

tortious liability without fault. It is somewhat discon-
certing for a banker who has forgotten the amount
which stands to his customer's credit to find himself
bracketed with a man whose dog has bitten a sheep.

The genuine instances of quasi-delict would seem,
therefore, to be reducible to (*a*) strict liability, and
(*b*) vicarious responsibility. Strict liability is a strong
illustration of it, for there a man may be held liable not
only in the absence of intention or of inadvertence[1] on
his own part, not only for the misdoings of his servants,
but also for the wrongs of an independent contractor, a
person over whom he has no control whatever so far as
the details of executing the contract go. Vicarious responsibility does not go quite this length, but it goes
far enough. It is best illustrated by the liability of an
employer for the torts of his servant. Here, it is common
knowledge that, provided the tort is committed in the
course of employment, the employer is liable even if he
has expressly forbidden the particular misconduct of
the servant of which complaint is made.[2] His personal
intention or inadvertence is beside the mark. The
"course of employment" is determined by the courts
irrespectively of either. Yet the analogy to tort holds in
all other respects, and that would justify the use of
"quasi-delict" or "quasi-tort" to describe the employer's liability.

So far we have taken Professor Isaacs on his own
ground. The main plinth of his argument appears to be
an acceptance of the theory "no responsibility without
fault" as the basis of genuine liability in tort, and upon
that he builds a very reasonable theory of quasi-delict
in order to find a shelter for breaches of law which are
commonly treated as torts, but which exhibit responsi-

[1] But some of the exceptions to the rule in *Rylands* v. *Fletcher* seem to
turn upon absence of inadvertence. *Post*, chap. xii, p. 244.
[2] *Limpus* v. *L.G.O. Co.* (1862) 1 H. & C. 526.

216 TORT AND QUASI-DELICT

bility even where there is no fault.[1] Whether, on practical grounds, it is worth while to create a sub-department of the law, and to baptize it with an unfamiliar term, is a disputable matter. Even if the balance of opinion welcomed the change, it would not release anyone who contemplates writing a book on the Law of Tort from including in it the law relating to strict liability or the general principles of vicarious responsibility, though the Workmen's Compensation Acts could—indeed must be—omitted.

A more vital objection to making quasi-delict an independent head of the law is this. Is it really possible or practicable to make the formula "no responsibility without fault" an integral factor in describing liability in tort? Professor Isaacs freely admits that what we include in quasi-delict must depend largely on how we define tort. That opens the door to our own definition of tort, which, it will be recollected, is silent as to mental culpability on the part of the tort-feasor. So far, then, we should have some excuse for putting aside quasi-delict altogether. But, as we have not the hardihood to regard the definition as canonical, we must suppose that there are some other analyses of tort which make "no liability without fault" an essential ingredient. On the English side of the Atlantic they are so rare as to be beyond our ken. And it must be confessed that there is nothing in the history of the law of tort or in its condition at the present day to warrant any incorporation of the mental element in a definition of it. It has never been admitted in time past, nor is it now the fact, that a universal element in tortious liability is intention or inadvertence. Far from it, the pendulum has occasionally swung so much the other way as to lead some writers

---

[1] Sir Frederick Pollock regards quasi-delict as both significant and appropriate to an owner's liability for the safe keeping of dangerous things. *Essays in Jurisprudence and Ethics* (1882), 17.

TORT AND QUASI-DELICT 217

to assert that in mediaeval, and even in later, law a man acted "at his peril". But this, it is submitted, is just as much an overstatement in one direction as "no liability without fault" is in the other.[1] It may not be easy to mark the boundaries that lie between tort and other species of liability, but it is possible to achieve this without reference to any mental element. That is no part of the external wall which separates tort from breach of contract, crime, or any of the other topics which have been handled in these lectures. In the region within the wall, the investigation of it is both necessary and helpful. It is important to know that assault and battery cannot be committed unintentionally, and that intention or inadvertence is (or is said to be) immaterial in some torts of strict liability; but that is not a valid reason for putting assault and battery inside the wall and torts of strict liability outside it. Criminal law affords an instructive parallel here. No definition of crime in current textbooks on English criminal law takes account of the mental attitude of the wrongdoer. Yet *mens rea* is always the subject of careful examination for the purpose of distinguishing various kinds of criminal liability. And there is a strong resemblance between some offences in which statutes have made it a matter of indifference whether any mental element accompanies the act or omission, and strict liability in tort. Yet no one has urged that they should be segregated and styled "quasi-crimes".

It is worthy of note that Dean Pound, although he is of opinion that the theory of liability for nothing except culpable damage had much influence in Anglo-American law during the last half of the nineteenth century,[2] nevertheless holds that the generalization of "no liability without fault" was "never adequate to explain

[1] 42 *Law Quarterly Review* (1926), 37–51.
[2] *Introduction to the Philosophy of Law* (1922), 162.

218 TORT AND QUASI-DELICT

all the phenomena of liability for tort in the common law".[1]

Various reasons have been advanced for the fact that quasi-delict is unknown in English law. So far as the duties imposed by law on the innkeeper and the common carrier are concerned, Sir William Holdsworth thinks that they might have been classed as quasi-tortious but for the fact that *assumpsit* was wide enough to embrace them.[2] Professor Isaacs, who gives quasi-delict a wider meaning, naturally adds several other causes for the neglect of the term in Anglo-American law. One of these is that

so long as every type of tort stood on its own bottom, so long as it was deemed useless to formulate a uniform law of torts, there was no particular reason for isolating the law of trespass or the law of trover or the law of libel or the law of slander, those instances in which an action traditionally lay in spite of the absence of elements generally present in torts.[3]

And his epitome of this paragraph is that quasi-delict is unknown in our law because hitherto there has been no need of it. We would respectfully add that there is no need of it now.

[1] *Interpretations of Legal History* (1923), 35.
[2] *History of English Law*, viii, 89.
[3] 31 *Yale Law Journal*, 580–581.

Chapter XI

STATUTES OF LIMITATIONS, AND JUDGMENT

THESE topics deserve a separate chapter for several reasons. First, there is scarcely any available literature on them in connection with the subject of these lectures. Secondly, they are rather wider in their application than would justify their treatment as a mere incident in the discussion of the relations between tort and contract. Thirdly, it is suggested that there are broad principles which will cover the relations of tort, not only to contract, but to several other branches of the law as well.

The problem is this. Where there are variant periods of limitation for barring different kinds of action (or different claims in the same action), between the same plaintiff and defendant, which period is the defendant entitled to plead? Facts which constitute a tort may also constitute a breach of contract, or a breach of bailment, or a quasi-contractual claim, or an injury to property, or a breach of trust. What is the position of a plaintiff whose claim is alive under one of the heads of the law and dead under another?

In the first place, the statutes themselves must be consulted. It must not be hastily inferred that no question at all arises if the periods of limitation be alike in any two departments of the law, for it does not follow that the rules for ascertaining the moment at which the period begins to run will necessarily be the same.

The principal statute relevant to simple contracts and to tort is the Statute of Limitations, 1623–1624 (21 Jac. I, c. 16, s. 3). Its effect, as amended by the

220   STATUTES OF LIMITATIONS

Mercantile Law Amendment Act, 1856, is that all actions on the case (except slander), actions of account, of trespass *quare clausum fregit*, of debt upon loan or contract without specialty, of debt for arrears of rent, of detinue, of trover, and replevin, must be brought within six years; actions of assault, battery, wounding and imprisonment within four years after the cause of action has arisen; and actions of slander within two years next after the words spoken. The reforms made by the Judicature Act, 1873, did not affect the Act of James I. One result of them was to alter in some measure the nomenclature of actions, but the Statute of Limitations still applies to the circumstances which constituted the actions named in it.[1] The Act of 1623–1624 says nothing of *assumpsit*, but it was held that both it and *indebitatus assumpsit* came within the equity of it.[2] This equates a large body of the claims on quasi-contract to claims on a simple contract, at any rate so far as the number of years goes; for *indebitatus assumpsit* was the remedy for most of the cases of genuine quasi-contract. Further, it will be seen from the express words of the statute that six years is the period not only for all simple contracts but also for most torts. That removes many possibilities of conflict where a plaintiff, on the same set of facts,[3] has alternative claims in tort, in contract, or in quasi-contract, but it does not remove every such possibility. The period for assault, battery, wounding, and imprisonment is four years. Suppose that conduct of the defendant which is any one of these torts is presumptively negatived (so far as the law allows such negation at all), by a contract with the plaintiff, as in

---

[1] *Per* Brett L.J. in *Gibbs* v. *Guild* (1882) 9 Q.B.D. 59, 67.

[2] *Roche* v. *Hepman* (1729) 1 Barnardiston, 172. *Chandler* v. *Vilet* (undated) 2 Wms Saund. (ed. 1871) 391. Cf. *In re Mason* [1928] Ch. 385, 393–394.

[3] It is important to emphasize this. E.g. the facts were not the same in *Gloucestershire Banking Co.* v. *Edwards* (1887) 19 Q.B.D. 575.

AND JUDGMENT 221

medical or quasi-parental restraint, or in lawful games, and that the plaintiff sues more than four, but less than six, years after the perpetration of an injury which he alleges goes outside the contract. Is the defendant entitled to plead that the action is statute-barred? There is no direct authority in answer to this, and indeed it is unlikely that, as a matter of tactics, the plaintiff would go to law at all upon such a stale grievance;[1] but if he did, it might be urged that the defendant's plea ought to be bad because, when parties have fixed their relations to each other by a lawful contract, a claim upon it ought not to be transferred, for the benefit of the defendant, to another branch of the law under which it would have fallen if there had been no contract. The defendant's liability here is certainly of longer duration in contract than in tort, but it might be said that he had brought it upon himself, and that if he chose to make a contract, he must take its usual legal consequences, one of which is that a right of action on a simple contract is not barred until six years have elapsed. But it may be doubted whether this line of argument goes to the root of the matter. A better test is "What was the substantial cause of the action?" If it was tort, then the tort period of limitation ought to apply; if it was contract, then six years would be allowable. A decision from which this test may be inferred is *Howell* v. *Young*.[2] The plaintiff had employed the defendant, an attorney, to ascertain the sufficiency of certain securities upon which the plaintiff proposed to lend money to X. He sued the defendant for negligent misrepresentation as to the value

[1] Note that staleness of demand, as distinguished from the Statute of Limitations and analogy to it, may furnish a defence *in Equity* to an equitable claim: *per* Lindley J. *In re Sharpe* [1892] 1 Ch. 154, 168. For laches as an equitable defence, see 13 *Laws of England* (Halsbury) §§ 203 *seq.*

[2] (1826) 5 B. & C. 259. See too *Brown* v. *Howard* (1820) 2 B. & B. 73.

222 STATUTES OF LIMITATIONS

of the securities. The action appears to have been framed alternatively in *assumpsit* (contract) or upon the case for negligence (tort). It was argued that if it were the former then the period of limitation ran from the moment at which the breach of contract took place, but that if it were the latter then from the moment that the damage occurred. It was held that the only question was "What cause of action did the declaration disclose?" Here the negligence of the attorney was the gist of the action and it mattered nothing whether the plaintiff elected to sue in tort or upon the contract. The time must be reckoned as commencing from the date of the occurrence of the negligence and not from the date of the accrual of the damage. The actual *decision*, then, was that whether negligence is sued upon as a tort or as a breach of a co-existent contract, the accrual of the cause of action is at the moment at which the negligence was committed, not that at which the damage arose. Beyond that it did not go. But the reasoning in the decision seems to indicate that the test for settling which of two competing periods of time ought to be adopted is "What is the substantial cause of action?" And Bayley J's touchstone for determining substantiality may be paraphrased in this way. If all reference to one cause of action were omitted from the declaration, would there still be enough left to support the other cause of action?[1] It is conceivable that *both* causes of action may be substantial. At any rate nothing is said in *Howell* v. *Young* in negation of this possibility. In the problem which we put with respect to assault, battery, and false imprisonment overlapping with contract, more would have to be known of the facts, and variant cases would have to be taken on their own merits. If the gist of the action were tort, then the four years period would apply; if it were breach of contract, then

[1] At pp. 263–264.

AND JUDGMENT 223

the six years period. If it were as substantial a claim in contract as in tort, then the plaintiff ought not to be deprived of the longer period; indeed it is difficult to see how he could be thus deprived without altering the Statute of Limitations by judicial legislation. Suppose a patient were kept unjustifiably in detention in a private hospital into which he had contracted to go until he was cured, and he sued an action for false imprisonment against the proprietor of the hospital five years after the detention had ceased; is his claim substantially in tort or on contract? It would appear to be on both. If so, the action is not repelled by a mere plea of the Statute of Limitations, whatever may be its fate on other grounds.

Similar problems may be imagined on other discrepant periods of limitation. The time for a contract under seal is twenty years.[1] Such contracts are repeatedly made by corporations. Assume that a corporation commits the tort of negligence in the execution of such a contract. Is the period within which the action must be brought twenty years or six years? Here the plaintiff might well come into court without creating an unfavourable atmosphere that he had slept upon his rights, for, as noted above, in negligence the period runs from the date of the negligent act or omission and not from the date of the damage, and he may have perceived nothing of the latter until long after the former had been perpetrated. Again, it is suggested, the test of substantiality ought to be applied.

Take again nuisance as a tort. Six years is the span within which the action for damages for it is maintainable. Is this prolonged to twenty years by a covenant under seal with the plaintiff, an adjacent owner, that the defendant will not create or suffer any nuisance on the premises which he occupies? Yes, according to one writer; but the authority cited in support of the opinion

[1] 3 & 4 Will. IV c. 42 s. 3.

224 STATUTES OF LIMITATIONS

is wide of the mark, and there is no discussion of principle which, we contend, ought to be that which is stated above.[1]

Another aspect of the same problem arises where the plaintiff waives a tort and sues in contract. This has been the subject of some litigation in the United States in jurisdictions where the statutes of limitation prescribe a shorter period for tort than for contract or *assumpsit*, and the longer period has been regarded as that applicable.[2] The general principle laid down was that "the statute of limitations applicable depends upon the nature and character of the action, and not upon its form."[3] This appears to be sound enough, and it might well be the rule in English law, though no direct authority on the point is traceable. It amounts in effect to the principle of substantiality already considered. There has been copious litigation on the particular moment at which the Statute of Limitations begins to run in claims of a quasi-contractual nature, such as those for money had and received and actions by co-sureties against one another, but none of it is of practical help in the present discussion.[4]

Nor is any direct decision discoverable on the period of limitation where the plaintiff waives a tort and sues in quasi-contract. There is some show of authority for the proposition that if trover be waived and an action for money had and received be sued, the time runs from the conversion, and not from the moment of receiving the money.[5]

[1] Banning, *Limitation of Actions* (3rd ed. 1906), 73.
[2] Keener, *Quasi-Contracts* (1893) 195, note 2. Cf. Woodward, *Quasi contracts* (1913), § 294.
[3] *Kirkman* v. *Phillips* (1872) 7 Heisk. 222.
[4] The cases are collected in 32 *English and Empire Digest* (1927) Limitation of Actions, 328 *seq*. See too 41 *Harvard Law Review* (1928), 1051–1055.
[5] *Denys* v. *Shuckburgh* (1840) 4 Y. & C. 42, 48.

AND JUDGMENT 225

Where bailment and contract co-exist, it is conceived that if the plaintiff frames his action on contract, the usual period of six years applies. That would be the same if he were to sue in tort, but detinue runs only from the date of demand for, and refusal of, return of the goods bailed.[1] What is the position where a breach of trust which is also a tort has been committed? A trustee's wrong-doing may often answer the description of the tort of negligence, or of conversion, or of deceit. The law as to limitation of actions against trustees is contained in the Trustee Act, 1888, which modified the old rule that a claim against an express trustee for breach of trust could not be barred by mere lapse of time. Sect 8 of the Act provides that all rights and privileges conferred by any Statute of Limitations shall apply as if the trustee or person claiming through him had not been a trustee or person claiming through him, and that if the action or other proceeding is brought to recover money or other property and is one to which no existing Statute of Limitations applies, the trustee can plead lapse of time in like manner and to the like extent as if the claim had been against him in an action of debt for money had and received. The Act does not apply where the claim (i) is founded on any fraud or fraudulent breach of trust to which the trustee was a party, or (ii) is to recover trust property, or the proceeds thereof, still retained by the trustee, or (iii) is to recover trust property, or the proceeds thereof, previously received by the trustee and converted to his own use. The section applies to constructive, as well as express, trustees. Apart from the exceptions mentioned, the Act covers cases in which the relief sought against the trustee is in the nature of damages for breach of duty by him in the conduct of the trust, e.g. for loss arising from his negligence.[2]

[1] *Wilkinson* v. *Verity* (1871) L.R. 6 C.P. 206.
[2] Lewin, *Trusts* (13th ed. 1928) 918, 919–920.

226 STATUTES OF LIMITATIONS

The trustee is entitled to the protection of the several Statutes of Limitations as if the actions or proceedings for breaches of trust were mentioned in them.[1]

If, then, an action for negligence be brought against a trustee, it is immaterial from the point of view of limitation whether the plaintiff sue as for a pure tort or as for a breach of trust. The defendant can plead the Act of 1623–1624 and the period will be six years either way.[2] If the action were for deceit or for conversion, then the older law applies and no Statute of Limitations helps the trustee. Of course if the plaintiff knows the defendant to be a trustee, he would not be so foolish as to sue him otherwise than as a trustee, but if the trustee were only a constructive one, he might turn out to be so only after an action of this kind had been commenced; in that event he cannot have the benefit of the Act of 1888, and he loses the advantage of pleading the ordinary period of limitation for deceit or conversion, which would have been open to him if it had never appeared that he was a trustee. We can deduce this from *In re Exchange Banking Co.*,[3] which was decided before the Act of 1888. It was held that directors who had committed a breach of trust could not plead the Statute of Limitations, for their conduct was impeached as a breach of trust and not as a tort, though they had certainly committed negligence, if not actual fraud.

Where the Trustee Act, 1888, does apply in the trustee's favour, it may be a question as to which of the various Statutes of Limitations ought to apply. Thus, if he undertook his trust by virtue of a covenant under seal, and he be sued for negligence, the period appropriate would presumably be that fixed for a contract under seal.[4]

---

[1] *How* v. *Winterton* [1896] 2 Ch. 626.
[2] See *In re Bowden* (1890) 45 Ch. D. 444.
[3] (1882) 21 Ch. D. 519.
[4] *How* v. *Winterton* [1896] 2 Ch. 626, 642.

AND JUDGMENT

As to actions for the recovery of land, there does not seem to be much probability of any difficulty arising from their coincidence with remedies in tort. The question of title to land might be raised incidentally in an action for trespass done to it. Under the Statute of 1623–1624, trespass *quare clausum fregit* is barred after six years, while under the Real Property Limitation Act, 1874, s. 51, an action to recover land is kept alive for twelve years. There can be no doubt that the longer period should be allowed where title comes in question in an action of trespass. The substance of the claim is the recovery of the land and it is the trespass that becomes of secondary importance in the primary point at issue, which is "Who was entitled to the land?".[1]

To sum up, it would appear that where disparate periods of limitation apply to claims founded alternatively on tort, contract, quasi-contract, bailment, breach of trust or ownership, the question as to which period is to be selected ought to be determined by settling which is the substantial claim, and that where several or all of the claims are equally substantial the plaintiff can rely upon that one which puts him in the most favourable position under the Statutes of Limitations. Mere juggling with procedure on the part of either plaintiff or defendant is just as likely to be discouraged by the courts in this connection as in any other part of the borderland between tort and other provinces of the law. As was said by a great master of the Common Law, the substance of the matter is to be looked at, and the foundation of an action consists in those facts which it is necessary to state and prove in order to maintain it, and in no others.[2] This may look like a truism, but it is one

---

[1] Cf. *Keyse* v. *Powell* (1853) 2 E. & B. 132. Darby and Bosanquet, *op. cit.* 298–299, 545.

[2] Bramwell L.J. in *Bryant* v. *Herbert* (1878) 3 C.P.D. 389, 390. So too A. L. Smith L.J. in *Turner* v. *Stallibrass* [1898] 1 Q.B. 56, 58.

15-2

228   STATUTES OF LIMITATIONS

that has not always been given sufficient prominence in the very scanty literature on the subject of this chapter.

There is, of course, no connection between the respective effects of statutes of limitations and of judgment on alternative claims, but judgment may be conveniently dealt with here. If a plaintiff sues upon one of two alternative claims grounded upon the same facts, and judgment is given in that action, can he afterwards pursue the other claim in a second action? The answer to this depends upon the rules as to *res judicata*. In general, judgment in the one action will prevent any later action. *Nemo debet bis vexari pro eadem causa.* If the same facts have given rise to substantially one and the same ground of complaint, no further action can be brought, and this is so even though there are technical and formal differences between the two causes of action, or the two remedies have different names. Unless the causes of action are essentially separable, judgment upon the one bars the other. There is no positive law (except so far as the County Court Acts have from an early date dealt with the matter) against splitting demands which are essentially separable; but the High Court has inherent powers to prevent vexation or oppression, and, by staying proceedings or by apportioning the costs it has always ample means of preventing any injustice arising out of the reckless use of legal procedure.[1]

It has been held that a plaintiff who elected to sue in trover for the value of his goods at the time they were wrongfully sold by X, and who had recovered judgment against X, could not afterwards sue Y, who had received the proceeds of the sale, for money had and received.[2] Modern examples of the principle seem to be scarce.[3]

---

[1] *Per* Bowen L.J. in *Brunsden* v. *Humphreys* (1884) 14 Q.B.D. 141, 151.

[2] *Buckland* v. *Johnson* (1854) 15 C.B. 145.

[3] See Spencer Bower, *Res Judicata* (1924), §§ 327–332. As to conduct amounting to election between contract and tort, see *Valpy* v. *Sanders* (1848) 5 C.B. 886, and cases therein cited. For election between tort and quasi-contract see *ante*, p. 176.

Chapter XII

OTHER DEFINITIONS OF TORT

BEFORE other definitions of tort are considered, a few comments on the one proffered in these lectures are necessary. It was stated that "tortious liability arises from the breach of a duty primarily fixed by the law: such duty is towards persons generally and its breach is redressible by an action for unliquidated damages".[1]

The words "primarily fixed by the law" serve to distinguish liability in tort from that arising on breach of contract,[2] and from breach of bailment.[3]

The statement that the duty is "towards persons generally" marks off tort from contract,[4] bailment,[5] and quasi-contract.[6] But, while this element in the definition is important and is sufficiently workable in the majority of cases, it must be admitted that the vagueness of it is open to objection. Every one would concede that the duty not to commit an assault, or a trespass, or a slander, is towards persons generally; and so with all torts that have acquired specific names. Every one, on the other hand, would classify a contract as setting up duties towards a specific person, or specific persons. It would be no real denial of this to urge that there is a legal duty on everybody to carry out his contracts, no matter with whom they are made, and that the duty is, in this sense, general. But this is merely a loose way of saying that when once I have entered into a contract with anyone I must fulfil it. There is no duty which the law will enforce unless and until such a contract is actually created

[1] *Ante*, p. 32. [2] *Ante*, p. 40.
[3] *Ante*, p. 99. [4] *Ante*, p. 40.
[5] *Ante*, p. 99. [6] *Ante*, p. 188.

230 OTHER DEFINITIONS OF TORT

with a definite person. You cannot get an injunction against me if, before I have contracted with you, I proclaim that I will not carry out any contract which I may make.

These examples, one on each side of the line, are plain enough; but troublesome intermediate cases are imaginable. Suppose that an Act of Parliament imposes upon X a duty towards the inhabitants of the parish of Y, a village with a population of twenty persons, and that breach of this duty is redressible by an action for unliquidated damages suable by any aggrieved inhabitant. The duty has every appearance of being one in tort except for the absurdity of describing it as being towards persons generally. The difficulty of course is that it is impossible to say accurately what the test of generality is, or who exactly are "persons generally". If we suggest that they are all members of the community who cannot, as parties to any legal relation, be identified individually at any particular moment while the legal relation subsists, we lay ourselves open to the criticism that the inhabitants of a parish as small as Y can easily be known at any particular moment, and that nevertheless any lawyer would describe X's liability to them as tortious. With a large city like London the practical difficulties of identifying the inhabitants at any given moment would be so great as to justify us in regarding them as "persons generally". But here the problem might recur in another form. The duty might be towards the mayor and corporation of a large town, and the artificial individual thus described would be ascertainable with even greater ease than the twenty inhabitants of Y. These instances must be deemed exceptional and not of sufficient weight to force us to sacrifice the ingredient of generality in the definition. After all, problems of exactly the same type arise in connection with the distinction between rights *in rem*

OTHER DEFINITIONS OF TORT 231

and rights *in personam*, and one of them was discussed in the chapter on Tort and Breach of Trust;[1] yet those terms are far too fundamental to be abandoned on that account.

The last requisite in the definition is that tort is remediable. by "an action for unliquidated damages". This distinguishes it from crime[2] and from breach of trust,[3] though, as has been already indicated, trusts are more conveniently separated from the law of tort by the historical gulf which lies between them and the Common Law rather than by the narrow line of a particular legal remedy. One example of judicial recognition of this factor of "damages" in tortious liability may be given. In *Hulton* v. *Hulton*,[4] a married woman brought an action against her husband for rescission of a deed on the ground of fraud. Now the Married Women's Property Act, 1882, s. 12, in general excludes husband and wife from suing each other in tort, and it was contended for the defence that this was an action in tort and was therefore not maintainable. The Court of Appeal, however, held that it was, because, though an action for damages for deceit would have been excluded by the statute as being an action in tort, yet an action for rescission of a deed was not of this nature.

Of course, an action for damages is not the only remedy for tort. Other remedies are self-help, injunctions, and actions for the specific restitution of property. The first and third of these are necessarily limited in scope and do not apply to all torts, but the second is more extensive than is commonly supposed. There are probably no torts which are not redressible by an injunction except assault and battery, false imprisonment, and malicious prosecution;[5] and, according to some authori-

---

[1] *Ante*, p. 111.   [2] *Ante*, p. 201.   [3] *Ante*, p. 112.
[4] [1917] 1 K.B. 813, 820, 822–823, 824.
[5] Maitland, *Equity* (1909), 261.

232   OTHER DEFINITIONS OF TORT

ties, even apprehended assault can be prevented in this way, though it is doubted whether the court would ever exercise its jurisdiction in such circumstances. More probably it would tell the complainant to go to the justices of the peace and ask them to bind over the defendant to keep the peace.[1] Moreover, it would not be correct to say that the difference between an action for damages on the one hand, and self-help and injunction on the other, lies in the fact that the former is the primary remedy for a tort while the latter are only secondary remedies. If X finds Y, a trespasser, in his rooms, he is entitled to eject Y with reasonable force then and there without waiting to bring an action at law against him. So with an injunction. If any practising lawyer were asked "What is the civil remedy for nuisance?" he would reply "An injunction", and he might add "and an action for damages". And precedents are to be found in books of pleading in which the first claim in an action in tort is for an injunction.[2] The real reason why an action for damages is one of the

[1] Clerk and Lindsell, *Torts* (8th ed. 1929), 716–717.

[2] Bullen and Leake, *Precedents of Pleadings* (8th ed. 1924), 204–205, 431. Odgers, *Pleading and Practice* (10th ed. 1930), Precedents Nos. 50, 58; pp. 437–438, 443–444. Historically, it is interesting to note that long before injunctions or Chancery jurisdiction were known, the courts could prevent various wrongs to property quite apart from awarding damages; Holdsworth, *History of English Law*, ii, 247–249. Further, the writ of waste and the writ of prohibition against waste were examples of claims in which recovery or restitution was more sought after than any claim for damages; Coke, 2 Inst. 299. And the writ of estrepement, which originally lay after judgment in a real action and before possession had been delivered by the sheriff, to stop the vanquished party from committing any contemplated waste, was emphatically not a claim for damages; Blackstone, *Commentaries*, iii, 225–226. These examples need not now trouble us, for they represent obsolete law; and, so far as waste is concerned, they could scarcely be put under tort, independently of the fact that the claim was not for damages, for waste is an infringement of a duty owed to a specific person, and not of a duty towards persons generally. It is nevertheless treated in several books on tort as if it were a tort.

OTHER DEFINITIONS OF TORT 233

touchstones of tort is not that it is a primary remedy, but that the possibility of suing it is fettered by none of the conditions which attach respectively to self-help and injunctions. The granting of an injunction is notoriously a matter for the discretion of the court, acting on well-settled legal principles.[1] Again, self-help has always been reckoned as a perilous remedy owing to the stringent rules against its abuse. But there are no restrictions on instituting an action for damages for tort except such as apply to vexatious civil procedure in general. Subject to them, the courts must at least hear what the plaintiff has got to say, even if they come to the conclusion that the defendant has, in the circumstances of the case, nothing to which he need answer.

We can now pass to other definitions of tort, and begin with the analysis of that *maître d'armes* of the Common Law, Sir Frederick Pollock. The following are the main points in it. A tort is a civil wrong; it is a breach of a duty which is a general one, i.e. which is owed either to all fellow-subjects, or to some considerable class of them; it is fixed by the law and the law alone; and it is redressible by an action.[2] It is obvious that our own definition owes a great deal to this analysis. Sir Frederick adds:

Again, the term (*sc.* tort) and its usage are derived wholly from the Superior Courts of Westminster as they existed before the Judicature Acts. Therefore, the law of Torts is necessarily confined by the limits within which those courts exercised their jurisdiction. Divers and weighty affairs of mankind have been dealt with by other courts in their own fashion of procedure and with their own terminology. These lie wholly outside the common law forms of action and all classifications founded upon them.[3]

Hence, unless an action were maintainable in the courts of King's Bench, Common Pleas, Exchequer (or

[1] Kerr, *Injunctions* (6th ed. 1927), chap. ii.
[2] *Torts* (13th ed. 1929), 1–3.   [3] *Ibid.* 5.

234 OTHER DEFINITIONS OF TORT

any one of them), as they existed before the Judicature Acts, it cannot be an action in tort. This rules out trusts, as they were within the province of the Court of Chancery; claims for salvage, which were appropriate to the Admiralty Courts; and matrimonial causes, which belonged to the old Ecclesiastical Courts and later to the Divorce Court.

It is very necessary that the historical side of the law of torts should be emphasized, and Sir Frederick Pollock shows clearly how the organization of our judicature on lines which have been simplified only within living memory has influenced the contents of this branch of the law. It might be argued, then, that our definition ought to conclude with "an action for unliquidated damages *in virtue of the Common Law jurisdiction of the court*". But, after some hesitation, it has been decided not to make this addition; for there are some qualifications upon it, even as a matter of history, which might make it misleading. Thus, it is true that during the greater part of our legal history breaches of trust could be redressed only in the Court of Chancery. Yet it seems that at one time a defaulting trustee could be sued for damages in the Common Law Courts, for breach of an implied contract. No doubt the courts were acting outside their sphere in entertaining such actions, but still they did exercise such jurisdiction once.[1] Again, no doubt at the date of the Judicature Acts an action for damages against the co-respondent in a divorce suit was maintainable only in the Divorce Court. It was not then, and it is not now, an action founded on tort. But, until 1857, it was represented by an action for criminal

---

[1] Lewin, *Law of Trusts* (12th ed.), 15 (this note has been omitted in the current edition). Pollock and Maitland, ii, 232. Spence, *Equitable Jurisdiction* (1846), i, 442, note (*c*); but his reference to Y.B. 4 Ed. IV, f. 8, does not support his statement that "feoffee to uses could maintain an action of trespass against his *cestui que trust*"; indeed, the case is the other way.

OTHER DEFINITIONS OF TORT 235

conversation which was suable in a Common Law Court. Nowadays, breach of trust and adultery by a co-respondent are better placed outside the pale of torts for other reasons—the former on grounds which have already been stated,[1] the latter because it is the breach of a duty towards a specific person, and not of one towards persons generally; for the claim upon it is merely ancillary to a claim which the injured party must make in the first instance against the adulterous spouse, i.e. the claim against the co-respondent is always tacked to the suit for divorce, and that suit is for breach of a duty owed only to the petitioner and not to persons generally. Again, other matters of ecclesiastical jurisdiction make the procedural test somewhat embarrassing. Before the Judicature Acts, at least one writer of respectable authority could see no reason why a wrong should not be a tort even if it were remediable only in an ecclesiastical court. He spoke of torts as either "temporal" or "ecclesiastical", examples of the latter being mere imputations of fornication, adultery, drunkenness, or other immorality, punishable only in the spiritual courts unless it could be averred and proved that actual temporal damage, such as loss of the society of one or more particular persons, had ensued.[2] Then the historical side of injunctions also makes the pro-

---

[1] *Ante*, pp. 113–115.

[2] Chitty, *Practice of the Law* (2nd ed. 1834), i, 13. In spite of the great dwindling of the civil jurisdiction of Ecclesiastical Courts in modern times, some civil actions are still cognizable there, e.g. those relating to the fabric and ornaments of the church, the churchyard and churchwardens. So far as can be ascertained, they lack one essential of actions in tort. They do not claim, or result in, pecuniary damages. The procedure for making good dilapidations resulted, apart from statute, in disciplinary measures only, and now under the Ecclesiastical Dilapidations Act, 1871, is so peculiar in the case of parochial clergy that it cannot be styled an action for unliquidated damages. Phillimore, *Ecclesiastical Law* (2nd ed. 1895), ii, 828, 959, 1254 *seq.*, 1271 *seq.* 11 *Laws of England* (Halsbury), §§ 985 *seq.*

236   OTHER DEFINITIONS OF TORT

cedural test an awkward one. It was possible at one time to sue for them only in the Court of Chancery. Such actions were therefore not founded on tort. But the Common Law Procedure Act, 1854, gave the Common Law Courts power to issue prohibitory injunctions at any stage of the proceedings, and now every Division of the High Court can grant an injunction. Bearing this in mind and also the fact that an injunction is often the primary remedy claimed for a tort, it would seem odd to define a tort by reference to a jurisdiction which once had no power to grant an injunction, but which in fact is now able to do so.

Take, again, Admiralty jurisdiction. Claims in respect of collision of ships are founded on tort, for though the cognizance of such cases was, and still is, exercisable by Admiralty Courts, yet it was, and still is, also exercisable by the Common Law Courts. In fact, until the law was altered by statute, the Common Law jurisdiction was wider than that of the Admiralty, for it extended everywhere, while in Admiralty it was confined to the high seas. Legislation has made Admiralty jurisdiction wider with respect to collisions, and it is the more popular of the two because of the advantages given by the process *in rem*. But the Common Law jurisdiction remains, and the same measure of damages is allowed in whichever court the action is brought. By the Supreme Court of Judicature (Consolidation) Act, 1925, the jurisdictional test of tort is made even more artificial. Sect. 22 gives the High Court "admiralty jurisdiction" over (*inter alia*) "any claim for damage done by a ship" and "any claim...in tort in respect of goods carried in a ship".

Enough has been said to shew that the inclusion in a definition of any reference to the Common Law jurisdiction of the court would not tend to greater clarity, however necessary it may be to explain the historical

OTHER DEFINITIONS OF TORT 237

anomalies which still appear in the fabric of the law of tort.

Sir John Salmond's definition, as slightly amended by his learned editor, Mr Stallybrass, who adds that no satisfactory definition of a tort has yet been found, is as follows:

A civil wrong for which the remedy is a *common law* action for *unliquidated* damages, and which is not exclusively the breach of a contract or the breach of a trust or other merely equitable obligation.[1]

The words italicized represent Mr Stallybrass's alterations. We have just shewn cause against the embodiment of the jurisdictional element in the definition. Further, it would appear possible to frame it less negatively than to say that a tort "is not exclusively the breach of a contract or the breach of a trust or other merely equitable obligation"

So far, the definitions considered have approached the topic from the starting-point of breach of duty. But others prefer to look upon tort as a breach of right. A definition which we have taught experimentally for several years and have abandoned with a good deal of reluctance is:

A tort is a civil wrong which infringes a right *in rem* and is remediable by an action for damages.

More briefly, but on the same lines, Sir Hugh Fraser, without committing himself to a definition, regarded the following as a good description for practical purposes:

A tort is an infringement of a general right or right *in rem*.[2]

The objections to these definitions are partly formal, partly substantial.

It may be said that the phrase "right *in rem*" is none

---

[1] *Torts* (7th ed. 1928), p. 7.

[2] *Torts* (11th ed. 1927), 1. So too Innes, *Torts* (1891), § 6. For other authors, see 30 *Harvard Law Review* (1917), 251, note 5.

238 OTHER DEFINITIONS OF TORT

too well-known in the law courts and has the prejudice of unfamiliarity against it. But there seems to be nothing in this criticism. While the terms used in definitions of legal topics ought not to be outlandish, there is a limit to the concessions which must be made to sheer conservatism, and, unless he has scamped his legal education, every practitioner must be well aware of the antithesis "right *in rem*—right *in personam*", though he might be excused for staring at "quasi-contract" and gasping at "quasi-delict". Perhaps a more valid formal objection is the tendency of legal classification to take as its basis duties in preference to rights.

On substantial grounds the difficulty is that, though the definition will cover most of the ground, yet it will not include some wrongs which are, or ought to be, reckoned as torts, but which are breaches of rights *in personam*. Such is the refusal of an innkeeper to receive a guest,[1] or of a common carrier to take goods for carriage.[2] My rights against such persons are rights *in personam*. They avail against specific persons, and not against persons generally, as do rights *in rem*. The difficulty does not arise if breach of duty is made the foundation of tortious liability, instead of breach of right. If torts be regarded as breaches of duties towards persons generally, then they include these refusals of the innkeeper and the common carrier.[3] Their duties might be styled "*in rem*", but the right of the prospective guest at the inn or of the prospective consignor of goods for carriage is not a right *in rem*.

Most other definitions of tort which bear any relation to the facts of English law[4] are variations of those

[1] Salmond, *Jurisprudence* (7th ed. 1924), § 169 (4).
[2] 30 *Harvard Law Review* (1917), 252.
[3] *Ante*, pp. 151 *seq.*
[4] Some of them bear very little; e.g. "Every person who on any occasion is required to use reasonable care and omits to use such reasonable care commits a tort". Markby, *Elements of Law* (6th ed. 1905),

OTHER DEFINITIONS OF TORT 239

which have been examined.[1] All of them are workable in practice, but with a certain amount of creaking which is incidental to our own definition quite as much as to them.

Other writers, however, take the Sadducean course of denying that it is possible to define tort at all. This pessimistic or negative school of thought includes scholars of considerable repute.[2] Their opinion is based on the assertion that there is no common affirmative characteristic which can be predicted of all torts.

The word "torts" is used in English law to cover a number of acts, having no quality which is at once common and distinctive.[3]

It is impossible to define the general term otherwise than by an enumeration of particulars...it is impossible to lay down any general principle to which all actions of tort may be referred.[4]

A tort, in English Law, can only be defined in terms which really tell us nothing....To put it briefly, there is no English Law of Tort; there is merely an English Law of Torts, i.e. a list of acts and omissions, which, in certain conditions, are actionable.[5]

These are fair specimens of this particular attitude towards the Law of Tort.

It may be said at once that we respectfully disagree

§ 715. The idea of a man omitting to use reasonable care when he seduces *A*'s daughter or calls *B* a swindler, knowing that *B* is an honest man, is grotesque.

[1] E.g. Clerk and Lindsell (8th ed. 1929), 1.

[2] Addison, *Torts* (8th ed. 1906), 1. Jenks in 30 *Harvard Law Review* (1916), 8–9; but editorially he accepts the definition of Sir John Miles in Jenks, *Digest of English Civil Law* (2nd ed. 1921), § 722. Markby, *Elements of Law* (6th ed. 1905), §§ 670, 713; but this did not prevent him from attempting the singular definition cited in the note, *supra*. For other writers who take the same view, see 30 *Harvard Law Review* (1917), 252–254.

[3] Markby, *op. cit.* § 713.

[4] Clerk and Lindsell, *op. cit.* 1, 3.

[5] Jenks, cited in 30 *Harvard Law Review* (1917), 253.

240 OTHER DEFINITIONS OF TORT

with the thesis that there is no English Law of Tort, but only an English Law of Torts, and that we have already given reasons for adopting a contrary view.[1] For the rest, it is not easy to understand this counsel of despondency. What ground is there for saying that the definition put forward in these lectures (which is substantially the same as that selected by many other authors) yields no common characteristic of torts? If it be applied to any of the nominate torts, where does it break down? As to innominate torts, i.e. those which are still in process of creation, or which are yet unborn, they depend on the principle that all harm done by a man to his fellow-subject is, in the absence of lawful justification, actionable. Of such wrongs it is impossible to prophesy exactly the detailed conditions subject to which the courts will allow redress, but why should it be denied that their broad outlines will conform to the general definition which has been adopted?

Probably two causes, neither of which is valid, have been responsible for the theory that definition of tort is impossible. The first is the tendency to speak of the law of tort in terms that would have been more appropriate two generations ago than now. If the historical sketch in an earlier chapter shewed anything, it was the late separation of the law of tort from other parts of the law. Until the net of procedure which enmeshed it had been cut by nineteenth-century legislation, nothing else could be expected. The important question for any plaintiff was "What action can I sue?" The number of actions was limited and the scope of several of them (e.g. *assumpsit*) took in claims which might equally well have been described as in contract or in tort. Hence, any attempt to define a tort must have been a cross-section through actions, the contents of which had scarcely been considered at all in scientific fashion. Even now we are

[1] *Ante*, pp. 32 *seq.*

OTHER DEFINITIONS OF TORT 241

not sufficiently liberated from these historical influences to ignore them in the law of tort, but we are free enough of them to make a tolerably correct definition of tort not only possible but also advisable. It is not without significance that in some of the treatises in which this is denied, modern editors merely continue to repeat opinions of their authors which had some weight seventy years ago, but which are obsolescent in the light of more recent developments.[1]

Secondly, some definitions of tort have been so negative in character as to justify the complaint that they afford no affirmative test. They tell us rather what a tort is not than what it is. "A favourite method of defining a Tort is to declare merely that it is not a contract. As if a man were to define Chemistry by pointing out that it is not Physics nor Mathematics!"[2]

However, there are many definitions which give positive tests, and there the objection fails.

We have been considering a theory which is really retrograde, chiefly because it has the dead hand of history upon it. We must now take account of one which is revolutionary. Like the first, it starts with the hypothesis that all existing definitions of tort are inadequate, but it does not stop there. It suggests that salvation can be found:

1. By discarding the former custom of grouping together under the general head of tort cases of liability without fault.

2. By recognizing the existence of the modern common law rule—that, generally, fault on the part of the defendant is requisite to constitute a tort. If this view is carried out to its logical result, the use of the term tort would be confined to cases of fault, and cases of liability without fault would be classed under the

[1] The first edition of Addison's *Torts* was published in 1860.
[2] Wigmore, *Select Cases on the Law of Torts* (1912), vol. i, Preface, vii.

WP   16

242 OTHER DEFINITIONS OF TORT

distinct head of absolute liability. Then it would be possible to state a common affirmative characteristic of actionable torts.[1]

Such was the line taken and pursued by Jeremiah Smith with his customary skill and energy in the *Harvard Law Review*.[2]

He explained "fault" in the expression "liability without fault" to mean "conduct which involves either culpable intention or culpable inadvertence",[3] and the main heads of his "absolute" (we prefer "strict"[4]) liability were:

Division 1. Cases of absolute liability which hitherto have usually been classed under tort. These include:

(*a*) Liability for non-culpable mistake.
(*b*) Liability for non-culpable accident.
(*c*) Vicarious liability for the wrongful acts of others.

Division 2. Cases of absolute liability which hitherto have been regarded as more nearly akin to breach of contract than to tort.[5] These are quasi-contractual in nature.[6]

Any suggestion originating from such a source deserves great respect. But, so far as current English law is concerned, we have put forward reasons in the chapter on Tort and Quasi-delict for thinking that the premises on which the theory is founded cannot be accepted. "Fault" has never been an essential ingredient in defining tort in English law.[7] Sometimes it is relevant to liability, sometimes (at least superficially)[8] it is not, but the contents of the law of tort have been determined without making the presence or absence of fault a prime factor. This, however, does not conclude the matter.

[1] 30 *Harvard Law Review* (1917), 254.
[2] "Tort and Absolute Liability", *ibid.* 241–262, 319–334, 409–429.
[3] *Ibid.* 259.
[4] Indeed, the learned author was not satisfied with the accuracy of "absolute". *Ibid.* 256.
[5] *Ibid.* 325.
[6] *Ibid.* 426.
[7] *Ante*, p. 216.
[8] *Post*, p. 243.

OTHER DEFINITIONS OF TORT 243

Jeremiah Smith was writing as a reformer and he admitted that he cherished no illusion as to the speedy adoption of any suggested changes of classification, though he said that some of them were based upon distinctions already recognized in some legal treatises.[1] We are therefore bound to estimate his suggestions without much regard to any jolt that they may give to established associations.

Division 2 had better be taken first, for it seems possible to dispose of it shortly by urging that Quasi-contract is almost sure to become a separate branch of English law and that the contents of it will probably be determined on the lines laid out in a previous chapter.[2]

The advisability of adopting Division 1 is somewhat doubtful from the teaching point of view. To separate torts of strict liability from other torts is not such a smooth affair as it might appear to be. At least two points need further explanation before a decision one way or the other is taken, and they both affect the proposed change at its very root, which is that strict liability depends on absence of fault, i.e. on absence of intention or inadvertence.

In the first place, all torts of strict liability do not exhibit the same degree of strictness. Thus, in the rule in *Rylands* v. *Fletcher*[3] the defendant is not allowed to plead that he took reasonable care to prevent the injury, but in the rule in *Indermaur* v. *Dames*,[4] the defendant is excused if he used reasonable care to prevent damage to the plaintiff from unusual danger of which he knows or ought to know; yet his duty is reckoned as a strict one, because he is liable for the default of an independent

[1] 30 *Harvard Law Review*, 241–242.
[2] *Ante*, chap. vii.
[3] (1868) L.R. 3 H.L. 330. Pollock, *Torts* (13th ed. 1929), 501 *seq.* Salmond, *Torts* (7th ed. 1928), § 88.
[4] (1866) L.R. 1 C.P. 274, 2 C.P. 311. Pollock, *op. cit.* 527 *seq.* Salmond, *op. cit.* § 122 (9).

244 OTHER DEFINITIONS OF TORT

contractor. Here, then, we have an example of strict liability which requires some sort of inadvertence on the part of the wrong-doer. Where is it to be classified under the new system? Is it to go under the ordinary law of tort or under the new department of the law which is to take in cases of strict liability?

Secondly, an equally puzzling question arises in connection with the rule in *Rylands* v. *Fletcher* itself. No stronger example of strict liability could be cited. Yet among the exceptions to the rule is the defence that the harm was caused by the act of a stranger. But that defence might just as well be described by saying that there is no inadvertence on the part of the defendant. If you state that John Smith is not liable for the act of William Jones, who, as a mere stranger, lets loose something of John Smith's which injures Henry Brown, you are in effect stating that John Smith is, in these circumstances, free from liability because there is neither unlawful intention nor unlawful inadvertence on his part. Nor is this the only exception to the rule in *Rylands* v. *Fletcher*, and nothing demonstrates more clearly the inaccuracy of calling such liability "absolute" than the existence of these exceptions.

It may be that these difficulties can be explained away, but at present the revolutionary school seems scarcely to have realized where its proposed reforms are likely to take it, while the pessimistic school has gone to the other extreme of overlooking the progress which has been made in the law of tort during the last half century.

INDEX

Abatement, 18
"Absolute" liability, 92, 208, 211, 242–244
Abuse of procedure, 18, 233
Accident, 242
Account, 19
  stated, 28, 167–168
Actio personalis moritur cum persona, 49, 150
Action
  "founded on contract", 43, 64, 76–78
  "founded on tort", 43, 64, 76–78
  joinder, 46–48
  joint parties, 54–62
  mixed, 25, 26
  "of contract", 43
  "of tort", 43
  personal, 19, 20, 22, 23, 25, 26, 27, 54
  real, 19, 22, 23, 25, 26
  survival of, 46, 48–54
  upon the case, 93–94, 96, 169, 172
Addison, 5, 8, 82, 86
Admiralty, Court of, 234, 236
Affreightment, 183
Agency, 147
  quasi-contract, 135–138
  unauthorized gains, 166–167, 177–178
American law. *See* United States
Ames, 13, 15, 110, 121, 180
Anson, Sir W. R., 106
Appeal of felony, 10, 19, 20, 27, 52–53
Architect, 66
Assignment of action in tort, 3
Assumpsit, 19, 21–22, 23, 28, 29, 44–46, 49, 60, 61, 66, 67, 94–96, 124–125, 180, 182, 214, 220, 222, 240
  origin, 14–15
Attorney, 59, 65, 151, 152
Austin, John, 110, 210
Average, general. *See* General average

Bailment, 92–103
  action upon case, 93–94, 96
  assumpsit and, 94–96
  Bracton, 92
  Britton, 92
  commodatum, 92
  consideration, 94–96
  contract and, 28, 65, 93, 94–103
  County Court Acts, in, 101
  definition, 21
  detinue, 96
  finding, 151
  Glanvill, 92
  gratuitous, 95, 99
  involuntary, 100
  liability, strict, 92
  Limitations, Statute of, 225
  married woman, 98
  minor, 98
  negligence, 92–93, 101
  possession, 99, 100, 101–103
  quasi-contract, 123
  remedies, 96
  right *in rem,* 102–103
  third party, 102
  tort and, 2, 21, 27, 29, 65, 92–103, 229
  trover, 96
  undertaking, 93–96
Banker, 213–214
Bankruptcy, 54, 212
Battle, trial by, 10
Bentham, 31
Blackstone, 13, 22, 23–31, 64, 129–130, 151–152, 193, 200
Bracton, 82, 92, 121–122, 208–209
Breach of peace, 20
Britton, 9, 92, 209
Brooke, 123
Buckland, Prof. W. W., 208
Burial expenses, 173–174
By-law, 180

Capias, 46–47
Cardozo, Chief Judge, 37
Carrier, common. *See* Common carrier.

246 INDEX

Case, action upon. *See* Action
Chafee, Prof. Z., 107
Chancery, Court of. *See* Equity
Chattels, servitudes on, 106–107
Cheshire, Dr, 204
Children, 83–84
Chitty, 29–30, 235
Chose in action, 27
Cinematograph, 83
Civil proceeding, 2, 3, 27, 190, 194–196, 202–203
Club, 180
Co-contractors, 44, 67
Codification, 4
Coke, 9, 23, 110
Common calling, 59–63, 147, 151–154
Common carrier, 47, 59–62, 70, 146–147, 151–155, 181, 238
 bailment, 94
 contract, 65
 quasi-delict, 210, 213–214, 218
Common counts, 66–67, 142, 159
Common Pleas, 190
Compulsory payment, 161–165
Conflict of laws, 150
Consideration, failure of, 156–157
Conspiracy, 20, 34, 83
Constructive notice, 212–213
Contract, 30, 40–91
 account stated, 167–168
 action "founded upon", 76–78
 actions, joinder of, 46–48
  survival of, 46, 48–54
 affreightment, 183
 agency, 177–178
 alternative claims, 220; to tort, 65 *seq.*
 bailment. *See* Bailment
 common carrier. *See* Common carrier
 constructive, 118
 costs, 78
 County Court Acts, 76–78
 crime, 83–84
 damages, 40–43
 distinguished from tort, 40–63, 64–65
 drunkard, 166
 executory, 45
 express, 28

Contract (*contd.*)
 fraud, 84
 history, 44–46
 implied, 28, 45
  by law. *See* Quasi-contract
  warranty of authority, 177–178
 inducing breach of, 34, 82
 innkeeper. *See* Innkeeper
 interference with, 82
 joinder of actions, 46–48
 joint, 44, 67, 163–165
  parties to action, 54–62
 judgment, 228
 lunatic, 166
 married woman, 82, 98
 minor, 80, 82, 98
  necessaries, 182
 necessaries, 165–166
  minor, of, 182
 nuisance, 85
 parties to action, 54–62
 personal, 54
 privity, 73–76, 105–108. *See also* Quasi-contract
 public policy, 86
 recognizances, 149–150
 record, 149–150
 social, 28
 standardized, 213–214
 Statutes of Limitations. *See* Limitations
 statutory, 181–182
 stranger to, 73–76, 147
 substantial claim, 68–72
 survival, 46, 48–54
 third person, 73–76, 147
 tort and, 2, 3, 21–22, 23, 27–28, 29, 40–91, 229
 trespass, 84
 trust, 76. *See also* Trust
 unlawful, 84–86
 volenti non fit injuria, 82–83, 84–86
 waiver, 213–214
Contribution, 117, 147, 163–165
Conversion, 15, 18, 79, 80–81, 145, 169–170
Conveyance, 102–103
Corbin, Prof. A. L., 76, 107–108
Costs, 43
Co-surety, 117, 147, 163–165

INDEX

247

County Court
Acts, 76–78
costs, 43
County Courts, 64
Court
Admiralty, 234, 236
Chancery. *See* Equity
Common Law, 233–237
County. *See* County Court
Divorce, 234–236
Ecclesiastical, 234–235
Courts
creation of new torts, 33–38
Covenant, 19, 44, 66
Creditor
defrauding, 212
Crime, 23, 51, 190–203
appeals, 195
compensation, 201–203
contract, 83–84
criminal cause, 194–196, 198
criminal matter, 194–196, 198
criminal proceedings. *See* Criminal proceeding
damages, 201–203
definition, 192–194, 200
evidence, 195
felony, 202
fine, 198–199, 201
imprisonment, 196, 198–199
judicial definitions, 193–194
mens rea, 217
offence, 199
pardon, 195, 196–197
penalty, 199
pleas of Crown, 190
public injury, 196–197
public law, 194
public offence, 195, 200
punishment, 195–199, 200–203
reward for detection, 202
sanction, 196–197
statutory definitions, 194
tort, 2, 3, 20–21, 26, 27, 29, 190–203
distinguished, 201
trespass, 190–191
volenti non fit injuria, 83–84
Criminal cause, 194–196, 198
Criminal matter, 194–196, 198
Criminal proceeding, 2, 3, 27, 190, 194–196, 202–203

Culpa, 208
Customary duty, 178–181

Damages
action for, 29
causation, 41–43
contract, 40–43
alternative claim, 78–80
conversion, 79, 80–81
crime, 201–203
direct, 41
exemplary, 40–41, 78–79
indirect, 41
liquidated, 184–185
nova causa, 41
remoteness, 41–43
tort, 40–43
alternative claim, 78–80
unliquidated, 3, 24, 52, 112, 183–189
in tort, 113–114, 231–233
vindictive, 40–41, 78–79
Damnum absque injuria, 37, 38
Dangerous chattel, 75–76
Dangerous operation, 35–36
Dangerous thing, 216
Death, 3, 46, 48–54, 150
quasi-contract, 145, 175, 176
volenti non fit injuria, 89
Debt, 19, 44, 45–46, 150, 181, 207
compulsory payment of another's, 161–165
See also Quasi-contract
Deceit, 13–14, 18, 20, 34, 66, 68, 113, 169, 170–172, 214, 231. *See also* Fraud
Declaration, writ and, 15–16
Delict, 209–210
Detinue, 15, 19, 93, 96, 207
Discontinuance, 18
Disseisin, 18
Disturbance, 18
Divorce Court, 243, 246
Dogs, 212–213
Dommage, 38–39
Drunkard, 166, 188
Duties, legal, 204–207
Duty, 26

Ecclesiastical Courts, 234–235
Education, legal, 30

248 INDEX

Ejectione custodiae, 19
Eldon, Lord, 129–130
Enticement
  of husband, 34
  of wife, 34
Equity
  Chancery, Court of, 234
  contribution, 163–165
  injunctions, 232
  laches, 221
  quasi-contract. *See* Quasi-contract
  trusts. *See* Trust
Escape, 18
Estoppel, 147, 178
Estrepement, 232
Executors, 49–54

False imprisonment, 18
Farrier, 59, 151–152
Fault, liability without, 241–244
Faute, 38–39
Fauxime, 18
Felony, 11, 18, 20, 27, 202
Finch, Sir Henry, 16–23, 26, 47, 64
Finder, 150–151
Fitzherbert, 13, 59
Fleta, 209
France
  Code Civil, 38–39
Fraud, 67–68, 84, 170–172. *See also*
  Deceit
Funeral expenses, 173–174

Gaoler, 151
General average, 139, 182–183
Germany
  Bürgerliches Gesetzbuch, 38–39
Gilbert, Lord Chief Baron, 46

Hanbury, H. G., 110–112, 130–131
Harvard Law School, 2, 7
High Court
  costs, 43
Hilliard, F., 9
Hohfeld, 108
Holdsworth, Sir William, 14, 15, 92–
  93, 95–96, 121, 123, 127–128,
  129, 180, 191, 192–193, 209,
  218, 232
Holland, Sir T. E., 120
Holt, Chief Justice, 92, 126, 127, 142,
  156, 170

Husband
  enticement of, 34
Huston, 110, 111

In consimili casu
  writs, 12
Incumbent
  action by, 179
Indebitatus assumpsit, 45, 48, 150,
  157, 158, 159, 170, 172, 174,
  175, 179–181, 220
  advantages, 141–146
  quasi-contract, 123–131
Indebitatus counts, 117
India, 34, 118–119, 151, 157, 161,
  166, 173, 174, 182, 183
  Inducing breach of contract, 34
Injunction, 231–233, 235–236
Innkeeper, 47, 59, 147, 151–155,
  181, 238
  quasi-delict, 210, 218
Insimul computassent, 168
Intimidation, 171–172
Intrusion, 18
Isaacs, Prof. N., 210–218
Italy
  Codice Civile, 38

Jenks, Dr E., 118, 120, 149, 168,
  173, 239
Joint contractors, 44, 162–165
Joint liability, 46, 54–62
Joint parties, 54–62
Joint tort, 165
Joint tortfeasors, 44–48, 54–62, 67
Jones, Sir William, 96, 97
Judgment, 228
  debt, 149
  foreign, 150
Jurisdiction in tort, 233–237
Jus naturale, 130
Justinian, 121, 208–209

Keener, Prof. A. W., 117–118, 149,
  187
Kenny, Prof. C. S., 192, 196–197,
  200
Knighthood
  fees for, 179

Laches, 221
Land law, 204–207

INDEX 249

Langdell, 110
Lee, Prof. R. W., 208
Liability, "absolute". *See* "Absolute" liability
  without fault, 241–244
Licence, 82–91
Limitations, Statutes of, 3, 219–228
  assumpsit, 220
  bailment, 225
  contract, 219–228
    under seal, 223–224
  Equity, 221
  indebitatus assumpsit, 220
  land, recovery of, 227
  negligence, 223
  nuisance, 223–224
  periods, 220
  quasi-contract, 220, 224
  substantial claim, 221–224
  tort, 3, 219–228
  trespass, 227
  trust, 225–226
  waiver of tort, 224
Littleton, 15
Lunatic, 166, 188

McNair, Dr A. D., 42
Maim, 18
Maitland, Prof. F. W., 11, 12, 13, 15, 23, 46, 54, 92, 109–112
Malicious prosecution, 34
Mandamus, 24–25
Mansfield, Lord, 49, 50, 51, 52, 56, 57, 126–134, 142, 143, 163, 190
Markby, Sir W., 238, 239
Marriage
  breach of promise of, 41, 52
Married woman
  contract, 82, 98
  tort, 82
Menaces, 18
Miles, Sir John, 239
Minor
  bailment, 98
  contract, 80, 82, 98
  necessaries, 181–182
  tort, 80, 82
Misdemeanour, 11
Misjoinder. *See* Joint
Mistake, 242
  money paid under, 157
Misuser, 18

Money
  had and received, 28, 52, 117, 149, 155, 157, 168, 181, 184, 228
  contract, where none, 140
  equitable action, 130
  waiver of tort, 143–146, 169
  See also Quasi-contract
  paid, action for, 155, 161, 173–174
  paid at request, 161
  paid on illegal purpose, 160
  paid under mistake, 157
Necessaries
  drunkard, 188
  lunatic, 188
  minor, 181–182
Negligence, 36
  alternative claims on, 63, 69, 81, 222
  bailment, 93, 101
  common calling, 154
  common carrier, 60
  contract, 63, 69
  duty in, 76
  finder, of, 151
  independent tort, 15, 34
  Limitations, Statutes of, 223
  quasi-*assumpsit*, 147
  trustee, 113, 226
Νομοτεχνία, 16
Non-joinder. *See* Joint
Nuisance, 18, 89, 223–224, 232

Omission
  liability for, 189, 210, 211
Ouster, 22

Pardon, 196–197
Parties, joint, 54–62
Payment
  compulsory, of another's debt, 161–165
  voluntary, on behalf of another, 173–174
Penalty, 199, 213
Personal property
  law of, 6, 206
Pleas of the Crown, 190
Plucknett, Prof. T. F. T., 11
Pollock, Sir Frederick, 2, 12, 33, 43, 70, 84, 86, 99, 115, 119, 133, 161, 173, 174, 207, 216, 233, 234

250 INDEX

Possession
bailment and, 100, 101–103
Pound, Prof. Roscoe, 217
Praecipe quod reddat, 22, 23, 47, 54
personal, 19
real, 19
Privacy, 34–35
Private wrong, 30
Privity
contract, 73–76
quasi-contract, 161–162
trust, 105–108
Prize-fight, 82, 83, 88
Procedendo, 24
Procedure, abuse of, 228
Prohibition, 24
Property, law of, 6
bailment, 100
Limitations, Statutes of, 227
personal, 6, 206
tort, 2, 3, 26, 204–207
Public calling, 28, 96. *See also*
Common calling
Public law, 194
Public policy, 37, 86, 88–91, 133, 156
Punishment, 195–199, 200–203

Quantum meruit, 117, 155, 157–160, 182, 187–188
Quantum valebat, 159–160
Quare ejecit, 19
Quasi-assumpsit, 146–148, 178, 210
Quasi-contract, 6, 21, 45, 46, 48, 53, 116–189, 242, 243
account, 122–123
account stated, 167–168
aequum et bonum, 128–135
agency, 135–138, 177–178
agent's unauthorized gains, 166–167
alternative, 148, 167–176
American law, 117–118
bailment, 123
benefit, 119–121, 122, 141, 149, 178
common calling, 151–155
common carrier, 60, 62–63, 151–155
common counts, 159
compulsory payment of another's debt, 161–165

Quasi-contract *(contd.)*
contract implied, 120, 124–129, 134–141, 151
implied by law, 119, 131
contribution, 163–165
co-surety, 163–165
County Court, 77
customary duty, 178–181
damages, 183–189
death, 150, 175, 176
debt, 122–123
compulsory payment of another's, 161–165
defined, 119–121
distinguished from tort, 188–189
doubtful, 148, 177–183
drunkard, 166, 188
enrichment, 119–121, 122
Equity, 127, 129–131
failure of consideration, 81, 156–157
finder, 150–151
foreign judgment, 150
general average, 139, 182–183
history, 121–147
Holt, Chief Justice, 126–127
husband, 165
implied warranty of authority, 177–178
indebitatus assumpsit. See *Indebitatus assumpsit*
indebitatus counts, 117
indefiniteness, 116
indemnity, 162–165
innkeeper, 151–155
joint tortfeasors, 165
judgment, 124, 228
land law, 126–127
Limitations, Statutes of, 220, 224
liquidated claims, 183–189
lunatic, 166, 188
Mansfield, Lord, 126–134
minor, 181–182
mistake, money paid under, 157
money, had and received. *See*
Money, etc.
paid, 155, 161
paid at request, 161
paid on illegal purpose, 160
paid to recover goods, 168
paid under mistake, 157
natural justice, 120, 128–135

INDEX

251

Quasi-contract (*contd.*)
  necessaries
    of drunkard, 166, 188
    of lunatic, 166, 188
    of minor, 181–182
    of wife, 165
  payment, compulsory, of another's
    debt, 161–165
  privity, 161–162
  of contract, 134–141
  pseudo-, 63–64, 148–155
  public calling, 151–155
  public policy, 133
  pure, 148, 155–167
  quantum meruit, 155, 157–160,
    187–188
  quantum valebat, 159–160
  quasi-assumpsit, 146–148
  recognizances, 124, 149–150
  record, contracts of, 149–150
  Roman Law, 116, 121, 130
  salvage, 139, 151, 155–156, 187,
    188, 234
  specific goods, claim for, 183–184
  stakeholder, 160
  statute, 141
  statutory, 188
  statutory duty, 181
  surety, 162
  terminology, 119, 125
  threat of proceedings, 161–165
  tort, 2, 29, 116–189, 229
    distinguished, 188–189
  tortfeasors, joint, 165
  trusts, 115
  unfamiliar term, 116
  unliquidated claim, 183–189
  waiver of tort, 168–176. *See also*
    Waiver of tort
  warranty of authority, implied,
    177–178
  wife's necessaries, 165
Quasi-delict, 208–218
  "absolute" liability, 211
  banker, 213–214
  common carrier, 210, 213–214,
    218
  constructive notice, 212–213
  creditors, defrauding, 212
  dogs, vicious, 212–213
  equitable restitution, 211–212
  genuine, 215

Quasi-delict (*contd.*)
  innkeeper, 210, 218
  omission, 210–211
  responsibility without fault, 211–
    218
  Roman Law, 208–209
  Roman-Dutch Law, 208
  Scots Law, 209–210
  statutory liability, 212–213
  strict liability, 211, 212, 215
  trespass *ab initio*, 211–212
  vicarious liability, 211–212, 215
  waiver of contract, 213–214
  warranty, 214
  waste, 211
Quasi-tort, 2, 6, 77, 155, 178. *See
  also* Quasi-delict

Rape, 18
Rationabili parte, 19
Real property, law of, 204–207
Recognizances, 150
Record, contract of, 149–150
Registrum Brevium, 13, 205
Replevin, 168
Res judicata, 228
Responsibility without fault, 211–
  218
"Restatement" of case law, 4, 76,
  107, 115, 149
Restitution, specific, 231
Rhodian Law, 183
Right, 26
  in personam, 102–103, 206, 231,
    238
    trust and, 108–113
  in rem, 205–206, 207, 230–231,
    237–238
    bailment, 102–103
    trust and, 108–113
    writ of, 207
Rights, legal, 204–207
Roman Law, 92, 116, 121, 130, 208–
  209
Roman-Dutch Law, 208

St German, 16, 22
Salmond, Sir John, 5, 33, 86, 110,
  204, 237
Salvage, 139, 151, 155–156, 187, 188,
  234
Schade, 39

252 INDEX

Scots Law, 209–210
Scott, Prof. Austin W., 110–113
Self-help, 231–232, 233
Servitudes on chattels, 106–107
Sheriff, 151, 152, 153, 154, 179
Shipowner, 65
Si fecerit te securum, 19, 20, 22, 23, 47, 54
Sitten, gegen die guten, 39
Slander, 18
Smith, Jeremiah, 5, 241–244
Specific restitution, 231
Stakeholder, 160
Stallybrass, W. T. S., 237
Star Chamber, 191
Statham, 14
Status, 3, 154–155
Statutes of Limitations. *See* Limitations, Statutes of
Statutory
  contract, 181–182
  duty, 181, 188
  liability, 212–213
  obligation, 146–147
Stephen, Sir J. F., 83, 192
Stone, Judge Harlan F., 110
Story, Judge, 97, 153
Street, T. A., 5, 146–148, 152, 210
Strict liability, 212, 242–244
Surety, 147, 162–165
Surgeon, 59, 65, 69, 82

Tailor, 151
Terry, Prof. H., 97
Threat, 161–165, 169, 172–173
Tithe, 24
Tort
  "absolute" liability, 242–244
  accident, 242
  action, "founded upon", 76–78
    personal, 22
  actions, joinder, 46–48
    survival, 46, 48–54
  alternative claims, 220
  assignment of action, 3
  bailment, 92–103. *See also* Bailment
  Britton, 9
  common carrier. *See that title*
  Common Law Courts, 233–237
  contract, 64–65. *See also* Contract
  contribution, 165

Tort *(contd.)*
  costs, 43, 77–78
  County Court, 43, 76–78
  courts in which redressible, 233–237
  crime. *See* Crime
  damages, unliquidated. *See* Damages
  dangerous thing, 216
  definition, 32–39
    details, 229–233
    none satisfactory, 5
    reasons for, 1–7
  definitions, various, 229–244
  derivation, 8
  doubtful, 34–36
  duty, fixed by law, 113, 229
    to persons generally, 25, 229–231
  ecclesiastical, 24, 234–236
  equitable, 112
  etymology, 8
  fault, liability without, 241–244
  first book on, 8
  foundation of liability in, 32–39
  High Court costs, 43
  history, 8–31
  injunction, 231–233, 235–236
  innkeeper. *See* Innkeeper
  innominate, 34
  intimidation, 172–173
  joinder of actions, 46–48
  joint, 44, 67
    parties to action, 54–62
  judgment, 228
  jurisdiction, 233–237
  land law, 2, 3, 26, 204–207
  law of "torts" or "tort"? 36–37, 239–240
  liability without fault, 241–244
  leave and licence, 82–91
  licence, 82–91
  Limitations, statutes of. *See that title*
  mandamus, 24–25
  maritime, 24, 236
  mental element, 217
  mistake, 242
  new, 33–38
  nominate, 34
  nuisance, 89
  parties, 54–62
  personal, 20, 54, 205–207
    action, 25

INDEX

253

Tort (*contd.*)
  private wrong, 23, 25, 30
  property, to, 205–207
  property law, 2, 3, 26, 204–207
  public policy, 88–91
  quasi-contract, 116–189. *See*
    Quasi-contract
  quasi-delict, 208–218. *See* Quasi-
    delict
  quasi-tort. *See* Quasi-tort *and*
    Quasi-delict
  remedies, 231–233
  reputation, to, 205–207
  right *in rem*, 237–238
  self-help, 231–232, 233
  source, 10
  specific restitution, 231
  status, 3
  statutory, 212–213
  strict liability, 242–244
  substantial claim in, 68–72
  survival of action, 46, 48–54
  threats, 169, 172–173
  "torts" or "tort"? 32 *seq.*, 239–
    240
  trespass. *See* Trespass
    ab initio, 211–212
  trust, 104–115. *See* Trust
  vicarious liability, 3, 211–212, 215,
    242
  volenti non fit injuria, 82–91
  waiver. *See* Waiver
  waste. *See* Waste
Tortfeasor, joint, 44–48, 54–62, 67
Tortious liability, 32. *See* Tort
Trespass, 169–170, 190–191, 207,
  227, 232, 234
  ab initio, 211–212
  against Crown, 18
  case. *See* Trespass upon the case
  civil, 11
  contra pacem, 20
  criminal, 11, 51–52
  de bonis asportatis, 11
  de clauso fracto, 11
  early meaning, 10
  felonies, 11
  goods, to, 19
  land, to, 19
  misdemeanours, 11
  origin, 10–11
  person, to, 19

Trespass (*contd.*)
  personal nature of, 49
  process, 46–47
  quare clausum fregit, 227
  quasi-criminal, 10
  tort, 9
  vi et armis, 11, 18, 20, 27
  writ, 10–11
Trespass upon the case, 11–15, 18,
  19, 21
  deceit, 14
  warranty, 66
Trover, 15, 96, 144, 145, 168, 169–
  170, 207, 228
Trust, 104–115
  agreement, 113
  American law, 115
  beneficiary's remedies, 109–113
  breach of, 22
    tort and, 2, 3, 27, 104–115
  Common Law Courts and, 104–
    105, 114, 234
  constructive, 113
  contract, 76, 105–108
  deceit of trustee, 113
  distinguished from tort, 108
  equitable tort, 112
  jurisdiction, 104–105, 114, 234–
    235
  Limitations, Statutes of, 225–226
  nature of right, 108–113
  negligence, 113, 225–226
  privity of contract, 105–108
  property law, 114
  quasi-contract, 115
  right *in rem* or *in personam*? 108–
    113
  third parties, 108–113
  tort, 29, 104–115, 234
  trustee's duties, 109

United States, 2, 4, 5, 8, 34, 76, 84,
  106–108, 115, 117–118, 164–
  165, 210, 224
Unliquidated damages. *See* Damages
Usurpation, 18

Valore maritagii, 19
Vexatious litigation, 18, 233
Vicarious responsibility, 3, 211–212,
  215, 242

254 INDEX

Viner, 29
Volenti non fit injuria, 82–91

Wade, E. C. S., 106–107
Waiver of contract, 213–214
Waiver of tort, 96, 117, 121, 168–176
  action for extorting by threats,
    169, 172–173
  action upon the case, 169, 172
  advantages, 143–146
  conversion, 145, 169–170
  damages, 186–187
  death, 176
  deceit, 169, 170–172
  election, 176
  fiction in, 140–141
  fraud, 170–172
  inducing breach of contract, 174–
    175
  intimidation, 172–173
  Limitations, Statutes of, 224
  proof of tort, 175–176
  tort
    capable of waiver, 169–175
    proof of, 175–176
  trespass, 169, 170
  trover, 145, 169–170
Warranty, 66–68, 147, 214
  false, 18
  of authority, implied, 147, 177–
    178
Warren, Samuel, 142
Waste, 26, 206, 211, 232
Wife, enticement of, 34
  necessaries of, 165
Wigmore, Dean J. H., 241

Williams, Joshua, 6
Woodward, F. C., 118, 149, 187
Writ
  account, 19
  assumpsit. See *Assumpsit*
  common pleas, 19
  conspiracy, 19
  covenant, 19, 44, 66
  debt. *See* Debt
  deceit, 13
  declaration and, 15–16
  detinue. *See* Detinue
  ejectione custodiae, 19
  estrepement, 232
  in consimili casu, 12
  mandamus, 24–25
  praecipe, 19
  procedendo, 24
  prohibition, 24
  quare ejecit, 19
  rationabili parte, 19
  right, 207
  si fecerit te securum. *See that title*
  trespass. *See* Trespass
  trespass upon the case. *See that title*
  valore maritagii, 19
Wrongs
  goods, to, 18
  land, to, 18
  person, to, 18
  possessions, to, 18
  private, 23, 25, 26, 27
  public, 23
  real, 18, 22
  with force, 18, 19, 20, 26
  without force, 18, 19, 20, 26

For EU product safety concerns, contact us at Calle de José Abascal, 56–1°,
28003 Madrid, Spain or eugpsr@cambridge.org.

www.ingramcontent.com/pod-product-compliance
Ingram Content Group UK Ltd.
Pitfield, Milton Keynes, MK11 3LW, UK
UKHW010851060825
461487UK00012B/1039